LIVING MY BEST LIFE, HUN

following your dreams iS <u>No</u> <u>Joke</u>

LONDON HUGHES

GRAND
CENTRAL

New York   Boston

Grand Central Publishing
Hachette Book Group
1290 Avenue of the Americas, New York, NY 10104
grandcentralpublishing.com
twitter.com/grandcentralpub

First Edition: September 2023

Grand Central Publishing is a division of Hachette Book Group, Inc. The Grand Central Publishing name and logo is a trademark of Hachette Book Group, Inc.

The publisher is not responsible for websites (or their content) that are not owned by the publisher.

The Hachette Speakers Bureau provides a wide range of authors for speaking events. To find out more, go to hachettespeakersbureau.com or email HachetteSpeakers@hbgusa.com.

Grand Central Publishing books may be purchased in bulk for business, educational, or promotional use. For information, please contact your local bookseller or the Hachette Book Group Special Markets Department at special.markets@hbgusa.com.

Library of Congress Cataloging-in-Publication Data

Names: Hughes, London, author.
Title: Living my best life, hun : following your dreams is no joke / London Hughes.
Description: New York : Grand Central Publishing, 2023.
Identifiers: LCCN 2022057935 | ISBN 9781538722435 (hardcover) | ISBN 9781538722459 (ebook)
Subjects: LCSH: Hughes, London. | Women television personalities—Great Britain—Biography. | Women comedians—Great Britain—Biography. | LCGFT: Autobiographies.
Classification: LCC PN1992.4.H766 A3 2023 | DDC 791.4502/8092 [B]—dc23/eng/20230411
LC record available at https://lccn.loc.gov/2022057935

ISBN: 9781538722435 (hardcover), 9781538722459 (ebook), 9781538758748 (signed edition), 9781538758755 (special signed edition), 9781538759325 (special signed edition)

Printed in the United States of America

LSC-C

Printing 1, 2023

To fourteen-year-old London Hughes,
she knew this would happen one day

Introduction

I bloody love birthdays: mine, other people's, it doesn't matter. I've always been a birthday person. I find it weird when I meet people who don't really celebrate the day they were born. I get the same feeling whenever I meet a straight man who dislikes going down on women. It's very confusing to me.

I guess the reason is that some people always have shit birthdays, so they just don't want to get their hopes up. Now, I totally understand that concept; I've had some of the WORST birthdays, seriously! Real, could-cause-depression-should've-gone-to therapy-type-monstrous birthdays, many of which ended with me crying alone at the end of the night.

Places I've cried alone on my birthday:

Pizza Hut
A karaoke bar
A Jacuzzi
My living room
My bedroom
My kitchen
An old Peugeot 206
The streets of London

But I never gave up. I always had hope—hope that one day I'd have the most epic of birthdays to end all epic birthdays, and I'd only be crying genuine tears of complete ecstasy. I used to watch this show called *My Super Sweet 16*, where rich kids would let MTV film their insanely lavish birthday parties, every birthday took place in a huge nightclub, there was always a performance by a famous rapper or R & B superstar and the night usually ended with the kid getting a Ferrari! It was my favorite show; I watched every episode, and I was in complete awe of those spoiled little bitches.

I always wanted a birthday like a super sweet sixteener, a fabulous soiree filled with jealous friends, a free bar, celebs galore, paparazzi, and everyone in attendance completely adoring me.

Well, after thirty-two years of living through failed birthday attempt after failed birthday attempt, it finally happened: I finally had the epic birthday of my dreams!

June 7, 2021: Hughesy's birthday extravaganza! It was INSANE! Five crazy jam-packed nights that started off at Dave Chappelle's house in Ohio and ended with me on an IV drip in the presidential suite at the Waldorf Astoria in Atlanta. It was so beyond epic that I have zero problems relaying to you that I didn't catch a single dick the whole time and I didn't even care. #Growth. I was so fucking happy I even wrote parts of the night down in my journal (lol, okay iPhone Notes app) so I wouldn't forget it. Here's what I wrote:

Fucking Dave Chappelle just got up and gave a speech about me to everyone at the party! Afterwards he took me to one side and literally said the words London, you're going to write about this night in your autobiography one day! Fucking hell, should def include in my book!

And then I wrote

Marianna infused macaroni cheese! Insane! Would recommend

(I was drunk, and potentially high on marijuana.)

So I basically wrote this whole book to tell you how a young Black British female comedian from Thornton Heath, Croydon, managed to follow her dreams, move to the US and spend her thirty-second birthday partying in Ohio with one of the greatest comics in the world! Well, it's a hell of a journey, it's a hell of a story, and you're gonna bloody love it!

Let's start at the beginning, shall we?

LIVING MY
BEST LIFE, HUN

Chapter 1

Three Lies and a Truth

I want to open this chapter with a statement so bad-bitchingly confident that it just leaps off the page, something like, I've always been funny. I've always been cute. I've always been confident. I was born to do this shit.

But in reality, only one of those four things is true.

I'VE ALWAYS BEEN FUNNY
(Lie Number 1)

My dad, Mr. David Hughes, will confirm that I only became funny at around the age of eight. Some people might think that's normal, but for the hilarious Hughes family I was seriously slacking on the hahas.

You see, I come from a family filled with jokers. There's my older brother, Joel; imagine me but in male form, way taller, and ten times more charming. Joel is the funniest man I know: his comedic timing is impeccable and he's devastatingly witty, with a brain that can mine comedy out of any situation.

When he was a kid, around eleven or twelve, Joel got hit by a car, really badly. A driver ran him over whilst he was crossing the street and he literally flew through the air. I was so upset when I heard about the accident and remember imagining the worst as I rushed to the hospital to visit him. When I got there, I expected him to be lying in a hospital bed, all bandaged up, barely breathing. Instead, he was sitting upright doing impressions, all the nurses gathered around him laughing at his jokes. The man is a top-tier clown.

So is my father. He's the man responsible for my epic taste in comedy, and he made sure I was well versed in all the comedy greats from a young age. He taught me about the US stand-up legend Richard Pryor, but he also made me watch tons of classic British comedies like *Fawlty Towers*, *Keeping Up Appearances*, and *Dad's Army*. In the car we used to listen to BBC Radio comedies, so I was the only ten-year-old in school who could quote jokes from Kenneth Williams in *Round the Horne*. It's like a ten-year-old today quoting Norman Lear—I was clearly a comedy connoisseur.

My dad thrives on embarrassing his children; he does it so well he should truly have his own sitcom. I got a taste of my sitcom dad when I was about twenty-seven and I brought a boyfriend home to meet him and the rest of my family. I was quite anxious, mainly because my dad hadn't particularly liked my previous boyfriend. There was A LOT of pressure riding on this first meet.

So to ease the tension, my father decided to greet said boyfriend and me at the front door wearing my stepmum's wig and church dress. "All right, mate, nice to meet you," he said to my boyfriend, shaking his hand but staying very much in character.

I was mortified. I could see that the rest of my family were just as shocked as I was, but they decided to hold in their laughs and play along with the charade for maximum entertainment. My dad, getting carried away, started pouting and flicking his wig, whilst my poor polite boyfriend continued trying not to acknowledge it. After what seemed like hours, my dad eventually broke character and the whole family cracked up. Actually, we still crack up about it to this day.

The next joker of the group is my grandma Myrtle (ninety-six and still going strong). She's hilarious, too. A fabulous wise-cracking, attention-demanding diva, she even managed to have the whole family laughing at my granddad's funeral. My grandma is such a professional she made up a joke she uses solely for family weddings. If you're ever at a wedding reception with Grandma Myrtle, without fail you will see her grab the mic and tell this same joke, and we all have to laugh like we haven't already heard it before. Here it is:

[Said in a posh Jamaican accent] *You see, in a marriage there are three rings. You may think there are only two but there are indeed three! See, there's the engagement ring, then there's the wedding ring, and then . . . there's the suffer-ring!* [hold for laughter and applause]

And then there's my mum. God bless my mum. I wouldn't call her funny *per se*, as I'm yet to laugh at a single joke she's actually made on purpose, but she's definitely got a good sense of humor. It's just sometimes things go over her head. I always say, if everyone's laughing at a joke, my mum's laughing, too, but she's laughing at the hat the guy who told the joke is wearing.

Honorable mentions go out to my brother Alex, who truly has the best laugh ever, my younger sister Sakilé, who is definitely *not* the funny one but she'll say something so savage you'll have to laugh unless you'll cry, and my youngest sister, Maya, who, with time, has the wits and smarts to eventually out-funny us all.

My fun-filled family teases each other all the time, but I hated it when they teased me when I was younger. For some reason, I was late to the funny train because I wasn't able to take a joke. Don't get me wrong, I ABSOLUTELY LOVED laughing at other people's expense: if you fell over or said something stupid, that was me gone, I would have a complete laughter fit. No remorse. But I ABSOLUTELY HATED it when other people laughed at me. I would throw mini tantrums and sulk if anyone so much as snickered in my direction. Funny how things worked out.

Due to my lack of hilarity, it was no surprise that when my first-ever joke finally left my mouth, my family was flabbergasted. They truly didn't think the day would ever come, and not only was it a funny joke, it was also an original one that I completely made up myself. It went like this:

What do you call a Rasta man that wears glasses?...
Rasta-four-eyes! [Said in a heavily Jamaican accent to sound like the word Rasta-far-Is, which is the Jamaican term for a Rastafarian—high level stuff, mate.]

A little niche, sure, but my dad exploded, he was so happy for me. My brother stared at me, totally impressed, probably for the first time ever. I'd finally made it; I'd finally done a funny. And it felt great.

I'VE ALWAYS BEEN CUTE
(Lie Number 2, Although My Parents Would Dispute This and Say I Was Born Extremely Cute, but I Definitely Didn't Feel It)

I grew up Black in a predominantly white country in a predominantly white neighborhood in the nineties. My favorite popstars were white, my Barbie dolls were white, my best friend was white, but I wasn't white, and I used to HATE IT.

It wasn't as though I wanted to be a white person. I loved being a Black person, and I loved everything that came with my Blackness: the heritage, the culture, the food, the music, possessing natural rhythm...I bloody loved being Black, but what stumped me was how my Blackness equated to beauty—it didn't.

I used to think that my kind of Black skin was unattractive. I wasn't light enough to be considered biracial, and in the nineties and noughties, a light skin tone was the only Black skin tone that I considered beautiful—and for all of this, I solely blame the British and American media.

First of all, there were no beauty campaigns for women of color when I was growing up—nothing at all, none of this Fenty shit! If on the rare occasion your fave makeup brand did come in a darker shade, it was either caramel or chocolate, and I was too dark for caramel and too light for chocolate. Oh, how I longed to be able to wear effortless shades like "snow" or "peachy cream" just like the white women did in the commercials.

It was also made very clear by the British press who they deemed to be attractive. There was always a new It girl on the scene that teenage girls like me aspired to be, whether it was Rachel Stevens from S Club 7 or Cheryl Cole from Girls Aloud or Jordan the Page 3 model. None of these It girls were Black, and I heavily bought into the notion that that was because Black girls just weren't attractive.

And can we talk about Rear of the Year?! The honorary British award for celebrities who are considered to have a notable posterior. Excuse me, none of the skinny white women who won even had great bums! It was all very confusing.

I find it quite hilarious now that my favorite Spice Girl of all time was Ginger Spice. She's the one this little Black girl wanted to be! I thought she was by far the prettiest. I used to think redheads were just white people and I didn't know that being "ginger" was a whole different category in itself. I thought Geri Halliwell was called Ginger spice because she really liked ginger beer, and I bloody loved ginger beer; it was one of the many reasons why I wanted to be her. But when my friends and I pretended to be Spice Girls in the playground, it was my redheaded best friend at the time, Amy, who got to be Ginger after several heated arguments. As the only Black girl in my school friendship group, I was doomed to spend the rest of my playground years being the token Scary Spice.

Also, while we're here, can we touch on how problematic the

name Scary Spice is? The Spice Girls were given their names by a white female journalist early in their careers before their personas had been fully formed. All their names made sense at the time: Sporty loved football, Ginger was a redhead, Posh was posh, Baby was the youngest... But what exactly made Mel B scary? Nothing about her was scary; she was just a loud, energetic mixed-raced girl who wore her natural hair. She only started wearing leopard prints and roaring at the camera after her nickname was coined. Scary? Wild? Nah, I reckon that journalist was just scared of a Black woman living authentically in her own skin.

Anyway, back to me. I'm eleven, and at this point I'm so obsessed with whiteness that I literally remember praying to God every night asking for long blonde hair instead of the dry frizzy bird's nest I currently had growing out of my scalp. I hated my big Black features; they were the opposite of sexy to me, especially my lips. There are actual pictures of me as a teenager folding my mouth in as I smile to make my lips appear thinner. God, I so wanted them sexy thin white girl lips.

As time went on, I started to gradually accept my beautiful Black skin tone, but then American TV shows made me start to believe that I was the wrong shade of Black.

If you were a fan of most eighties and nineties Black US TV shows and movies, the formula for Black female characters often went like this:

Cute/educated/girl-next-door/pretty/virginal/calm/quiet/
     kind/married = light skin tone.
Slutty/single/loud/uneducated/unattractive/wild/aggres-
     sive/intimidating/brash = dark skin tone.

There were some exceptions to this rule of course, but the most obvious example of this was in two of my favorite Black TV shows of all time: *The Fresh Prince of Bel Air* and *My Wife and Kids*.

In early seasons of *The Fresh Prince of Bel Air*, Aunt Viv was played by a dark-skinned Black woman named Janet Hubert. Her version of Aunt Viv was fierce. She wouldn't take any shit, she stood up for herself, wore the trousers, and wouldn't hesitate to put a family member in their place. Who could forget the iconic dance scene where she absolutely slaughtered those young girls in her dance class with a routine I'm still trying to perfect thirty years later! She was the epitome of sass and could intimidate the hell out of anyone.

But when she was later replaced by a light-skinned actress (Daphne Maxwell Reid), Aunt Viv's character changed completely. She had less to say and became more timid, sweet, and kind. Sure, she might give Uncle Phil or the kids a few looks when they messed up, but all that sass, fierceness, and intimidation were completely gone.

The same thing happened in *My Wife and Kids*, when the dark-skinned version of the character Claire Kyle (played by Jazz Raycole) was replaced by a much lighter-skinned actress (Jennifer Freeman). Claire Kyle went from a no-nonsense schoolgirl who even her brother's bullies were afraid of, to a ditzy, clumsy girl-next-door type the whole football team wanted to date.

I often identified with the darker-skinned characters a lot more, in looks and in personality, but society made me believe that having lighter skin was more attractive, more palatable. This resulted in me wearing makeup two shades too bright for me and putting a yellow jumper on my head and pretending it was my own long blonde hair. I was a lost cause.

I'VE ALWAYS BEEN CONFIDENT
(Lie Number 3—A Big One)

Well, it's no surprise—considering up until the age of twelve, I wanted to be a blonde white woman—that this frizzy-haired Black girl was not the bundle of confident energy you read before you. I thought I was ugly. I also had mild forehead eczema, acne, and asthma, and for a month or so some serious puberty-driven BO, which I remember the kids severely teasing me about. Ah, secondary school was so fun.

The crazy thing was, I was confident on the inside. I knew I was funny, I was kind, I was nerd-level smart, the teachers liked me, even I quite liked me. I should've been a confident kid on the outside, too! The only problem was, I relied way too much on how other people saw me, and how they saw me shaped my view of myself.

Again, I blame American television. On all the TV shows I used to watch as a kid, you were a nobody unless you were popular; being popular made you a somebody and I really wanted to be a somebody! The popular girls got all the hot guys, they were invited to prom, they went to the mall after school to shop and sip smoothies. I wanted to go shopping at the mall and sip smoothies! But I couldn't because I WAS NOT POPULAR, nowhere near, no matter how hard I tried.

Let me give you an insight into why twelve- to fourteen-year-old

London Hughes didn't have many friends. First, she was not the Urban Dictionary definition of "cool."

"Cool" back then was wearing Juicy Couture or Baby Phat tracksuits with Nike trainers. It also helped if you wore short skirts and real gold jewelry, spoke fluent slang, had insanely braided hairstyles or hair filled with chemical relaxer, used gel to slick down your baby hairs, and listened to Dizzee Rascal and/or Sean Paul.

London Hughes did absolutely none of these things. London Hughes wore British Home Store tracksuits, shuffled around in Reebok trainers, had terrible hair because her mum didn't know how to braid, couldn't manage to keep her thick baby hairs down no matter how much gel she used, wasn't allowed chemical hair relaxer until she was eighteen, wore annoyingly long skirts, spoke German for fun, had 100 percent plastic jewelry, and listened solely to Avril Lavigne. The popular girls annihilated me, and I would do almost anything to seek their validation.

I went to a very high-achieving all-girls' school in Thornton Heath in Croydon. Thornton Heath is now famous for its mild gang violence and being the birthplace of rapper Stormzy (and now myself, of course), but back then it was only really famous for its twenty-four-hour Tesco supermarket—the first in the area!

I was a great student. My favorite lessons were English, PE, and the occasional lunch, and most days I found myself looking forward to going to school.

That was until this incessant need to be popular took over my life well into secondary school, resulting in me being savagely bullied all the way up until university (more on that later).

I don't believe I became this confident badass bitch version of myself until around the age of twenty, and the main reason I got so confident was thanks to the wonderful world of stand-up comedy. Which leads us nicely to my next statement, the only true statement:

I WAS BORN TO DO THIS

Chapter 2

I Was Born to Do This

Sounds wanky and bigheaded, but I really was. I truly am doing exactly what I was put on this earth to do: entertain you bitches. And I knew this, I've always known it, even from a young age.

Now, let's be clear: like I said before, I haven't always been funny, but what I have ALWAYS been is obsessed with fame.

Television was my best friend growing up. I have no idea why I adored it so much, but I was obsessed with it—my obsession was so bad that, at age five, I tried to get into the TV by climbing around the back of it and attempting to crawl inside (I almost electrocuted myself). I figured out pretty quickly that to be on TV you had to be famous, so that was my next goal.

Apparently when I was seven, I told my mum that I didn't want any kids until I had a star on the Hollywood Walk of Fame. A bold statement. She probably thought I was joking. I'm now thirty-two, no star—no kids.

The goal of being famous took a lot of practice, planning, and preparation. A lot of time and energy went into it, more than you may think a seven-year-old girl would have been able to handle, but I was ready, mate. I pushed myself.

WAYS IN WHICH YOUNG ME PREPARED TO BE A STAR:

I. Popstar Training

Like I say, at this time in my life, I knew very well I was going to be a famous celebrity—I just didn't know what for, so I prepared myself to be good at everything and anything: singing, dancing, acting...the works. I was doing Saturday dance classes: I trained in jazz, tap, modern, and even kathak-style Indian dancing—baby girl had range.

Sidenote: You really haven't submerged yourself in culture unless you've been the only Black girl in an otherwise all-Hindu Indian dance group. I learned to speak Hindi, wore a sari and bindi, and danced to kathak music with gold bells on my feet like a bad bitch. I loved performing kathak dance. I miss my Hindu crew—we completely shut down the Asian Mela in Hyde Park in '97!

At home I did what I like to call popstar training. I would take over the living room, put the TV on The Box, the only music channel at the time, and sing whilst making up a freestyle dance to every single song that came on. From the Beastie Boys and the Prodigy to Aqua and the Spice Girls, I would perform the songs like I wrote them (I nearly sprained my neck dancing to "Firestarter"). There was a part of my living room where the carpet joined together, creating a straight line that ran the length of the room. On one side of the line was the audience, and on the other side of the line was my stage. I performed on that stage forty to fifty times a night.

Whilst performing to a Janet Jackson music video on The Box, I noticed that Janet had the most insane six-pack. I decided there and then that if I was going to be famous, I needed to get a six-pack, too, so I started doing sit-ups. I started at like ten, then twenty, and then I tried to do them for a minute, then during a full advert break, and before I knew it I was doing sit-ups throughout the duration of every advert break of my favorite TV shows (and I had a lot of favorite shows).

It was sit-ups every fifteen minutes during *The Powerpuff Girls*, *That's So Raven*, *Dexter's Laboratory*, *Sister, Sister*, *Kenan & Kel*, *Clarissa Explains It All*, *Rocko's Modern Life*, *Sabrina the Teenage Witch*, and *Are You Afraid of the Dark?* After two weeks, I had a noticeable two-pack, but I had to go to the doctor because I couldn't lie on my stomach without being in extreme pain. Definitely overdid it.

2. Writing

If you've watched my Netflix stand-up special *To Catch a D*ck*, you would know that I used to write myself into episodes of *Frasier* for fun! I played Denise, Frasier's charming Black British adopted daughter; Frasier loved the fact that I was British, and he would use me and my accent to help get him the ladies. I in turn would date their sons—we were a Seattle dream team! I used to love writing; back then it wasn't even called fan fiction, it was just a normal Thursday night for me! (Sidenote: If you haven't seen my Netflix special yet, please put my book down and go watch it! Thank you!) Nobody knows that the real reason I wrote fan fiction is because I thought it would be a way to get myself onto television shows. I figured out at a very young age that I'd have way more chances of getting on TV if I did all the hard work and actually wrote myself into the episodes, so I did.

Frasier was one of many. The first was *The Fresh Prince of Bel Air*, as at the time Will Smith was my EVERYTHING. (Well, pre-slap Will Smith.) He meant more to me than any living celebrity and was the sole inspiration behind my career. I wanted to be Will Smith. The first time I saw *Fresh Prince*, it shattered my tiny mind, mainly because at the time, Black families didn't dominate UK comedies (they still don't). The UK had only four TV channels when I was growing up, and Black people were on none of them.

I grew up at a time when TV funding for ethnic minorities had been cut. Black British comedy shows like *Desmond's* and *The Real McCoy* had previously had specific government-ordered diversity funding allocated to them for the advancement of Black British talent, arts, and culture. Eventually that funding got cut and the government said, "We're not going to specifically fund Black shows anymore, we're just going to include more Black characters into our white shows. Simple!"

The only problem was, they didn't. Which meant that there was a time when Black British TV shows completely disappeared, and we only got one Black man added to the cast of *EastEnders*. I was watching so much white television that it wasn't until *The*

Fresh Prince of Bel Air got syndicated and aired on BBC Two in the late nineties that I saw my first-ever Black woman on TV: Aunt Viv. I thought Will Smith's comedic timing and clowning was so engaging that I found myself completely copying his whole persona. I would do his and Jazz's famous high five with my friends and say all his catchphrases, like "Jean Claude Van damn, I look good!" I knew the theme tune by heart (even the extended version; they always forget about the extended version), and, coolest of all, I used to dance like him. Yes, I had the rhythm of a male African American teenager from the eighties. I was fresh to def, mate! Totally slammin'!

I decided that I was going to be famous by getting on an episode of *The Fresh Prince of Bel Air*; all I had to do was write it! What I didn't know was by the time I was watching it, the series had been long canceled.

I wrote myself into a three-episode arc (I love that even while I'm imagining, my dreams are still completely realistic. Hey, I knew my strengths, but I had school, so I didn't want to completely ruin my education!) in which I play Ashley's (Will's little cousin) English tutor. Will then falls completely head over heels for me, we have a brief secret fling but then decide to break up because Ashley's education has to come first. How noble of me!

I also wrote a spin-off of *That's So Raven*, in which my character, Magpie, can see into the past; "That's So Magpie" was a cult hit in the Hughesy household—the mind-bending crossover episode where Raven looks into the future and sees Magpie for the first time was especially groundbreaking!

I also wrote stories for fun. I liked to imagine myself in cute scenarios where I was usually rich and famous and lived in America. There was one where I was Oprah's niece, and my friends and I were house-sitting for her whilst she had a boob job. We were supposed to be looking after her two dogs, Cookie and Cream, but instead we threw insane mansion parties and invited *NSYNC!

My writing got grittier as I got older, and at fifteen I wrote a three-part drama called "Street Life," which I got my cousins to star in alongside me. To this day, my cousin Leanne will tell you it's the best thing I've ever written and swears that accused and now-canceled writer Noel Clarke must've found it and used it as inspiration to write his hit movie *Kidulthood*.

3. Parental Pressure

You read all these horror stories about child stars and how their pushy overbearing parents forced them into the entertainment industry. WELL, I REALLY WISH MY PARENTS HAD DONE THAT. I was the one constantly telling *them* that I wanted to be famous, and they did next to nothing to help.

I remember having a very serious conversation with my mum, informing her that Britney Spears's career had been kicked-started after she made it onto *The Mickey Mouse Club* at twelve years old. I was already eleven and a half, so I truly believed in my heart of hearts that I had six months before I'd be too old to make it.

Of course, when I told my mum this, she laughed in my face. I remember being confused as to why my parents couldn't see what a star I was, or why they had no interest in helping me become one. I realized that I was clearly the only one willing to take my career seriously, so I sought out professional representation instead.

4. Getting an Agent

Ten-year-old me knew that most famous people had things called "agents." What I didn't know is what they were, or how you got one. But a small detail like that wouldn't stop me.

So in the nineties, before the internet, we couldn't just Google our favorite celebrity, find their agent, and track down their email. I had to really think long and hard about how to get an entertainment management company to notice me, and then it hit me. The one place all people go to find companies? The Yellow Pages! I stole my mum's Yellow Pages and looked under "agents."

Now, for future reference, there aren't any actual entertainment agents in the Yellow Pages, but there are . . . estate agents. Of course I did not realize that an estate agent literally had nothing to do with getting me onto an episode of *Barney*, so I rang every single estate agent in that phone book, put on my deepest, most professional voice, and asked if they could make me a superstar Black Britney Spears or a female Will Smith. It ended in Foxtons Estate agents banning my landline number from their call list and my mum grounding me for running up the phone bill.

5. Stalking Celebrities

Desperate times call for desperate measures. After all my writing, training, singing, dancing, and phoning, I had finally reached the age of twelve and I still wasn't famous. I had no choice but to do what I did next: write letters to celebrities and beg them to put me on their TV shows.

The first celebrity I decided to write to was Will Smith— hey, might as well start at the top. Now, I knew after the estate agent fiasco that there was no way that my mum or dad had Will Smith's address, so I was going to need to source that information myself.

I watched every episode of *The Fresh Prince of Bel Air* for clues and after nearly six seasons and over one hundred episodes, all I could deduce was that Will Smith lived with his aunty and uncle in a mansion in Bel Air. But then I noticed that after every episode, the end credits would flash up on the screen pretty fast. I assumed that that must have been because they showed the actors' and actresses' addresses, and they probably did not want everyone to see them. So one day, I got a pen and paper, sat as close to the TV as possible and tried my best to make out the graffiti yellow and pink wording as the end credits flashed on the screen. I did this several times.

It was a very hard task, but one day I clocked it: I saw a logo and the words Buena Vista Studios flash up on the screen. I immediately wrote it down and figured that **Will Smith, Buena Vista Studios, Bel Air, America** would be enough for the postman to get this letter directly to the Fresh Prince himself.

Now all I had to do was write the letter. To this day I don't remember exactly what I wrote, but I remember exactly how I felt; and at that time I felt that all Will Smith had to do was know who I was and he'd immediately make me a star.

I just had to use the letter to convince him to meet me in person, and once he'd done so he would put me on the show. I even included my three-episode story arc as proof of my professionalism and to show him who my character could be. I stole one of my mum's stamps from her letter drawer and posted it in my nearest mailbox. I was so fucking excited I couldn't sleep. That week, whilst I waited for a response from Will, I trained extra hard for my six-pack, and I even made sure I knew *The Fresh Prince of Bel Air* theme tune rap by heart, just so when fame came a-knocking, I was ready to open the door!

A week went by with no response. That's fine, America is far away, I'll give it another week. Another week goes by—totally fine, he's a busy guy, I'll give it until the end of the month. Three months went by and by then I was absolutely distraught. That was it. My dreams were over, I was never going to be famous in America and I was never going to meet Will Smith.

I grew up a lot in those three months. I realized that my American dream may have been too much of a huge reach, and then the walls all came crumbling down when I found out that *The Fresh Prince of Bel Air* had ended. My dreams were dust. I couldn't be on a show if it doesn't exist.

I cried and cried and cried. My mum thought I was overreacting. Looking back, she probably thought I was crying because I was a brain-dead television-obsessed hormonal preteen. My mum was a workaholic and she believed that the only way to achieve anything in life was through hard work. She used to hate that my brother and I watched so much television, so much so that whenever she saw us zonked out in front of the tube, she would yell, "Why are you still watching the TV? Those people on the TV screens are working—they're actually doing something with their lives! What are you doing with your life?"

Bit of a harsh thing to say to a twelve-year-old; it's not like I could exactly go get a job! But what my mum didn't realize was I *was* doing something with my life: I was essentially planning my future career. But now I was devastated because I'd just lost my meal ticket.

6. Celebrity Stalking Part 2

A few months went by, and my American dream disintegrated and turned into an English hope: I focused on getting on an English TV show, but not many English TV shows had people of color in them. My best bet was *EastEnders*, but they already had a Black child character named Billie. After a while, I realized that I'd probably missed my chance—I couldn't think of any British TV show that would want or need a twelve-year-old Black girl from South London.

But then I came across *Lenny Henry in Pieces*. *Lenny Henry in Pieces* was a late-night BBC One comedy sketch show hosted by Sir Lenny Henry and featuring some of Britain's best Black comedic talent—and on that show was a wonderful comedian named Gina Yashere. Gina was the first-ever British comic to make me laugh. Like I said before, back then, there were few to no Black people on UK television. So much so that when they did pop up on TV, it was an event! I remember the whole family and our neighbors gathering around ours just to watch the first Black contestant on *Gladiators*. You would have thought we all knew the man the way we cheered for him when he did well, and then all gasped in horror when he finally got caught by the big bad Wolf!

I was in awe of Gina Yashere. She had her own segment on *Lenny Henry in Pieces* and did this sketch where her character's punchline was "I don't think so!" It was so hilarious. She was the funniest woman I'd ever seen. Plus, she had a thick London accent and she looked just like me. She was a dark-skinned Black woman on TV being funny! Seeing her on that show did more for me and my hopes and dreams than any BBC diversity outreach program ever could. I would say her catchphrase over and over again to make my school friends laugh. I wanted to be just like Gina Yashere. I needed to get on that Lenny Henry show.

Now, after being well and truly burned by Will Smith, my heart couldn't take any more celebrity rejection, so I spoke to my mum about it—and to my surprise, she assured me that not only did she know Lenny Henry, but she also had his address! I was beyond happy!

FYI THESE WERE ALL LIES.

I'm sure at the time my mum probably thought it was cute to lie to her daughter. A bit of harmless fun, like I was sending letters to Father Christmas or something, but what she didn't fully realize was that I was trying to lay the foundations to cement my future career in entertainment and she was being the enemy of progress!

I wrote a deep and meaningful letter to Lenny Henry telling him why I would be great on his show, and lo and behold, Sir

Lenny Henry wrote me back (in my mum's unique handwriting, not that I noticed). He told me to never give up and to always work hard and follow my dreams.

Well, Lenny, that wasn't quite the answer I was looking for, so I wrote to him again, this time making it FULLY clear that he needed to meet me and put me on his show. He wrote back saying that he promised he'd do that one day.

And that, ladies and gents, was enough for me! A handwritten confirmation that Lenny Henry himself would have me on his show in the near future. I'd done it! After years and years of training and hoping and wishing, I'd finally done it! I was going to be a comedy star on BBC One with Lenny Henry and Gina Yashere!

I started writing sketches for them to include in the show, I started practicing all my impressions (I could do a really good one of Scooby-Doo). And very soon I was ready; I was ready to make my BBC One debut.

Lenny Henry In Pieces aired for two series and then got canceled. There was no word from Lenny.

I cried again. Years later, my mum eventually confessed that she had been the one writing the Lenny letters, and then five years after that, the real Lenny Henry hired me to star in his sketch series. But more about that later.

Chapter 3

I'm a Lover, Not a Fighter

THE POPULAR PEOPLE IN SCHOOL NEVER GROW UP TO BE THE POPULAR PEOPLE IN LIFE

...Is a sentence I repeatedly told myself throughout secondary school. It's true—some of the most famous people in the world were unpopular at school, from Lizzo and Mark Zuckerberg, to even the fabulously amazing female comic London Hughes—but that doesn't mean I believed it back then.

I think everyone deals with bullies in their own way, but as far as I knew, I really had only three options: ignore them, tell a teacher, or fight them. Now, I'd already tried these options several times and none of them worked well for me.

Parents always tell kids to ignore bullies, but how are you supposed to ignore someone that you legally have to see five days a week!? Fighting a bully was not in the cards for me, either, as I have very tiny wrists. I'm a lover, not a fighter; the only things I'll fight are parking tickets and sleep. And the one time I tried to tell a teacher that a girl was bothering me, the girl denied it and we both ended up in detention—and then she bullied me whilst in detention!

So it'll be no surprise to you that in order to deal with the bullies, I had to invent a new technique: I decided to make them laugh.

As you know, I was inspired by hilarious comedy legends and confident and charismatic on-screen TV heroes, who as far as I could tell were fazed by no one and marched to the beat of their own drum. I wanted to be like them so badly, but I didn't have the confidence of the Fresh Prince or the sassy charm of Raven Symone. After all, I was an eleven-year-old girl with asthma, mild eczema, and previously mentioned very tiny wrists. I knew that if I was going to be like the badass characters I saw on TV, I had to try to emulate them in real life. To do this, I had to completely reinvent myself, but that was easier said than done.

The problem with trying to reinvent yourself at age eleven is you have no idea who you really are yet—and to figure out who I was going to become, I first had to figure out who I was, which meant me and my parents had to endure several weird and wonderful phases of me simply figuring this shit out.

WHO WAS LONDON HUGHES?

Eleven-year-old London Hughes was definitely a white girl named Emily. Emily was my best friend at the time, and I thought she was cooler than a Charizard Pokémon shiny! Emily was a swimmer, so I swam (okay, tried to swim; I was very good at drowning); she listened to alternative pop rock, so Avril Lavigne lived in my head rent-free for most of the summer holidays. Emily was tall and blonde and looked like some of my favorite idols; you know, the usual suspects: Britney, Christina, Sabrina the Teenage Witch. Blonde white women were deemed the "popular ones": on TV, and my God, I craved popularity like Donald Trump craves attention.

It's this hunger for popularity that led to my first-ever best friend breakup. You see, even though Emily had all the physical attributes that would make her popular in a '90s sitcom—tall, blonde, white, pretty, and super smart—by school social standards she was a total nerd (or neek, as we called them back then), and if Emily was a nerd, that meant that by association I was a nerd, too! We were at the bottom of the school social hierarchy, but I had a plan to change that. I was going to make us both popular by becoming popular myself first. It was foolproof.

The popular girls were a bunch of terrifyingly mean but drop-dead gorgeous Black girls, and, reader, I vowed to become one of them.

Thirteen-year-old London Hughes was a Black girl named Latoya. Latoya was my primary school frenemy. I hated and worshipped her with equal measure. She was stunning and smart, boys liked her, she had the best trainers, her mum let her use relaxer on her hair, and she wore real gold jewelry to school. Latoya had been popular from birth; I'm pretty sure she walked out the womb with the latest Nike backpack. She was everything thirteen-year-old me dreamed of being! Latoya was so popular that when she announced to the class which high school she would be going to, every girl copied her, myself included. I hadn't even heard of the school, but I knew that if that's where Latoya was going, then that's where I needed to be.

I used to be friends with her in primary school because her little brother was in the same class as my little sister and hanging with Latoya was an adventure. She could be sweet and then salty: she was the type of girl to help you with a math question and then openly mock your "busted" school shoes. Even though at any moment she could make me feel completely worthless, I adored being in her orbit. I'd felt the warm glow of her popularity shine on me a couple of times when I was around her and I bloody loved it.

By the time we got to high school, Latoya's popularity had completely blown up. She even had her own entourage, a rotating group of beautiful badasses that she rolled with who were Rihanna-eating-an-ice-lolly-in-a-Gucci-bikini cool. It was pretty clear to me that Latoya was in the big leagues, and my league, by comparison, was as tiny as my wrists. I had to level up.

To get in with Latoya and her crew I had to first observe them. Oh, how I loved to observe them. They were typical South London schoolgirls: short skirts, short ties, hair gelled to perfection, a Chupa Chups lollypop positioned in each afro ponytailed puff, acrylic nails with the latest designs, and Clark's Wallabee shoes on their feet. Iconic. They oozed cool from their nails and their hairstyles to the way they spoke and the music they listened to. I knew if I was going to fit in, I had to move just like they did; knowing the words to "Sk8er Boi" by heart just wasn't going to cut it, mate.

This is going to hurt a few feelings, but in the early 2000s if

you were a Black school kid in London, you were either Jamaican or pretended to be Jamaican. The worst thing you could
admit to being was African. I know! I know! But kids in the
early noughties were nowhere near as woke as they are now. For
whatever reason, being called African was an insult. I mean, it
didn't help that the media often likes to portray Africa as a third-
world continent full of Black people with flies on their faces,
instead of a rich and vibrant melting pot of culture and wealth. I
guess children pick that shit up! Anyway, being called an "African booty scratcher" was the highest form of insult. I didn't even
know what it meant, I just knew that if someone called you one,
the whole class would burst out laughing and you'd get to leave
school early due to being so distressed. Kids are cruel.

So being Jamaican or having access to Jamaican culture was
the only way to get respect. I figured it was because—and as a
Jamaican I may be being a bit biased here—1) we have the best
music, 2) we have the best food, 3) we have the best fashion, and
4) *Cool Runnings*. Latoya and her entourage were all Jamaican,
or at least claimed to be (I'm pretty sure Adenike was Nigerian,
but she could do a pretty spot-on Bob Marley impression, so
they let her slide). My mum was born in Jamaica so I had an
advantage, and I knew it would be my only way to infiltrate the
group.

The biggest bully in terms of capacity for cruelty and in bra
size was a girl (or should I say woman; she honestly looked about
twenty-six) named Amanda. Amanda was *very* Jamaican—she
was actually born there—so in school popularity ratings she was
basically the Pope.

At lunch, Amanda and her friends would take over the

classroom and dance to the latest Jamaican reggae, bashment,[1] and dancehall songs.

Amanda knew how to do every dance move to these songs to perfection and she'd show all the girls how to dance like a true bashment queen. I would watch on in awe as all the popular girls fawned over Amanda as she dutty wined, willy bounced, and logged on (all popular dance moves, look 'em up). Even though I had an extensive jazz, tap, ballet, and modern dance background (and killed it in the aforementioned all-Hindu dance troupe), I had never actually danced like an extra in a Sean Paul music video before; but I knew that the key to popularity was to watch and learn.

I went home that day and danced my ass off. I applied the same kind of determination to mastering those Jamaican dance moves as I did to trying to become famous. I danced all over the house: I was grinding and twerking on the stairs, on the sofa, on a chair. I even tried twerking while in a handstand and nearly broke the left side of my face! By the end of the night, after hours of what I can only describe as seriously sexual dancing, I'd mastered those moves. I was officially a Dancehall Queen! (Okay, Dancehall Princess; I still hadn't landed that twerking in a handstand move.) The next step was to show off my newfound skills in front of all the popular girls. Obviously, I didn't sleep that night.

---

[1] Sidenote: Early noughties dancehall music went through an era called bashment. Bashment songs were based on fun elaborate dance moves, which would be mentioned in the song, and you had to do them, a bit like a Jamaican Simon Says. For research, look up Elephant Man's "Pon de River, Pon de Bank" music video. Great times, sexy stuff; try not to hurt yourself.

I walked into school the next day with the confidence of a thousand naked Nicki Minaj's. When lunchtime finally came, Amanda was holding court in her usual spot and dancing to the very popular track "Get Busy" by Sean Paul. She had all the moves from the video down, but little did she know that so did I. A circle of girls soon formed around Amanda and I let her have her well-deserved moment before I tried to step into the circle myself. Bad move. Amanda pushed me out immediately and my heart instantly dropped into my vagina.

"Er, what do you think you're doing?!" To be honest, for a split second I asked myself the same question. Amanda was looking at me like I'd just spat in her hair and my inner voice was screaming at me: "Run! Leave! Dutty wine away!", but I stood firm.

"I can dance, too, Amanda," I feebly insisted, as my armpits started sweating uncontrollably. Amanda laughed in my face.

"This shit ain't the Spice Girls, this is Sean Paul!"

She pushed me away again and all the other girls in the circle fell over themselves laughing. Just the thought that I was even attempting a dance-off with Amanda was comical to them. My armpit sweat had fully saturated my school shirt.

Welp, you tried, I thought. That was more than enough confrontation for one day. I wasn't about to get beaten up trying to show Amanda my perfect willy bounce! My tiny wrists!

I retreated, embarrassed, tears building in my eyes, ready to give it all up and move to Jamaica myself, but then I heard a sweet voice. It was Latoya's.

"Nah, man, let her dance." It was the most beautiful sentence I'd ever heard. I turned around in shock and Latoya smiled at me. "Come on, then. Show us, innit." Another beautiful sentence.

Amanda kissed her teeth and gave me a dirty look, but she stepped aside. The other popular girls were already sniggering as Amanda started "Get Busy" from the beginning. I started nodding along to the beat. More laughter. I knew that if I didn't absolutely nail this routine not even the great Sean Paul himself could save me.

I had to go big or go home. The beat started to ramp up, so I wiggled my hips a bit. More laughter. But the laughter gave me an idea; I decided to use it to my advantage, so I started dancing badly on purpose: off beat, stiff, awkward, just terrible. Amanda nearly choked she was in hysterics and the rest of the girls were crying with laughter. When I felt that they'd all had sufficient time to catch their breath, I grabbed a chair and did the sexiest, most X-rated, wine, twerk dance move ever seen from a thirteen-year-old girl. Honestly, it looked like something out of *Magic Mike XXL*. Amanda looked like she'd just swallowed a goldfish and the whole room erupted! They were screaming, cheering, whooping, I think someone even threw their school bag in the air! They had no idea I'd had it in me, and to be honest neither did I.

Everyone started shouting, "BEWWW BEWWW!"

Out loud it sounds like booing, but in the early 2000s among Black school kids from South London, "BEWW" was the biggest compliment. It was the height of cool. I was the height of cool. I was finally popular.

Unfortunately, that popularity lasted only twenty-four hours because by the next day at school nobody cared. I kept trying to bring it up, like "Hey, remember the time yesterday when I out dancehall queened Amanda?!" But no; I was yesterday's news. The good thing was Latoya and her entourage slowly started acknowledging me in public, and I was confident it wouldn't be long before they would let me in their crew. I didn't know it then, but by the end of that year I'd achieve everything high school me had ever I wanted: I'd eventually become popular, I'd have my first kiss, I'd have my first fight and end up leaving that school for good. But I had a few challenges to get through first.

I'VE GOT VERY TINY WRISTS

I used to hate confrontation. I was petrified of it. It was so bad that I'd let myself get walked all over, then I'd replay the encounter back in the shower the next day and absolutely demolish my opponent with my imaginary comebacks. There were many times at school that I should have stood up for myself, and my inability to do so would follow me all the way into adulthood and into my comedy career (more on that later). It was a shitty time, but hey, it makes the story all the sweeter when I eventually come out on top.

THE POPULAR GIRLS VS.
THE PEPPERONI PRINCESS

Disclaimer: This is an experience of bullying, and you may end up feeling sorry for me after you've read it. Please don't; it was shit, but it was character building. I know I seem amazingly confident now, but I wasn't always, and I want you to know that if you relate to the girl in this story right now, it doesn't always have to define you. You will become the badass king or queen you want to be, I assure you.

It was my thirteenth birthday, and my mum said I could have a party at Pizza Hut with no adults! Having a Pizza Hut party was the more sophisticated, grown-up version of a McDonald's party. It was a rite of passage, plus they had an all-you-can-eat ice cream station, which is the childhood equivalent of a free bar. That, plus zero adult supervision, equals a very, very classy party. I could picture it perfectly: just a bunch of independent gals, gossiping and munching on pizza like a scene from *Sex and the City*!

My mum said I could invite ten friends and I was over the moon—but there was a catch. She couldn't afford to pay for all ten meals, so she agreed to give me money to pay for everyone's drinks and ice cream, but not for all the individual pizzas. Now, we were all teenagers and got pocket money, and pizzas were only £4.99 back then, so I didn't think that asking my friends to pay for their own pizzas would be an insane ask; but I'd forgotten one important thing: teenage girls are bitches.

In my attempt to be popular (yes, I was always trying to be popular), I asked my actual friends and some of the popular girls to come. My friends were all excited and had no problem with paying for their pizzas, but the popular girls weren't exactly thrilled at the idea; actually, they were downright insulted.

"We ain't going to no cheap birthday party!" Even though that sentence didn't grammatically make sense, it still cut me deep. The thought of going to Pizza Hut and having to pay for their own pizzas was "disrespectful," so they all turned down my invite. I didn't tell my mum what they said. I decided to shrug it off and enjoy the day come what may. I just hoped most of my friends would turn up and I'd have a good time regardless.

The day came and I got to Pizza Hut, put on my birthday crown, and waited patiently for my table of ten to arrive. I had deliberately over invited in case some people didn't show up and expected maybe one or two empty seats. I had nine empty seats. It was just me, my then-bestie, Emily, and my deep crust Pepperoni Lover's pizza. Apparently, word had gotten out about my "disrespectful" birthday invite, and the popular girls had made it their mission to convince the rest of my classmates not to go. It worked. An hour went by, and I was sitting amid lots of tear-soaked pizza crusts, feeling very full and very sorry for myself. But then it got worse.

My mum turned up to surprise me and, as she arrived, I burst into tears of embarrassment. I didn't want my mum to see me this way, surrounded by carbs and empty seats. At the same moment, the door swung open and about twenty of the popular girls and every other girl I had invited to my party piled in. At first, I was so happy; they had changed their minds and finally come to their senses and realized they were being childish and . . . Oh no, actually: the exact opposite.

All the girls had come to embarrass me further. They sat at the table opposite mine and mocked my pitiful attempt at a party. They literally showed up just to mock me—and here's the kicker: they then all ordered and paid for their own pizzas! What did I say: bitches. They laughed and pointed at me until my mum grabbed my things and escorted me out of the restaurant in tears. I didn't even get to eat my free unlimited ice cream!

As I cried in the shower the next day, I acted out what I would have said to those heartless beasts. I felt so sorry for myself, but when I reflected back on that time later on, I realized they were the ones I should have felt sorry for, because even at thirteen years of age, there was something about me just being myself that got to those girls. I think they might have been jealous, but at the time I believed I truly had nothing to be jealous of—my parents were comfortable but they didn't make the most money, I was nowhere near the cutest, I was a nerd, and I had really tiny wrists—but for whatever reason something about me bothered them. What was it about me? I didn't know, but whatever it was would continue coming up through my school years, into university, and beyond.

Chapter 4

The Boy Is (Not) Mine

The second time I should've stuck up for myself involved a boy: a very cute Year 8 boy all the girls fancied named Jaden. I went to an all-girls' school, and if you didn't know, all-girls' schools are filled with horny girls, lesbians, and horny lesbians. Whenever the boys from the nearest boys' school showed up outside our gates, it created absolute teenage girl hysteria.

One of the main focuses of our collective obsession was a Black Justin Bieber-gone-bad hunk of a fifteen-year-old named Jaden. I had never seen Jaden in real life, I'd just heard of him; he was mythical, like Black boy Bigfoot, but apparently he was "buff," which was South London girl slang for "hot" and he was in a gang, which basically meant he was Tupac. He was like schoolgirl catnip and essentially the opposite of me in every way. I was not considered buff or "fine," although I did have a very fine eczema rash on my forehead and neck that no amount of Diprobase cream could control. I was, however, in a gang. It was a library gang. We called ourselves the

Roald-Dawgs, as speed-reading Roald Dahl's books was our forte. There was even one summer where we read *Esio Trot* backward. Fucking cool.

All that to say Jaden was hot and I was not, which is why I was surprised when, as I was walking to school on a gray Thursday morning, I heard a young man's voice: "Excuse me." I carried on walking; he couldn't have been talking to me. Boys didn't talk to me—the most action I'd had was when old Pastor Humphries gave me a long hug goodbye in Bible class. "Oi, miss. Excuse me, I'm talking to you." Was he actually talking to me? I was the only miss around. I slowed down.

"Oi, browning!" Okay, he was definitely talking to me.

When boys found girls attractive back then, they would put them in categories according to the color of their skin (I know, terrible). So there were "lighties," lighter-skinned mixed-race or Black girls; and there were "darkies," a derogatory term for darker-skinned Black girls. Being called a lighty was a compliment and being called a darkie was an insult, and then there were "brownings." A browning was the range between light and dark skin and being called one was often seen as a compliment. I'd been referred to as a browning before but never by a boy. I stopped in my tracks.

"Are you talking to me?" I stuttered.

"Yeah, babes. Couldn't you hear me calling you buff ting?"

BUFF TING. Never in the history of man has a phrase so penetrated my prepubescent soul.

I instantly became moist, everywhere. But there was more.

"I'm Jaden, what's your name?" My tongue immediately

went dry and got caught in my throat. THE JADEN RICH-ARDS had just called me A BUFF TING. I looked around thinking it was some kind of joke and I was on an episode of *You've Been Framed!*, but no, we were alone, and in real life one of the hottest boys in Thornton Heath went out of his way to call me, London Hughes, the girl who wasn't quite sure if she'd even remembered to put on deodorant that morning, a "buff ting." Jaden asked me for my number, I gave it to him, he said he'd text me. I floated all the way to school.

School went by like a blur. It had been a couple of weeks since my dancehall infiltration and the popular girls were starting to give me the time of day. I was still doing my best to impress them, walk like them, talk like them, and dress like them, and although I was a bit rusty, to the untrained eye it actually looked like I was fitting in. I knew they would just die once they heard this Jaden story. It would be like getting a badge (or vaj) of honor.

I was bursting to tell them, but I had to drop the news in the best way possible for maximum cool points. I thought about the delivery over and over again, but in the end it all came out in my food technology class whilst I was no doubt burning some Cornish pasties. My Nokia 3410 buzzed, it was a text from Jaden: FINKIN OV U :-) X

Poetry, pure poetry. Amanda was my partner in class and noticed my huge grin. "Er, what man are you texting?"

I guessed now was as good a time as any, so I went for my big reveal!

"Jaden chirpsed me on my way to school this morning!" I beamed ("chirpsed" was South London slang for someone asking you for your number). I was just happy that I used the word correctly and in context; I was firing on all cylinders today!

"Jaden who?" Amanda scoffed. What a bitch! She knew exactly which Jaden I was talking about. I guess she still hadn't forgiven me for the dance-off.

I fired back with "Y'know, Jaden. Jaden, innit." Again, 10/10 for delivery and execution.

I was trying my best to seem aloof about the whole thing, like hot high school bad boys asked me for my number all the time, but Amanda wasn't buying it.

"There ain't no way that Jaden Richards asked you for your number, no offense."

Ooh, the no-offense technique. It's the perfect way to deliver an insult so cutting and deadly without actually having to apologize for it afterward. The no-offense technique is how high school girls have been arguing for centuries. I'm sure early cavewomen would have said "no offense" right after insulting their neighbor's cave decor.

"Well, he did. He even texted me." I showed Amanda the text, and she immediately whipped out her phone to check the number, paused in shock and then burst out laughing. She whispered something to the popular girls who happened to be eavesdropping nearby and they all giggled whilst I fidgeted in my seat.

"He only chirpsed you for a joke," Amanda snapped back. "He don't like you. You're butters, no offense."

Translation: He got your number for a joke. You are extremely ugly. Don't take offense. Well, offense was taken, hun. I could feel the spikes of tears at the back of my eyes, but I stopped them because I know that I definitely didn't imagine what Jaden had said! I looked down at my feet as I thought up a defiant reply, but Amanda chimed in again.

"Okay, I'm gonna text him." Amanda sent Jaden a text asking him if he liked me, and in true fuckboy fashion, he denied it!

Jaden texted back: NO WAY, SHE'S BUSTED* (*See: butters). Amanda showed his reply to all the girls in the class and they fell over themselves laughing. Come to think of it, kids laughed at me a lot back then—no wonder I'm a comedian.

Amanda smiled as she delivered the final blow: she told me that Jaden was coming after school to tell me in person to delete his number from my phone. I left class in tears. My Cornish pasties were burned beyond recognition.

Word got round of mine and Jaden's interaction and the rest of the day was filled with girls sniggering, pointing, and immediately going silent as I walked by. Matters got worse when Jaden did indeed show up after school. Amanda took me by the shoulders and marched me up to him like I was a prisoner about to meet my maker. He looked gorgeous, and slightly nervous, which isn't surprising since we were surrounded by about twenty popular girls, who goaded Jaden to publicly humiliate me. He snatched my purple Nokia 3410 out of my hands and deleted his number from it. I could tell he felt bad, but the little prick still did it. He could have stood up to them or had my back, but I guess his popularity meant more than my feelings.

Amanda was grinning from ear to ear. I kept telling myself to do something or say something. I really wish this was like the part of a coming-of-age movie where the main character stands up for herself, but instead I just ran home in tears. I saw Jaden a few times after that, but he never had the guts to say anything to me that even resembled an apology, even though I could see on his face that he was sorry. Whatever, I bet he's got a tiny dick.

Although the whole experience was truly harrowing, it did make me realize one thing: I was actually attractive. I know it's sad that I looked to the likes of Jaden Richards for validation, but even though those girls were mean to me, it didn't take away from the fact that the hottest guy I'd even spoken to had asked me for my number. Something changed in me after that day. I realized that I had an effect on the opposite sex, and maybe in time I may be seen as cute, pretty or, dare I say it, sexy.

TRYING TO BE SEXY

I loved sex. For someone who hadn't ever had it or seen it up close, I was obsessed with it. Some kids wanted to be a doctor, or invisible, when they grew up, whereas I wanted to be a . . . hoe!

My actual hoe phase wouldn't come until much later, so I call this part of my life "pre-hoe." I knew that when the time came for me to have sex, I needed to actually be good at it, so I decided to do my research.

BARBIE DOLL BUKKAKE

I used to share a room with my older brother and sometimes I would dig out the old porno mags he kept under his bed. I was fascinated by them. It was all just so . . . SEXY! I couldn't name the feeling I got when I saw them, but my heart would beat faster, and I'd giggle to myself. Overall, looking at naked ladies made me feel SEXY and empowered. I got the same feeling the first time I heard the song "Don't Let Go" by En Vogue; now that is a very sexy song. I remember swinging my hips, popping my nonexistent boobs out to the beat, and strutting around the living room like a dominatrix. I got a similar feeling whenever I saw Jet from *Gladiators* or Pamela Anderson—they were just sexy. And up until Jaden had asked me for my number, I thought I was not.

My sexy research led me to Channel 5 at 11:00 p.m. on Friday nights, which is where I discovered the word "erotica" and the term "blue movies."[2] The late-night Channel 5 blue movies were beautiful, and bingeing on them as a kid shaped how I view porn today. They were so romantic, there was always a good storyline and a strong buildup toward the actual sex—you'd always know it was coming because you'd hear a saxophone playing a sweet melody in the background. Nowadays, if my porn doesn't have a solid backstory, I'm not watching it. I need to know why the wife is sleeping with her husband's best friend while he's at work. What inciting incident led her to that point?!

My mother was and still is a bit of a Prudy Judy, so it's no wonder that I was so into sex. She'd always tell me that I could talk to her about sex whenever I wanted, and yet whenever a

---

[2] Also, I want to give a special mention to the weird porn-based chat show *Eurotrash* on Friday nights on Channel 4; to this day I have no idea what that show was actually about, but boy did I learn a lot from it. I once saw a woman on that show put a baseball bat all the way up her vagina, and in that instant I learned 1) that women could do that and 2) that I never ever would.

couple so much as heavily kissed or started taking their clothes off on TV she would say, "Ooh, that's a bit much" and "Can they show this type of stuff on telly at this time?!"

My sex obsession was my little secret; well, mine and my Barbie dolls'. I used to have a very enviable Barbie collection, and for that I want to thank my grandma Doreen, God rest her soul. I had every Barbie imaginable: Beach Barbie, limited edition Esmeralda from *The Hunchback of Notre Dame* Barbie, Black Graduation Barbie with cap and gown and diploma included. Every single one of those Barbies ended up having wild sex parties with Ken. I only had one Ken and one of my brother's wrestling figurines, and those two tag-teamed the lot of 'em. Oh, the positions I put them in! The *Kama Sutra* ain't got nothing on a horny nine-year-old with an active imagination.

Once I got too old for Barbies, I moved on to my teddy bear. I had a giant pink teddy bear—it was huge, taller than me—and I don't remember his name, so let's just call him Marcell. I used to pretend Marcell was my husband. Marcell and I did things no one should do with a stuffed animal. To quote En Vogue, there was some "love making, heart breaking, soul shaking"! Well, at least that's what I thought I was doing; I'd never had sex and still hadn't seen it in full (the blue movies never actually showed the peen going into the vagine). Marcell and I had what eleven-year-old me interpreted as sex, which was me humping him repeatedly and saying "Oooh, baby." Great times, lots of fluff. I wonder how he's doing now?

The sexual fantasy going on in my head did not manifest itself in real life, even though I was a young sex goddess in training. Marcell and I were in a very loving relationship, but I still didn't know how to approach being sexy or even flirty with someone of the opposite sex.

That being said, I had many crushes, some of them way more intense than others.

The first major one I remember was on former UK prime minister Tony Blair. Seriously, Anthony Charles Lynton Blair lived in my eight-year-old head rent-free. I'd met him only once, but it was truly love at first sight.

I'm sure Tony won't remember me, but I sure remember him. We met the day he got into power, back in good old 1997. New Labour were doing a victory lap on a red open-top double decker bus around London, waving their red flags at all the supporters in the street. My mum was a huge Labour supporter (I feel like every Black person in the nineties was), and I remember standing on a busy street in Thornton Heath with her and waving a little red flag with a rose on it. At the time I hadn't a clue what was going on or why we were waving flags at a bus, but red was my favorite color and who doesn't love flags?! So I waved that thing around like I was doing a routine in the 1996 Olympics.

Well, my flag display must've caught Tony's eye, because all of a sudden the bus stopped right in front of me and a member of his team invited me and my mother on board. I walked up to the top of the bus, and there he sat, a pale, thin-lipped, sweaty white man. He seemed so happy, so friendly. I was in love. We posed for a picture, he shook my hand, and I sat on his lap. He smelled like peaches and success. My eight-year-old brain knew from that moment that he was the man I was going to marry. I was totally into politics after that. I was all in, I even had a Tony

Blair poster on my wall. My love for Tony went all the way up to the Iraq War. We had some good times, Tony and I.[3] It's a shame it ended the way it did.

After my love affair with Tony, I had to move on to more attainable suitors. It started off with cartoon characters at first. I had an on-again-off-again fling with Ace from the Gangreen Gang in *The Powerpuff Girls* and worked my way up to Shia LaBeouf in the Disney show *Even Stevens*. In these imaginary relationships my lovers and I would write letters to each other, have lots of sex, and travel the world, but in reality, if a boy I liked even so much as asked me for the time I'd choke on my Chupa Chups! I'd had many boyfriends in primary school well before I discovered my sexiness; we'd play Mums and Dads and get married with Hula-Hoop wedding rings. I even had an ex in Year 3 named Steven, who used to make me flowers out of pencil shavings. But as I got older and more mature, Marcell was still the closest I'd ever come to actually kissing and humping some-one's brains out; but that all changed once I finally became... popular.

It was a few months after the Jaden incident, and all was well with world: the popular girls were talking to me again, I'd forgiven them even though they hadn't apologized, and I was doing everything I could to stay on their good side. It's weird, you'd think after all the shit they put me through, I'd never talk to those Clarks-school-shoe-wearing-fake bitches again, and I'm

---

[3] Sidenote: I want to take this moment to apologize to Cherie Blair. Cherie, hun, I know you don't know me, but I literally hated you for years for no reason other than I wanted your man, and for that I apologize.

sure I probably told myself that I would do that. But even after all the tears I cried over them, the moment they smiled or said hi to me, it was like none of it ever happened. All was forgotten. I didn't care about the past, I was far too busy enjoying my new-found popularity and learning to gel down my baby hairs with a toothbrush. I was so in with the cool girls that I was actually getting invited to their parties now! And there was one party that I'll never forget.

I had been invited by Sandra, another one of the popular girls, to a party at her house. There weren't many of us—maybe eight or nine fully developed, sexually liberated fourteen- and fifteen-year-old girls (I was the only one there who had never worn a thong). I have no recollection of what we did at the party before the drama but I assume it was the usual fourteen-year-old girl stuff. We were all in Sandra's room, blah blah *NSYNC, blah blah charm bracelets, blah... when in walked a real-life dick-swinging human boy.

His name was Kane, and he was another bad boy from the school near ours. After what happened with Jaden Richards, I didn't even dare to make eye contact with Kane, but he was equally as cute and even more popular. The girls all laughed and joked around with him whilst I watched and said nothing. This went on for a while until Sandra's mum called us all downstairs. Kane was ordered to wait in Sandra's bedroom, as he'd snuck in without her mum noticing and she had no idea there were boys in the house. I was the last to leave Sandra's bedroom, but as I did, Kane grabbed my arm.

"Where are you going?" he asked, in such a sexy tone that—combined with his touch on my arm, and his scent of

Lynx Africa—did more things to me than Marcell the bear ever could.

I don't think any words had even left my mouth before he asked, "Are you ticklish?" He stood up, pushed me onto the bed, and started tickling me. I was a very ticklish person. My brother used to pin me down and tickle me all the time and I hated it, but when Kane did it, it felt like ecstasy.

"Stop it, Kane!" I giggled and he did just that: he stopped and then just lay on top of me, staring deeply into my eyes. I felt his boner poke me through my jeans. I don't think I even knew it was a boner at the time, I probably thought it was just his Sony Discman.

He straddled me, grabbed my arms, and pinned them down on the bed. "You sure you want me to stop?" he asked with all the sex appeal of a thousand post-*NSYNC Justin Timberlakes. I couldn't breathe, mainly because of my mild asthma, but also because I was incredibly scared and incredibly horny. I was scorny. I was alone in a room, on a bed, with a hot bad boy, and he could do anything he wanted to me. What if he wanted to have S-E-X? Would he be able to tell I'd only ever done it with my giant teddy bear? My heart was beating through my tits as he slowly lowered himself onto me and gently kissed me on my lips. My first-ever kiss from a real boy and not a teddy bear, my hand, or a Tony Blair poster! I'm not even sure if I did it correctly—my lips were definitely dry and my mouth was open from shock—and just as my lips were losing their virginity, Kelly walked in and Kane immediately jumped off me. Kelly was automatically suspicious.

"What are you two up to in here?"

Kane shrugged it off. "Nothing. Stop being so nosy, man."

I didn't actually have any breath left in my lungs to say any-thing, so I just silently left the room. Kane didn't look at me for the rest of the day.

The next day Kelly interrogated me on the way to school. "What were you and Kane doing in Sandra's bedroom?!"

At first, I just denied it, I didn't want a repeat of what hap-pened with Jaden, but this time felt different. Kelly was one of the nicer popular girls, I'd known her since primary school and even though she was mean-adjacent, I didn't think she was truly that bad. I thought I could tell her the truth, so I explained everything that went down.

"Oh my God, I can't believe he did that! Were you scared?"

Was I scared? Actually, I had been—I'm sure at the time my heart and vaj were beating too wildly to notice—but, yes, I was very scared.

I told Kelly the truth. "Kinda, yeah. I didn't know what he was gonna do to me! Thought he was gonna rape me or something!"

Okay, it was a poor choice of words and I was definitely exag-gerating. It wasn't rape. I didn't really know what rape was, but that was the closest I'd come to experiencing anything remotely like it.

Kelly was shocked and seemed very concerned. "Are you okay?"

I was okay; more than okay. I felt better for saying what had happened out loud to someone, because to be honest I was beginning to think I had imagined the whole thing.

"Don't tell anyone, please!" I begged Kelly.

"I won't," she replied. "You can trust me, it'll be our secret."
The lying little shit.

By lunchtime, every single girl in my class was talking about
me. "I can't believe she's chatting shit about Kane and saying he
raped her!"

It was the talk of the girls' toilets. I knew this because I
was sitting in a toilet cubicle when I overheard someone say:
"Rolanda is so vex with London for chatting shit about Kane,
she's gonna beat her up after school."

I fell off the toilet seat. The words "beat," "her," and "up"
really triggered me. I'd never been in a real fight before—like I
said, I'm a lover not a fighter. Also, getting beaten up because
a hot boy straddled me seemed completely unfair; but I'd completely forgotten about ... Rolanda.

Rolanda was a bully in training; she'd not quite got her full
bullying license yet, but I knew she'd been practicing, and she
was more than capable. Bottom line: Rolanda had a huge crush
on Kane, and even though Kane wasn't her boyfriend, and they
hadn't even kissed (I'm not sure he even really knew who she
was), she felt the need to defend him and score Brownie points
by smashing my fourteen-year-old head in. Good old girl code.

The fight was set for after school, and even though I tried
to avoid it, it was right there waiting for me. I walked out of the
school gates with two other popular girls who had taken pity
on me after my breakdown in the girls' toilets. "Rolanda won't
touch you! We've got your back." They sounded pretty convinc-
ing; I only wish it was true.

I was shoved in front of Rolanda as almost all the Black
girls in Year 9 circled around us. She was small at only four foot

seven, but she was mighty like a tiny Black Michelin woman. I was already crying as I begged Rolanda to leave me alone, but she was adamant that I was chatting shit about her man and for that I needed to get "boxed up."

She was goading me to hit her first, people were yelling "fight!", but I refused. I said, "I don't want to fight you. This is so stupid!" but she wasn't having it. She punched me right in my jaw. I stood firm (I've always had a very strong jaw) so she punched me again. I'm sure those punches hurt, but the adrenaline pumping through me meant that I couldn't feel a thing. All I remember saying is "Why are you punching me? Stop punching me!" We got into a sort of headlock situation that I quickly wriggled out of.

All of a sudden the schoolgirl onlookers gasped, and I looked up to see that, lo and behold, Kane had showed up on a bike, like my knight in shining armor coming to save me—or so I'd hoped.

Rolanda stopped attacking my head for a moment and Kane approached me, still on his bike. "London, did you say I raped you?" He looked very angry, although I couldn't tell what was real anger and what was for show.

"No, I didn't, I just said I thought you were going to…" I wanted to be honest, but then Rolanda got a second wind and decided to punch me again. She pushed me backward and a punch-push combo ensued. God, she was like Goku from *Dragon Ball Z*! I found the courage to push her off, but then the most shocking thing happened: Kane balled up his fists and punched me. I was so taken aback that I immediately dropped my school bag and took off running. Rolanda and half the crowd of girls around us chased after me, and so did Kane, still on his bike. Kane, not intent on just assaulting me, went even further and took off his belt, which had spikes on it, and started wielding it at me like a twisted slave master. I was running for my life. What the actual fuck.

Eventually, either because Kane got distracted or maybe I was just that fast, I reached the top of the road and he was gone, as were most of the girls. It was just me, Rolanda, and a few onlookers. Kelly had caught up with me and gave me my school bag that I'd dropped. "Kane was going to smash your phone, but I saved it," she announced, like I should have been grateful! She was the reason I was in this situation in the first place! I was a blubbering mess, and Rolanda seemed pretty pleased with herself.

"Stop crying, man. I'm not gonna hurt you anymore," she said, as if this had all been a complete overreaction on my part. And that was it. The drama was over. I'm not sure what it achieved, but I tried to control my tears as the remaining girls, Rolanda included, walked me home.

I told my parents what had happened and within days the police wanted to know if I wanted to press charges, but I didn't. My dad did make a visit to Kane's and Rolanda's home addresses, taking me with him so I got to watch them cry and squirm as their parents told them off. They were both grounded and suspended for a few days. My dad asked me to name every girl who either helped me or intervened in the fight so he could reward them. Kelly got gifted a twenty-pound WHSmith book voucher.

That fight signified the beginning of the end of my teenage years in South London. The writing was on the school wall because at that time, unbeknownst to me, my aunty had bought a hotel in Brighton, and she was begging my mum to move out there with her and help her run it. My mum was seriously considering the move to Brighton, but she wasn't sure if she should disrupt my schooling. After the fight, however, she knew Thornton Heath wasn't for us anymore—and to say I was excited to leave was an understatement.

Chapter 5

Brighton Rocks (Off)

Before moving to Brighton, I'd been there only for the odd weekend and to be honest I wasn't that impressed. First, it didn't have a sandy beach, which I think should be a prerequisite for anything called a "beach," and second, it was lacking Black people. When we first moved there, the only people of color were me, my mum, and Countdown Dave (the first Black man on *Countdown*). I was worried at first about whether I'd fit in, but my mum insisted that immersing myself into Brighton life would be a good thing. "It's good to experience different cultures," she told me, and she was right, because up until then I really had only hung out with Black people. My old school was about 75 percent Black and Asian, and the only white people in my life were Tony Blair, my ex-best friend Emily, and . . . My Grandparents.

I HAVE WHITE GRANDPARENTS!
(RIP Doreen and Bill)

I love telling the story of my white grandparents. One day I'll write a comedy based on their lives, because they are the definition of absolute legends. Having them in my life shaped how I view racism in Britain, and they are one of the major reasons I'm so vocal about race and diversity in my career. I couldn't kickstart a chapter about moving to the completely colorless town of Brighton and Hove without telling you about them first, so here's their story.

My dad was adopted when he was a baby. He never met his biological parents, but thanks to Doreen and Bill Hughes, he never needed to. My grandma Doreen loved children; she worked at a children's home and had fostered children of all races over the years. Eventually she decided to have a baby of her own, who grew up to be my incredibly wise, pipe-smoking, Cambridge University alumnus, Uncle Leigh, the literal definition of an English gentleman. After Leigh was born, my grandma was told she couldn't have any more children, so she and my granddad decided to adopt.

The only problem was that the children they decided to adopt were Black. Now, being Black in England at any time has its problems, but in 1959 it was terrible. Racism was rife, as were clashes with the police, the National Front, and the "No dogs, no Blacks, no Irish" ideology—all that bad stuff. There were the racists who'd call you the N-word in a malicious way, and then there were the racists who'd say racist things because they were ignorant and didn't know any better—but either way you looked at it, Britain was (and still is) racist.

My dad was a Black baby without a family in 1959, and if my grandparents hadn't adopted him, who knows what his future would have been. My dad believes he wouldn't have the amazing life or kids he has now if it hadn't been for them, and for that I'll be eternally grateful.

The other problem was that interracial adoption was illegal at the time. My grandparents went to court several times to adopt my dad before they eventually helped get the law changed and became the first white couple to adopt a Black child in the whole of Sussex. Told you they were absolute legends! My grandma told me her reason for adopting a Black child was because she knew their lives would be much harder. The woman at the adoption agency told her, "Oh, nobody adopts the colored children," and my grandma knew right then and there that she was supposed to adopt my dad.

Doreen and Bill adopted two Black children, my dad and my aunty Marion, and fostered many more over the years— much to my grandma's mother's horror. She was a very racist woman—the malicious kind, not the ignorant kind. She actually had a cat named Nigger, and when she heard that my grandma was adopting "nigger children," she disowned her. In fact, all my grandma's friends and family washed their hands of her and my granddad. My great-grandma didn't want anything to do with my dad or aunty Marion; she loved only my white uncle Leigh and made a habit of telling my grandma not to bring the Black kids over when she visited. My great-grandma was such a racist, petty bitch that at Easter she would buy only one Easter egg and would give it to my uncle Leigh in front of my dad and aunty. My grandma would then split the chocolate egg up and share it among the children. She let her mother know early on that she would have to welcome ALL her children, or else she would never see her grandson Leigh again—that's the only way my dad and aunty Marion were allowed into her home.

The racism was so real, but my grandma and granddad knew right from wrong. And let's be clear, Doreen and Bill Hughes weren't some woke revolutionary white people. They weren't part of any anti-racist group. They didn't even have any Black friends! They were just pretty ordinary, kind, generous people, who'd lived through the Second World War, had never left England their whole lives, and raised my dad to be an intelligent and proud Black man with traditional English values; that's what makes them so special.

Being Black with white grandparents shaped my view of Britain in ways I could never have imagined. I learned so much about British culture from them, the kind of stuff I just couldn't get from my Jamaican grandparents on my mum's side. Even when it came to race there were things I only noticed with my white grandparents; for example, my Jamaican grandma, Myrtle, was perfectly happy to buy me white Barbie dolls and I was happy to receive them—we saw nothing wrong with it! The Westernized image of whiteness was so acceptable and marketable that even a Black woman born in Jamaica felt that gifting her Black granddaughter a tiny plastic blonde white doll was perfectly fine.

My grandma Doreen, on the other hand, went out of her way to make sure I had Black dolls. There was one time when we were shopping in Gamleys toy shop (Crawley's version of

Hamleys—Crawley was where my dad grew up, a very white town near Gatwick Airport with not much going on) and she couldn't find any Black baby dolls. She asked the manager where all the Black dolls were and he looked confused and said they didn't stock any, to which she replied, berating him, "What doll am I supposed to buy for my Black granddaughter? They're all white! Don't you see the issue here?!" I never really saw the issue myself until she pointed it out.

My grandma Doreen was always doing things like that. My dad said when he was a kid, they were walking along the promenade in the seaside town of Margate, and some white ladies came over to him and started playing with his afro. They were poking and prodding and laughing in the usual 1960s Karen way—oh, the caucacity! But my grandma soon put a stop to it. She walked straight over to the Karens and started excitedly putting her hands in their hair. "See! How do you like it when someone does that to you!" she asked like a woke badass. The Karens, mortified, apologized and scuttled off. What a queen!

She even took on Sainsbury's. When my aunty Marion was eighteen, she applied for a job as a checkout girl at their local store. She got an interview, but when she showed up, they told her the position had been filled. The next week my aunty saw that Sainsbury's had taken out another ad, STILL looking for a checkout girl. It was pretty obvious that when Sainsbury's saw "Marion Hughes" on her CV, they assumed she'd be white, but decided she wasn't suitable when they saw her. When my grandma found out, she took it up with Crawley's race relations council, which was their first-ever case! In the end, Sainsbury's was made to apologize and give my aunty a job. She went on to be one of the best checkout girls that Sainsbury's had ever seen! My grandparents once heard a customer say they preferred going to the "colored girl on till number five" because she was quicker than all the others. You're bloody welcome, Sainsbury's!

I loved having such a diverse family, but Christmas was when I really noticed just how cool it was. Christmas was fun with white grandparents, as it meant I actually got to experience a White Christmas! Now, don't get me wrong, Caribbean Christmases are great, too—they're loud and fun and the food is ten times better—but Caucasian Christmases at my grandparents' were just like the ones I used to see on TV, even if the chicken did need way more seasoning. When we were all together, with my dad, Uncle Leigh, his family, and their parents, I'm sure we looked like some kind of Black elderly outreach program, but it didn't matter to us.

We'd love it when people tried to guess what linked us all together, although it was very awkward when people got it wrong. My grandma had lots of pictures of us all on her wall, and I shit you not, when people came over, they'd sometimes ask if we were her cleaners! To which she would reply, "No, they are my family, and I'd like you to leave!" My grandad Bill passed away in 2005 and my grandma Doreen passed in 2019. I miss them more than words can say. Total Legends.

THE HUGHES FAMILY TREE

Speaking of my diverse family, here's a bit of Hughes family history. My parents divorced when I was five years old and I'm so glad they did. I truly believe they were only meant to be together to conceive me and my brother Joel and had no business actually being married in the first place. David and Veronica (my mum and dad) are the total opposite of each other; they are both kind people with great morals and common values, but that's where the similarities stop. I always joke with my dad about how I can't believe they were a couple, and he always says, "See, that's why you should never make life choices about your partner when you're still in your twenties." He's right, I guess my twenty-year-old dad couldn't see just how different they really were. For starters, my mum's seven years older than him and was born in Jamaica. She moved to England when she was nine and with that move came a hard immigrant outer shell, so as soon as my mum could she prioritized hard work so she could provide for her children. My dad also worked hard, but he definitely prioritized spending time with his children.

My mum and I didn't have much fun together when I was a kid—we had birthdays, holidays, and special occasions—but day in and day out she was always working, which often meant I didn't see as much of her as I wanted. She was the manager of a retirement home, and three times a week she had to stay there overnight. On those days, my brother Joel and I went up the road to stay at my dad's house. He was a social worker, and he loved working with kids and spending time with his children, but he was way stricter than my mum was. He didn't tolerate any disrespect—to this day I have never raised my voice or even sworn in my dad's presence, and he in turn has never raised his voice or sworn at any of his kids. Also, my dad gave much better presents at Christmas. One year he got me a Sony PlayStation whilst my mum got me some knickers. My dad felt it was important to give kids presents they want, and my mum thought it was important to give kids presents they need; two different parenting styles, both great parents. I'm happy to say that they are now both remarried to the loves of their lives, and I got two amazing stepparents and two epic half-sisters out of their split.

Let's quickly break all the siblings down. I have two older brothers and two younger sisters—in age order they are:

ALEX (same mum, different dad)

JOEL (same mum, same dad)

SAKILÉ (same dad, different mum)

MAYA (same dad, different mum)

Maya, Sakilé, and I all have different mothers. Yes, I know it sounds like a storyline from *The Jerry Springer Show*, but we actually all get along. Our mothers are friends and I've always felt like I have three mums and two dads. Despite the many complicated branches, we're a very close family. Sakilé's recent birthday was a sight to behold; we were all together for the first time in a while and my dad watched on in horror as his wife, ex-wife, and baby mother all danced together to Sister Sledge's "We Are Family"!

We were a close, unconventional family, which is why my mum and I moving to Brighton and disrupting all that was a big deal. If it had been down to my dad, I would never have moved to Brighton; he felt it was too far away from London, and he didn't want to live more than five minutes away from any of his children. Luckily, he still had my brother Joel, who moved in with him to stay close to his high school. But as for me, my mum quit her job at the retirement home, packed all our things into a van, and we left Thornton Heath for good.

FROM LONDON TO BRIGHTON

I saw moving to Brighton as an opportunity to reinvent myself. I'd tried being popular and all that got me was beaten up, so this time I just tried . . . being myself.

It was very interesting moving to a seaside town after living in London. Brighton is so small in comparison; there's one road where all the clubs were, one shopping center, and one beach, so after a week I felt like I'd completed it. And it's small in other ways, too. The thing about people in small seaside towns is that some of them are quite small-minded. As I said before, we were two of the maybe three Black people in Brighton in the early 2000s and, boy, didn't we know it.

My new school was the biggest culture shock for me. It was called Falmer High School and it was in a very lower working-class white area called Moulsecoomb (which the locals had affectionately renamed Mouls-scum). It was the second-worst school in Brighton until the worst school burned down, and then it became the worst school in Brighton. It was so bad it didn't even have a proper school uniform; it was the first time I'd ever seen kids allowed to wear trainers to school. My dad was worried that leaving my problematic yet high-achieving all-girls' school and moving to Mouls-scum would hinder my good grades; he was right—it did—but luckily I didn't need them to become a world-famous stand-up comedian.

I was the only Black kid in the school, which proved confusing to the other kids. They thought I (on my own) was a gang! Okay, I'm exaggerating, but I did manage to convince several members of my class that I was a member of So Solid Crew. The kids at Falmer weren't smart at all; they made Gemma Collins look like Neil deGrasse Tyson. When I joined in Year 9, the head teacher told me I was one of the smartest kids in the school, full stop. Kids with grades like mine didn't go to schools like Falmer, but it was the only school that would accept me in the middle of the term. I decided to make the most of it and embrace it all, so I got to know the kids and they tried to get to know me. One thing that came up A LOT was the color of my skin.

Some of the Questions I Was Asked in My All-White School About My Blackness

"Why are you called Black when you're brown?"

"Your hair is spongy, is that what the inside of pillows are made from?"

"When you tan, do you go lighter?"

"Why can't I say the N-word?"

"Do you know Patrick from *EastEnders*?"

"Are you from Africa?"

"What's a 'bumbaclart'?"

"Did you get here by boat?"

"Is it okay if I say the N-word when I'm singing?"

"Have you ever heard a gunshot?"

"Why are your lips so big?"

"Have you ever been stabbed?"

I couldn't believe it! I'd left bullies in South London behind only to be met with racists in Brighton! I couldn't catch a break! The kids in my school in Brighton were so ignorant that my dad reckoned I experienced more racism at school in the 2000s than he did in the whole of the sixties! My friends at Falmer would call me Golliwog[4] all the time and I let them—I had no idea it was offensive. I had no idea what a Golliwog was; when you go to a predominantly Black school, you get to miss out on all the cool new racism.

My school was no less racist than its pupils; they were always getting it wrong. They once decided to celebrate Black History Month, because now they actually had a Black student (me), and they asked me and for some reason Vruiti, the only Asian girl in the school, to do an assembly on Black history and slavery. You ever seen a Hindu girl completely butcher Martin Luther King's "I Have a Dream" speech? Well, I have.

Racism aside, I quite enjoyed my time at Falmer High School. I stuck to the plan of just being myself and quickly made friends. I was always making my friends laugh, so much so that they started calling me Little Miss Jocelyn after comedian Jocelyn Jee Esien, who had a popular comedy show on BBC at the time. Now, this could be because they thought I was funny, but it could also have been because we were both Black women; I'll never know, but I loved the compliment all the same.

---

[4] The Golliwog was a big and Black and scary and sometimes dangerous fictional character made famous by Enid Blyton in her popular Noddy and Big Ears books. In one of the books, the Golliwog even stole Noddy's car. For some reason, Britain took a shining to the Golliwog characters and even made them into dolls and featured them on jam jars in the seventies.

What I didn't realize at first was that being Black in Brighton automatically gave me a "cool pass." To them, being Black WAS cool. I was the new Black girl whose family owned a hotel on the Brighton seafront, and it doesn't get any cooler than that.

Chapter 6

Hoe-Tel Life

The first hotel my aunty and mum ran together was called Pebbles Guest House. It was this huge eighteen-room boutique hotel, and my mum and I shared a bedroom in the manager's quarters. Looking back, I'm not sure what teenager would want to go from having their own room in London to sharing a room with their mother, but I really enjoyed it. My mum and I got closer, I was in a new town with new possibilities, and I just remember the whole thing feeling like one big adventure.

Pebbles was cool, but the fun really started when my mum bought her own hotel a few years later. It was called Ainsley House Hotel, and it was bigger and even more beautiful than Pebbles. It was right on the seafront and overlooked a private garden. I was so proud of my mum the day we moved in, and I just knew that we'd be happy there.

Around the time we moved, US rapper Cassidy had a hit song called "Hotel," which was all about bringing girls back to his hotel until six in the morning. That song became my unofficial anthem, and I'd devised a plan to somehow lose my virginity in my hotel. I was going to do it in Room 4, as it was the nicest room with its own Juliet balcony that overlooked the square. I wanted to lose it to someone cute and famous so all my mates would be jealous, and I'd finally become a sexy hoe.

It became increasingly clear to me that I wanted to be a hoe. I wanted to be the type of girl who had a crazy fun sex life and boys lusted after, but the reality couldn't have been further from that. I was still a virgin and had hardly been kissed, but thankfully I'd thrown out Marcell the teddy bear. Meanwhile, the one thing everyone I knew seemed to be doing was having sex. Everyone in my school was doing it—there's nothing to do in seaside towns but fuck! It got so bad they had to make a special sex education video especially for teens on the south coast, because girls in my class kept getting pregnant and dropping out of school. When word got out that my V-plates were still fully intact, I was given the nickname Fourteen-Year-Old Virgin. Kids are so cruel.

Even though I was absolutely obsessed with sex, the truth was I was way too scared to actually have it. The thought of a man's thingy fitting into my tiny hole excited, frightened, and outright confused me. I didn't understand how it wouldn't hurt. I used to watch women moan and groan in sex scenes on TV and think *There's no way that she's enjoying that! She must be faking!* But my new seaside friends and I talked about sex all the time. They'd all lost their virginity in very creative ways—in back seats of cars, car parks, and the toilets at McDonald's—but the most romantic place to lose your virginity was underneath Brighton Pier.

"If he likes yah, he'll finger yah under the pier," a friend said to me at the time. She made it sound so beautiful and romantic, but I wasn't quite sure. I didn't want anyone to finger me anywhere—just the sound of it hurt!

Brighton Pier is constructed of wooden planks and long steel beams planted deep into the sea, and all that was underneath the pier were those beams, freezing cold waves, and hard rocks and stones—hardly the place to be swept off your feet. Thankfully, I was never asked to get off with anyone down there; if I had I would have had to decline because I hate the cold and can't swim. But most of my Brighton friends had hooked up underneath the pier, and I would listen to all their sexy, cold stories. My mate got the nickname Dribbles because she gave head underneath the pier and dribbled excessively. To this day, I don't know her real name. I think it's Mary?

Anyway, I learned all about sex from my friends, which was a relief, because I wasn't getting much intel from my mum or dad. I had an honest group of female friends that were certified, fully-fledged hoes, and I was so jealous of them! They would teach me all about giving head, fingering, sex positions, and the art of having lots of sex without getting pregnant. They had it all figured out.

MY FIRST BLOW JOB

I was always told I had blow job lips, so I really wanted my first blow job to live up to the description. My blow jobbing skills used to be so pitiful because I had no idea what I was supposed to do! The first time a guy I liked got his dick out, he weirdly asked me for a "hand blow," which I think was supposed to be something between a hand job and a blow job. I literally took his dick in my hands and gently blew on it. He actually looked like he was enjoying it! But when I told my mates about it afterward, they burst out laughing. I don't know what they were laughing about to be honest—he still came, so job done, mate!

After that blow job fail, I practiced on cucumbers and Coke cans, and learned these crazy techniques you were supposed to know, like breathing through your nose and wrapping your tongue over the top of it! Sucking dick was hard! But I practiced and practiced and practiced to perfection, so that by the time I gave my next BJ I was so good at it, they nicknamed me The Seagull (because seagulls swallow their food whole. I think you get the picture).

B-TOWN BOYS

I never had an actual Brighton boyfriend. Not only was I still a virgin, but sixteen-year-old me soon realized another thing about living in Brighton: every kid my age had already had sex with everybody else in the neighborhood! If I so much as mentioned I even liked a guy, there would be two or three of my friends who had already been fucked or fingered by him. It felt too much like hoes stepping on toes, plus I did NOT find the typical Brighton boy attractive. Brighton boys were white wannabe bad boys who listened to rap and hip-hop, smoked weed, and wore Nike tn Air Max trainers—they just weren't cutting it for me. They weren't edgy like Kane and Jaden, none of the boys in my school were anywhere near smart enough, and a lot of them were gay! So I never really dated any B-town boys. To be fair, they didn't rate me in return. I was a nerd-turned-So-Solid-Crew-gang member who used to write *Frasier* fan fiction for fun.

I still loved writing stories. I would come home from school and let my brain transport me to different worlds. In my stories I was knee-deep in dude dick, I could be as confident as I wanted, fall in love, fall out of love, and be the leading lady of my own life. I wished that my life was as simple as my stories, but in reality I was still getting over the drama from my previous school, putting up with racial ignorance in my current school, trying to get an education, and sum up the courage to get a boyfriend and lose my virginity so I could become a fully-fledged hoe! Living in imaginary worlds was a lot easier by comparison.

I did, however, have one advantage. In Brighton, the unwritten teenage law was that your coolness was judged by your proximity to London and being from London meant you were the coolest, so my girls and I would wait for London boys to come down to Brighton on their weekends.

Every Saturday we'd dress up and head to Brighton Pier, and we'd spend all day there on the dance machines in the arcade, riding the roller coasters, eating candy floss, and waiting to be chirpsed by sexy London boys. The summers in Brighton were the best—they were all so wild! Weeks and weeks of house parties, beach bonfires, underage drinking, drugs, and so much sex. (Not me, I was still a virgin, but some of my mates made *Skins* look like *Antiques Roadshow*!) London boys seemed excited by us Brighton girls, probably because we were relatively easier than London girls, but we owned it! You'd hear so many stories of a London boy coming down to Brighton one weekend, getting a Brighton girl pregnant, and then whisking her back to London to live happily ever after. That was partly my dream. I definitely didn't want to get pregnant—the prospect of having a baby was worse than getting flaming herpes to me—but I did want to move back to London.

After living in Brighton for a few years, I found myself longing for a bit more adventure, and everything that had anything to do with London excited me, especially the cool new wave of music coming out of East London.

BRIGHTON GIRL IN DA CORNER

Brighton me was obsessed with Black British music. There's something about being Black and moving to a white area that makes you want to hold on even tighter to whatever you feel your Blackness is. My Blackness basically equated to Dizzee Rascal. The first-ever album I bought was Dizzee Rascal's *Boy in da Corner*. It was fresh and raw UK grime at its finest and I was in love.

I used to rap one bit of the song "2 Far" all the time—*Don't tell me about royalty 'coz / Queen Elizabeth don't know me, so / how can she control me when / I live street and she lives neat?*

When I rapped those words, I really felt them. For some reason they resonated deeply with me. Moving to Brighton made me rebel against my old life, and this was my new phase. I wanted to be a youth from a council estate in London. When my mum heard me she'd laugh and say, "You live in a hotel in Brighton!

You're hardly street," and she was right. I wasn't street, I was more like pavement or cobbled path! But I thought acting like this would get London boys to like me more. All I wanted to do was find my London Dizzee Rascal–rapping prince charming. After a couple of years of looking for him on Brighton Pier, I decided to widen my search—to the internet.

DIAL-UP DATING BEFORE IT WAS COOL

Now, everyone who was born in the eighties and nineties will tell you they had a huge internet phase. We are MSN Messenger, we are LimeWire, we are burning CDs, we are waiting for the modem to finish making that noise so the internet could start, we are waiting two days for a movie to load, we are Myspace, we are Bebo, we are Freewebs, and we are MP3s. (If you didn't understand any of what I just said, you are way too young to be reading my book. Put it down and go watch some TikTok videos.)

Meeting boys on the internet back then was more exciting to me than a theme park full of London boys! It was like opening up a whole new world of virtual dick. It was all too easy. You'd sign into MSN Messenger and talk with friends and then friends of friends, and friends of friends of friends until your whole chat list was filled with sexy new strangers you'd talk to every night. I was dating about seven boys at once through MSN alone! They all thought I was their girlfriend, because on the internet I had what traditional fuckboys in real life would call "game."

I was very good at striking up conversations and making boys fall for me through the internet, because chatting online was like an extension of writing fan fiction. Online I could pretend to be whatever character I wanted to be! I was Diamond who worked at Foot Locker, Lacey who had two labradoodles and aspired to be a forensic scientist, and Dawn the slut. The boys were putty in my hands; they had no choice but to fall for me.

One time I got so caught up in MSN boy talking that I had to fake that I was on holiday in Barbados and go offline for two weeks just to manage it all! Having internet boyfriends made me feel like a virtual hoe and I loved it. Eventually I would be honest and tell them who I really was—a sixteen-year-old virgin—and surprisingly they were still interested! A lot of my online boyfriends lived in London, so online talk moved to texts (thank God for T-Mobile's five-day pass), which progressed to late-night phone calls, and before long I was paying ten pounds for a London-to-Brighton roundtrip train ticket to go and "link" (a fun slang word that means "to link up, or to date romantically") my potential suitors.

I was an almost-having-sex machine! Linking about three or four different London boys was starting to get really expensive, BUT I was getting all the sex research I could possibly ask for. All the things I used to do with Marcell the teddy bear, I was now doing with real-life human boys with tiny boners—it was so exhilarating! I even managed to get a boy back to Room 4 in my mum's hotel. We did some over the bra boob holding, but then my mum came home, and I had to sneak him out over the Juliet balcony before we could get to any of the juicy stuff.

After a couple of years my sexual confidence grew. I had dated some cool London boys, gave a few perfect hand blows,

BUT I was still an eighteen-year-old virgin. By now I was desperate to lose my V-card! I'd got pretty close a few times: there was the time I got fingered on the 250 bus and then the guy pulled out his dick and asked me to hop on top and I panicked and had an asthma attack; then there was the time I thought I'd actually had sex, but it didn't even go in, it just went around it and near my bum hole; and the time where, after giving head, I got lockjaw and accidently bit his dick. There was just never the right moment. After a while my friends sat me down for a very meaningful "you can't go to university a virgin" talk, with real concern on their faces.

So that was the plan: to just lose it before I started university. I remember thinking that being a virgin was too much of a burden, like a huge weighty dick on my shoulders that I just wanted to be free of.

LOSING MY V-PLATES

Women always get a served a raw deal when it comes to losing their virginity. Men are allowed to lose it anyhow they want, but women are built up to believe it has to be this super-romantic, mind-blowing, life-altering experience. It doesn't have to be; it really can be whatever you want it to be. Don't give it so much power over your vagina!

After all the buildup, I ended up losing my virginity in the most blah way. I don't actually remember his name or what he looked like. All I can recall is that he was a London boy who asked me for my number in Brighton one weekend. Let's call him Sheldon. Sheldon asked me for my number, but so did his best friend, Ace (told you I was becoming a bit of a player). After chatting to both of them for a while, I'd started getting closer to Sheldon, and—after my friends had given me the serious sex pep talk—I decided that he'd be the perfect guy to give my virginity to.

After hours of late-night talking on the phone, Sheldon invited me to his place in Streatham, in southwest London. I took the train up to his house, and at first we were just watching *The X Factor* in his room while his parents were downstairs—and then it just happened. He put a condom on, and we had about two minutes of unimpressive sex. I was staring at the dude crooning his heart out on TV the whole time. He came, I faked it, it was over, and I was so relieved. The next day I was so careful and cautious that, even though he wore protection, I still popped to Boots and got the morning-after pill. (So cool, so responsible.) And that was that; I'd slayed the virginity dragon and become a woman! It was simple! Or so I thought.

A few weeks after my extremely uneventful sex adventure, I was speaking to Sheldon's friend Ace on the phone and he told me that he and Sheldon had bet on who could take my virginity first. It had been a twenty-quid bet, and I guess Sheldon won. When I heard that I was mortified, so I rang Sheldon and screamed at him. I remember being more angry than upset. He apologized, but I never spoke to Sheldon again. I think that's why I don't remember his name or his face for that matter; it was probably my brain and vagina's way of dealing with the betrayal. If his moves in bed weren't bad enough, he'd totally ruined that experience for me by being a dick. What gives me peace is knowing that his claim to fame will always be that night, all terrible two minutes of it, whereas I don't even remember who he is!

After losing my virginity for a twenty-quid bet, I decided to maybe not have sex anymore. It wasn't that great and it hurt! I didn't groan "Oh God" at all, not even once! For a while, my fascination with sex started to wain and I stopped being boy crazy. I just got on with my life. Part of me felt a little bit cheated, like society had lied to me; it wasn't this huge and meaningful event, and I didn't even come!

Little did I know that sex can be an amazing thing, and I was just doing it wrong and with the wrong person. But now that I had sex out of the way, it did clear my mind to focus on the thing that had always been the most important to me: BEING FAMOUS.

BACK ON THE FAME TRAIN

Moving to Brighton had kind of derailed the fame train, so I hadn't made that much progress. The most famous things that had ever happened to me whilst living in Brighton were:

- starring in a school sex education video called Swings and Roundabouts,
- being an extra in an episode of the cult Channel 4 lesbian drama *Sugar Rush,*
- joining Brighton's first-ever street dance crew, the Funkstarz,
- bumping into Peter Andre and Jordan in a chip shop,

- and getting rapper Big Narstie to perform at my eighteenth birthday party (a step up from my traumatic thirteenth at Pizza Hut).

So let's just say I needed to up the stakes in the fame game! I decided to set myself some goals, real ones that I would stick to, like "By the time I'm twenty-five, I'm going to be a movie star with a house in Miami and be married to Tinie Tempah."

Sure! Easy goals, very doable. It was no surprise that I wanted to live in Miami, even though to this day I have never even been. I've always been in love with America; almost all my fan fiction was set there and most of the imaginary jobs I gave myself were either a popstar, movie star, or cheerleader. All the media I consumed as a child made me feel like America would always be my endgame; it was my Mecca. I didn't know how I was going to be rich and famous and American, but I just knew that one day I would be, and I also knew I couldn't do it by hanging around Brighton Pier with my mates all day drinking Lambrusco (the cheaper version of Lambrini); I had to get refocused.

I chose to apply to a London university because I assumed that nobody famous came out of Brighton (boy, was I wrong—two years after I left, Rizzle Kicks became a thing). Every part of my body was telling me that in order to make my dreams come true, I had to move back to London and be around Black people again (no offense to the white people of Brighton—apart from the mild racism, you lot were golden). I just needed to be back with my people. So I enrolled at a university with a high population of Black students and got accepted. Thank you, Kingston University.

Chapter 7

Getting a Reputation

Everything was going to change for me after I got accepted at Kingston. I just knew university would be my breakout moment. Brighton had been a four-year detour where I could find myself, but now London Hughes was back in London town!

I was armed with a newfound confidence now that I'd finally lost my virginity, grown into my face, and my mild eczema had cleared up. I was ready to take university by storm! I wanted to devour the whole experience, take it all in and do and see everything—and everyone! It was going to be different this time; I was starting a new chapter, a new life, and I'd be the most badass version of myself, standing up for myself and—I'll stop right there. I totally got bullied again. It was horrible.

But before we get into all that, let's have a bit of fun. Before I'd even got to university, my plan to get famous had already taken me to some unusual places. I met some guys on Brighton Beach that were filming a rap music video one day, and they asked me and my friends to be in it. That led to me becoming somewhat of a music video vixen, popping up all over the place in low-budget rap music videos on Channel U, I shit you not. I, London Hughes, was a sexy music video model. Take that, Amanda, I told you I could dance.

I definitely did not get paid for them, but it was a start. It was so glamorous, showing up to set, sitting in the girls' toilets, and doing my own makeup with the other lovely, cocoa-butter-scented girls—gosh, I felt like Kendall Jenner! All I had to do was look pretty and dance in front of cameras, so the job was basically a dream! I was nervous at first, as there was still a part of me that felt like the ugly girl with eczema; I don't think that ever leaves you.

After a while, I got comfortable with my surroundings and the people on set. We'd have a lot of downtime between takes, and I spent it trying to make the cameraman, rappers, and other video girls laugh, for no real reason other than boredom and my incessant need to impress people. I was even making the rappers laugh on set, and you may not know this, but that is a huge feat. Rappers are some of the most serious people in the world; they've lived life and seen some things! And here was this girl making them laugh with her Scooby-Doo impressions! "Oi, you're proper funny, y'know," said Badman G, one of the absolutely blinged-out rappers, on set one day. He's in prison now.

In the past I'd used comedy to try to be popular, but on set I was just being myself, and I guess people liked it. I got an amazing feeling whenever I made anyone laugh; it felt like electricity. That was the first step I took toward truthfully being confident in myself.

FROM VIDEO VIXEN TO BABESTATION

All that joking around on set led to my first television job. One of the other video girls presented on a cable television show on the side and she told me they were looking for new presenters. I remember thinking to myself that THIS WAS IT. This was the moment that my life would finally change: someone would see me presenting on this cable channel and I'd get an agent and then get booked in America and marry Tinie Tempah by the age of twenty-five and live happily ever after. Well, as you can imagine, that didn't quite work out, because the cable television program she wanted me to audition for was Babestation.

Babestation back in the early 2000s was basically a live porn channel. I'm not quite sure what it is now, but I'm sure your dad can tell me. I had recently lost my virginity and, even though I had the inner sexual confidence of a young Madonna in her prime, I wasn't quite ready to get my tits out on national TV. My friend assured me that no nudity would be involved, because this show was on in the daytime. You see, even though Babestation is a late-night live porn channel, it still needs to be on during the day to pay the bills—and that's where I would come in. My segment was called "Flirt UK," and it was my job to sit fully clothed and keep viewers entertained by essentially flirting through the TV.

At the bottom of the screen there'd be a rolling messenger chat, which before the days of Twitter enabled you to talk to random strangers. It would look something like this:

897: Who here wants to party?

678: ASL?

773: I'm into redheads, anyone into redheads?

445: 332, are you single?

I'd be pictured in the live feed above it, reminding people of the number to text and randomly putting up pictures that viewers would send in. I would say things like:

"Hey, you're watching 'Flirt UK, with London Hughes' and this is Clive! Clive is forty-seven and likes sexy, big-busted blondes half his age. If you're into flirting with Clive, text the number below!"

I did this from 4:00 p.m. until 10:00 p.m., and then I'd be replaced by topless ladies fingering themselves on live TV. I was essentially the fluffer, the opener, the prequel to the main event, fully clothed and earning twenty pounds an hour.

I learned a lot working at Babestation. Sometimes after finishing my shift, I'd wait behind to watch the nude girls do their thing. I'd see grown, topless women talking to men on the phone and fingering themselves screaming "Fuck me, Daddy!", and then in the next breath they put those "daddies" on hold and answered calls from their kids. "It's okay, hun, Mummy's just at work. There are some chicken nuggets in the fridge!" It was a crazy time. Those girls made seventy pounds an hour and they all looked like absolute bombshells. Younger, still-virgin me would have been insanely jealous of these glorious women, but this new me was a bit jaded by sex, so the thought of telling any man to "Fuck me, Daddy" made me want to become a celibate lesbian.

Now, even back then I knew never to let an opportunity pass me by, and I honestly thought that although I was on a show with only seven viewers on channel 879, somebody, somewhere would see my talent and make me a TV star. So even though the show had nothing to do with me and the viewers were just waiting for the porn to come on, I turned "Flirt UK" into the London Hughes show! I would make jokes and tell fun stories about my past dates, and I did a LOT of improv. Most of all, I'd just give the audience a bit of entertainment, and I think it worked, because I'd get a few compliments here and there, although mainly I just got comments from the foot fetish dudes telling me to stop talking and "get my toes out." Still, our viewership went up from seven to ten, so I was technically a hit!

I loved presenting on Babestation; it was live, it was in front of real cameras (well, one: a tripod that I had to operate myself, but still), and it really felt like I was going places. I even created my own mini segments, like Hughes's Shoes, where I spoke about riveting things like the shoes I was wearing that day. I started to get a loyal following and I had a few regulars that would tune in to every show.

There was one particular regular that I mentioned earlier: Clive, forty-seven, loves women half his age—remember him? Yeah, Clive was a handful. That bastard got me fired.

Clive would always text and email, asking me to put his photo up so he could "connect with the hot laydeeez." Clive wasn't that hot, bless him, but he was nothing if not persistent. I frequently obliged and put his photo up, but none of the hot laydeeez ever messaged him. Now, that may have been because none of the people watching Babestation in the daytime were hot heterosexual women, but who can really say.

I eventually grew tired of posting Clive's picture every week, so one day I decided to politely decline his email requests. Clive did NOT like that, and so he decided to take his revenge. One afternoon during my shift, I was in the middle of telling this hilarious dating story, which ended in me doing my rapper-certified impression of Scooby-Doo, when I got an email from Clive. Clive asked me to post a very special picture, but all I could see when I looked at the fuzzy JPEG image was that it wasn't a picture of Clive—it seemed to be a picture of me. I'd never had a fan send me literal fan art before, so I was honored and quickly shared it with the viewers. I should say that behind the scenes at Babestation, I controlled everything. I was in a dark, tiny room with a tripod camera pointing at me and a laptop on a table to my left. I could simply post a picture on TV by uploading it onto my laptop. This is exactly what I did, and within thirty seconds the picture of me went live on Babestation at four in the afternoon. The problem was it wasn't just a picture of me.

Clive had got his revenge in the worst way possible. He had paused his TV (shout-out to Sky+ for being invented that year) at a moment when my mouth was wide open; he then got out his penis, put it next to my on-screen mouth, and got a mate to take a photo. That was the picture he sent to me. If you just so happened to be watching Babestation that Thursday afternoon, you would have seen a picture of a Black girl with a dick in her mouth, and the real-life version of that Black girl screaming at said picture.

In my panicked state, I left the picture up way too long, and somebody saw it and complained to Ofcom—the British television complaints board! What weirdo complains to Ofcom about seeing porn on a porn channel!? Surely I was doing them a favor! Anyway, I instantly got the sack from Babestation for "lowering the tone of the show." Goodbye fame, goodbye twenty pounds an hour. But hey, not many people can say that they've been fired from a live porn channel for being too explicit. I can!

After being dropped from Babestation, I was absolutely devastated. What I didn't know at the time is that I'd be sacked from one more job before I would stumble upon my dream career. But for now, my TV dreams were over, and I was nowhere near to getting that house in Malibu. Luckily, I had university to fall back on.

A DEGREE OF JEALOUSY

As I said before, I was really up for uni life, mainly because I'd seen a lot of it in American TV shows and films and I thought it would be exactly like that in real life. It wasn't—mainly because this wasn't Hollywood, it was Kingston upon Thames. There were no sororities, no frat houses, no late-night ragers with keg stands. But there were a lot of parties.

I mentioned earlier that I got bullied at university and yes, I did, severely. Now, I've been bullied a lot so far in this book (there are even some stories I've left out), but I don't want you to think that I'm a victim or a weak bitch. When kids bully you, it could be for a number of reasons—their home life, their own frustrations, their own insecurities, etc.—but whatever it is, they're either jealous of you, something about you makes them feel bad about themselves, or both.

We've all had insecure moments in life; I know I have. There was a time that I wasn't too fond of Rochelle from pop group the Saturdays. It didn't matter what she said or did, I just didn't like her. It was only because I wanted to be where she was in life, up there dancing on *GMTV* next to Frankie and Una. As a kid I'd auditioned for S Club Juniors and I didn't get it, but she did and that was it. I didn't like her; I was a bloody jealous bitch! I actually met her years and years later and thought she was drop-dead gorgeous and charming, and I had no idea why I'd spent so much of my childhood having a problem with her. To be fair, I was a child and children can be stupid. But in the UK, once you hit eighteen you are considered an adult, and to some of these adult women at Kingston Uni, I was their Rochelle from the Saturdays. The only difference was that I wasn't in a cool pop group, I was just a normal girl from Croydon via Brighton with tiny wrists. But for whatever reason, they just couldn't stand me. And reader, did they let me know it.

I remember getting a lot of attention from boys at uni, mainly because 1) I'd grown into my face and 2) I could dance. I mean, I could really dance, none of this TikTok foolishness. I was that girl at Oceana nightclub, swinging on a stripper pole or getting sucked into a dance battle and dropping into a split, my signature move. I loved the attention, and it always seemed to find its way to me.

I would never rush home at the end of a night out—instead I'd hang back and put all my online dating skills to good use by talking to all my future potential suitors. I was just so excited to be surrounded by so many hot Black guys. I was a girl deprived! Zero Black guys went to my high school, so I needed my melanin man fix. I humbly apologize if you were a white guy at Kingston University at the time: I honestly didn't even know you existed. Now, I don't dick-scriminate—when it comes to love, anyone can get it—but by the time I got to Kingston University my milkshake was bringing all the Black boys to the yard and I loved it!

The only challenge was that, in the four years I'd been in Brighton, the culture around British Blackness had shifted a little bit. When I left London, it was very cool to be of Jamaican descent; Jamaicans were everywhere and influenced everything, from food to music. If you went to an underage club or house party and the DJ said, "Make some noise if you're from Jamaica," the whole place would erupt. Jamaica was always in the building! That was the London I was used to. But since then, Black London had changed and there was this whole influx of West African culture that had taken over and become the more dominant Black culture. Now being from Nigeria or Ghana was seen as the epitome of cool and Africans completely bossed the new scene.

The West African takeover in London was such a culture shock to me. I didn't know much about being from Ghana or Nigeria, so I had to learn fast for fear of sounding ignorant. I did my research and learned the names of their capital cities, their most popular foods, and the dances to popular African songs. I loved being around Black boys, in all their beautiful shapes and sizes! I didn't necessarily want to have sex with them, but I wanted to know what made them tick, what they liked, what they disliked, what they liked about me. I just wanted to talk. I loved talking!

I'd be outside the club most nights chatting them up for sure, but that's all it was—chatting. Most of it was innocent, most of it was just me being a bit of a flirt, but what I didn't know was how it looked to some of the other girls. To them it didn't look good; apparently, I was starting to get...a reputation.

Chapter 8

A Hoe-Fessional

A reputation in terms of what is or isn't considered "hoeish behavior" was such an interesting concept to me. In my old high school in South London, you'd be called a hoe[5] if you even looked at a boy too much, but in Brighton, nobody was called a hoe at all—and there were girls literally going around sleeping with guys in math cupboards and having threesomes with their boyfriends and their mates at lunch.

I was starting to get a name for myself at Kingston University, and not a good one. Apparently, everyone was talking about my hoeish ways! I had no idea I was so relevant! I came home from lectures one day and my four judgy housemates literally staged an intervention. Anyone would think I was on drugs, not dick!

"London, you're talking to way too many men."

"You're making too many friends."

---

[5] I'm using the term "hoe" in a derogatory manner here, but I've since reclaimed it and now use it to describe someone who loves to have sex. FYI, I'm currently living my best hoe life right now and I suggest you do the same.

"We don't like the way you're carrying yourself."

What a complete 180! I had gone from the girl with mild eczema who guys wouldn't even admit to talking to, to the hoe who now apparently had too many guys talking to her! I was so confused by the confrontation, and I got this weird feeling in my stomach, the same one I used to get in my old school when the popular girls would bully me. These girls were supposed to be my new friends, and I clearly wasn't making a great first impression. I just wanted them to like me. As you'll know by now, I hate confrontation, so instead of telling them to fuck all the way off, like I should have done, I listened to what they said and followed their advice. For two of the most miserable weeks of my life I stopped talking to boys, I stopped trying to make them laugh, and I stopped having dance battles in the club.

Reader, it gets very tiring living for anyone but yourself. I really didn't like the person they wanted me to be—she was sooo boring! She was quiet and sad most of the time and nothing like the real me who loves to dance, make people laugh, and talk to boys. In the past I'd tried to emulate other girls to fit in, but I didn't want to be like my housemates. I wanted them to like me, but not enough to stop being who I really am. Why did those girls deem talking to the opposite sex as a negative? Why did they automatically assume I was a hoe when really, I was just very charming! I tried to ignore my housemates, but this wasn't the end of it. Oh no, these girls would go on to make my university life absolutely miserable.

But for now, I had hope. I was loving the educational side of uni life and I'd even landed a waitressing job at TGI Fridays for five pounds an hour! It certainly wasn't show business, but I learned to make balloon animals, I got to sing happy birthday to cute boys, and eat all the secret recipe Jack Daniel's sauce I could get my hands on. I was living the student dream! But the girls I lived with just wouldn't let me know peace. There was always something I was doing or saying wrong, and I could just tell that deep down, for whatever reason . . . they hated me.

This was confirmed when one night I came home from doing the late shift at TGI Fridays to a house party that I WAS NOT invited to. Imagine turning up to your own house and finding tons of so-called friends having a rager that you knew nothing about. When I got there, the girls told me that it was their party and I wasn't actually invited, so I locked myself in my bedroom and spent most of the time trying to drown out the noise with my Will Young CD (his first album is literal art). He had a song called "Changes" that I used to listen to on repeat whenever I was unhappy. It was a beautiful song about Will hoping his life changes because he's desperately trying to get out of the situation he's currently in, and it became the soundtrack to my early depression.

So I bedded down with Will for the night and thought the worst was over. But the next morning I was summoned to a very important house meeting to discuss the fact that, during the soiree, someone had apparently knocked the bathroom door clean off its hinges, and we had to decide who did it and who had to pay for it. Every finger pointed at me being the culprit. I was completely innocent! The truth was that one of the boys who lived in the house next door had broken it by having sex up against it, but he didn't want to admit that, so instead said he'd seen me leaving the bathroom with a guy. I couldn't fucking believe it! It was like a game of Clue—yeah, sure, it was London Hughes, in the bathroom, with the doggy style!

All my housemates believed his story immediately.

"How could I have broken it when I wasn't even invited to the party and was in my bedroom all night?" I protested through tears.

"If that's the case, then why where you seen leaving the bathroom with a boy?! Just face it! You broke it, you have to pay for it," one of the girls snapped back.

They were all adamant that I had to pay, but I refused. The girls decided to punish me for not paying up by giving me evil looks, completely ignoring me, or the worst, leaving all their dirty dishes in a container outside my bedroom and telling me I had to wash them up.

It wasn't a fun time living with those young women. They were some of the meanest people I've ever encountered in my life, and they made that year one of the worst years of my life. Looking back, it's no surprise I went through several bouts of what I now know was depression. There would be times when I wouldn't get out of bed for days; I'd just lock myself in my room and cry. Thank God it was only a year (the university eventually kicked us all out of the house because we had too many noise complaints). Luckily, the next year I moved into a new flat with a bunch of much nicer girls. But in the meantime, the bullying got worse, and this time, it went viral.

KINGSTON UNIVERSITY UNCOVERED

The internet in the early 2000s was a magical place. I bloody loved it and still have fond memories from the people I met through it. I remember chatting with my MSN boyfriend Aaron who lived in Jamaica and setting up a Myspace music account just so I could add Tinie Tempah and put him in my top eight friends. The internet back then was mostly a place for good, but what I didn't anticipate was that it could be used for evil—and it all started with a little invention called Facebook.

I don't mean to brag, but I am the Facebook generation. I was in my first year of university in 2007 when it launched in the UK, and back then you could only have an account if you had a university email address. It used to be specifically for students to interact with other students from universities, and it was super cute at first—friend requesting the guy in your class to see if he's in a relationship, tagging your mates in pictures of them throwing up after a night out. Fun, harmless stuff. I used to spend hours and hours on it.

But when Facebook got into the wrong hands, that's when you got things like Kingston University Uncovered. It was an anonymously run Facebook page and its sole purpose was to "uncover Kingston University's biggest hoes." The page got sent to everyone at uni, so it had thousands of members, and guess who was its poster child? Yep! Whores truly.

In 2023 internet bullying happens all the time, but 2008 was way before Twitter trolls and viral abuse. Facebook wasn't the weird depression website it is now, only used by your aunties and Trump supporters. I'm not exaggerating when I say it was the most popular website ever. University libraries were packed full of kids spending all day on Facebook. This meant that the Kingston University Uncovered page was so in your face that everyone knew about it, everyone read it, and everyone could see that I was allegedly the university's biggest hoe. The headlines:

> "This girl is the biggest hoe in the world. She does TV and media studies and has given head to every man on campus. She once got gangbanged in a Lidl car park by fifteen Peckham boys and then they stole her phone. She works at TGI Fridays and likes to take her customers home and fuck them for extra tips. Even her own house-mates say that whenever they bring boys back to their house, they always see them leaving her room in the morning."

It then had quotes from people I'd allegedly slept with and horrible comments from so-called friends, as if it was some kind of TMZ exposé. At the bottom of the long and carefully crafted article, there was my picture and a link to my personal Facebook page. I was horrified that anyone would do this to me. And none of it was true! There aren't enough negative words in the world to describe how low it made me feel. I've been in Twitter wars with racist Trump supporters who were kinder to me than that Facebook page.

A REPUTATION
(Part Two)

If I wasn't completely sure before, I now 1000 percent knew that I had a scarlet letter stamped across my forehead and vagina.

Sure, I was a flirt and talked to a lot of boys, but I wasn't actually sleeping with all of them! I'd only recently stopped having clothes-on sex with my teddy bear! What a turn of events! I only wish that I'd been having as much sex as they claimed I was. I knew some girls at the uni whose vaginas were really living their best lives and I certainly wasn't one of them. But it didn't matter, it was on the internet for everyone to see, and if it's on the internet it must be true. So it stuck. Congratulations, I was Kingston University's biggest hoe.

I confronted my housemates about it, and they denied being involved. In fact, everyone denied it. Nobody knew who'd made the page and eventually it got taken down. I never got an apology from my housemates, I never found out who did it, and I never got closure. I just thank the universe that I've never seen any of those girls ever again—although five years later one of them had the audacity to message me on Facebook and tell me they were "proud of how well I'm doing."

If any of those girls are reading this right now, I need you to know from the bottom of my perfectly formed vagina that you were a bunch of evil bitches, but I forgive you. I didn't pay for the broken bathroom door, but you did have to pay for this book—and that, my friends, is closure.

NEW FRIENDS, AND A NEW BOY

After the Facebook page fiasco, nobody spoke to me, and I couldn't trust the ones that did, so I started making new friends and dating guys outside of my university. Kingston used to throw events with neighboring universities Roehampton and Brunel, so I could meet students who didn't already have a pre-conceived idea of me. I got to know some amazing people, and the connections I made were key to my comedy journey.

The boys at Kingston were all dead to me. In fact, I was done with student boys full stop, so I started dating a civilian named Leon. Leon was the closest thing I had to a boyfriend: We were together all the time, we'd go clubbing together, I knew all his friends, and we got on really well. The main thing I liked about Leon was that he didn't care what people thought about him; he knew who he was and would never let other people get to him. I wished I was more like him. Leon could do no wrong in my eyes, except when he was playing on his PlayStation. Every girl my age knows that when we were eighteen/nineteen, a specific game took over the minds of every young man in our lives: *Pro Evolution Soccer.*

I HATED THAT GAME! He would play it whilst on the phone to me, whilst I was with him, first thing in the morning, last thing at night, and just whenever he had a smidgen of free time. To Leon there was always a perfect time to play *Pro Evo* (that's what they used to call it). And it wasn't just him—all the boys were doing it. It was everywhere, faster than any omicron variant! They would go over each other's houses and play it in groups, have tournaments, all-day events. If you thought you were in a loving relationship around that time, trust me you were wrong: your man wasn't dating you, he was dating his PS2.

One day I'd had enough and let loose on Leon. I went on a massive rant about how infuriating the game was and when I was done, he just looked at me, laughed, and said:

"You're really funny! You should do stand-up comedy, you know!"

A light bulb went off. Sure, I'd been told I was funny in the past—Badman G the rapper said that I was "proper funny," the girls in school in Brighton would call me Miss Jocelyn—but nobody had ever suggested that I could be a stand-up comic. I brushed it off at first.

"Nah, what would I even make jokes about?"

"You're even funny without trying to be! You could literally go onstage and say what you just said to me about *Pro Evo*, and it'd be sick!"

Hmmm. He really gave me food for thought, and that night I couldn't stop thinking about what he'd said. Could I be a stand-up comedian?

I'd never been to a live comedy show before, so I had no idea how to start. My new friends from Roehampton University didn't have the answers, but they did tell me about an event in central London called the Sunday Show. It was a weekly variety show with all the hottest up-and-coming talent. There'd be poets, stand-ups, singers, rappers, the lot. I figured it was worth checking it out. Who knows, it could lead to a completely life-changing career in British comedy (wink).

Chapter 9

Getting on the Telly

But before I get to the origin story of the Princess of Comedy who took the UK stand-up world by storm, let's take a quick ride back on the fame train. After all the housemate-related trauma, I kept my head down and tried to take my degree seriously. I mean, I was studying television and media and cultural studies because I wanted to be on TV, so what better course is there to help me on my journey to inevitable stardom, right? Wrong! Reader, if you want to be on TV, don't study it at university, just go out and do it. After two years into my degree, I couldn't tell you how to use a teleprompter, but I could definitely tell you who invented it (shout-out to Hubert Schlafly). My degree was starting to feel like a waste of time; I wanted to learn about auditions, being on set and how to have an on-screen romance, but instead they made us write dissertations on old episodes of *Desmond's*.

The good thing about my degree was all the extracurricular opportunities we had access to, like applying to be extras and stand-ins on TV shows. I obviously jumped at the chance to be on a set, a real one, with lights and a stage and a camera crew, not just a laptop and DIY tripod.

ALAN CARR'S CELEBRITY DING DONG

Students required as stand-ins for the recording of untitled show

I nearly choked on my salt and vinegar McCoy's when I saw the email. I didn't even know what a stand-in was, and there was clearly no pay, but I would get to be on set of an untitled show! Wow. Marcell the bear would have been so proud!

I turned up extra early at the BBC Television Centre, as I was just bursting to get inside. I was in awe as I wandered around the halls and thought about how many other famous people had breathed this very same air. There were pictures of all the British television history greats surrounding me, ones I grew up watching, dead ones, ones I'd never heard of. It was like my TV had thrown up all over the walls with me inside it. I stopped dead in my tracks when I saw a giant black-and-white picture of Sir Lenny Henry. Lenny and I had history, and I still wasn't quite over it. I wondered what I would do if I saw him. Would I mention all the letters I'd sent him? What would I say? Unfortunately, I never bumped into him, but it didn't stop me from keeping an eye out for him.

As I walked past the famous faces plastered all over the walls, I realized that not many of them were Black, and hardly any of them were Black women. The only Black woman I remember seeing there was a CBBC presenter named Angellica

Bell. Angellica was the first Black British woman I was officially obsessed with.

My obsession started off like any other day: Eleven-year-old me was watching CBBC, ready to see what good old Tracy Beaker and her pals were getting up to this week, when suddenly they announced they had a new presenter joining the team, and that they would give us a clue as to who she was. Up pops a cartoon clip of Angelica from *Rugrats*. I was hooked. *What? Angelica, my favorite baby-themed cartoon character, is joining CBBC? What in the Tommy Pickles is going on?* But the actual reveal was even more surprising and ten times more exciting, because at the end of the clip, there stood a beautiful dark-skinned Black woman. "Everyone at home, meet Angellica, your new CBBC presenter." My mouth hung open. As you know, I'd never really seen a Black woman on TV before, besides Aunt Viv on *The Fresh Prince of Bel Air*, so when this young, gorgeous dark-skinned woman appeared on my screen, I was completely in love. I wanted to be her, and I wanted to be on TV just like her. For the first time ever, she made me believe it was actually possible.

Walking onto the set of my first-ever proper TV show made me feel alive, better than any fan fiction I could ever write or any scenario I could make up in my mind. This was MY real life. The untitled show turned out to be a late-night game show called *Alan Carr's Celebrity Ding Dong*. It revolved around comedian Alan Carr pitting celebrity teams against each other. It was my job as a stand-in to pretend to be the celebrities and stand on their marks so the camera crew and Alan could rehearse. Paying me to pretend to be a celebrity and being filmed on a TV set!?

I would have done it for free! Well, I was doing it for free, but that's not the point.

After a fun day of standing in, we were then allowed to sit in the audience and watch the whole show being recorded for real. I loved figuring out what everybody did, so I studied everything: the cameraman, the director, the floor manager, the makeup artists, even the dude who came out to warm up the crowd before the cameras started rolling. I was wide eyed and soaking it all up. I figured out quite early on that if I laughed extra loudly at Alan Carr's jokes during the show, the camera would cut to me in the audience, and bang there I was, laughing on national television. So, during every single recording that's what I did: I laughed. I laughed loudly and energetically, and I was featured on pretty much every episode of *Alan Carr's Celebrity Ding Dong*.

The show ran for six of the best weeks of my life, and by the final episode Alan was my first-ever celebrity friend. I've since drunkenly told him in a gay bar in Soho that he was an integral part of me getting into the British entertainment industry. Just as I'd done on the sets of low-budget music videos in the past, in between takes I would always try my best to make Alan Carr laugh—and it worked! He thought I was hilarious! (Unless he was just being nice.) I got so good at telling funnies that toward the end of the series Alan would ask me to help choose which jokes he did on the show. This was a comedy genius and here he was asking me, an eighteen-year-old TV and media studies student, for comedy advice! It felt glorious! I left that set every night with a new sense of purpose and confidence. I knew I was going to be just like Alan Carr one day and present my own TV show.

The thing is that, as a nation, us British people are not big dreamers. There's the American dream, but there's no such thing as the British dream. We're more "don't give up your day job" kind of people—a mentality I discovered when my dreams of presenting my own entertainment show were dashed the very next week.

I decided that if I was going to make my entertainment show dreams come true, I'd have to visit my future workplace and do some research. Still high off my *Ding Dong* endorphins, I applied to go on a tour of Channel 4 studios. The guy giving us the tour was an "industry professional," and we spent hours looking around the set and control rooms while our guide explained how to get into technical jobs such as lighting operators, sound engineers, editors, etc. After a while I got bored of learning how to be a behind-the-scenes person and asked what I'd have to do to become a presenter. He replied, very matter-of-factly, that there is only ever one presenter, and the chances of that being you are very slim. He suggested I forget presenting and focus on something more achievable. What a fucking bastard! But I'm glad he said it, because I decided right then and there that I was I going to prove that random guy whose name I don't even remember now wrong. My chances were slim?! I'd show him!

LOOKING FOR REPRESENTATION
(Attempt 2)

If I was going to be a TV presenter, the first thing I needed was an agent, and as you know I hadn't had much luck with agents in the past. But I was older and wiser and now that the internet was a thing, I could just google it! My search told me that all the UK agents I found wanted something called a show reel and a CV. I had zero idea what a show reel was, and so far my CV read:

Video girl for Channel U music videos
Fired from Babestation
Stand-in on *Alan Carr's Celebrity Ding Dong*

It wasn't going to cut it; I'd need to do more to get the agents to notice me! That's when I stumbled across an advert for an open casting call to be on the hot UK reality TV show, *Big Brother*.

DEAR DIARY ROOM

I was a HUGE fan of *Big Brother*. The thought of cameras on me 24/7 catching my every move was right up my street, plus being on the show could lead to me getting an agent. Hey, it worked for Brian Dowling! The casting call was a month away and I could hardly keep my excitement under wraps.

Auditioning for *Big Brother* was like nothing I'd ever imagined. You couldn't make it up! There were thousands upon thousands of hopefuls—it made the audition lines outside *The X Factor* look like the queue for the ladies' toilets. There were so many different types of characters: people dressed up, people dressed down, some people in costumes, some people completely naked. It was Britain's most weird and wonderful all in one place, and if I had to bet money on it, I would say around 70 percent of them were Geminis.

We were split up into groups of around twenty people, and we had mini thirty-second interviews and icebreaker games, like Two Truths and a Lie. Whilst we were playing, a bunch of important-looking people would observe us and write stuff down on their clipboards, and if they liked us, they'd put a sticker on us and we'd move to the next round. I made sure those clipboard people noticed the hell out of me. I was loud, brought lots of energy, and made all the other hopefuls laugh. It was a piece of cake. I got through round after round after round, and the groups got smaller and smaller. Once we were in the final round, we had to fill out a questionnaire the size of the King James Bible and have one-on-one interviews.

They were so intense. I had to sit in a dark, tiny room with a camera and a spotlight on my face, while a voice came out of nowhere and asked me questions. It's a blur, and the only question I remember was from a man, who asked what I wanted to do when I was older. I replied without hesitation that I wanted to be a TV presenter, which was met with a pause. "Are you sure...?" *Oh no, not again. Not another man telling me that I'm not good enough to be on TV.* And then he finished his question. "Are you sure... you want to be on *Big Brother*? You're really fun and have great energy, so you've probably got more chance of being a presenter without this show."

I couldn't believe it. This was the only solid plan I had to break into television, and here is this random man I can't see telling me that I don't need to do it! As I silently pondered over what he said, he continued. "Being on a show like *Big Brother* could potentially hurt your chances of being a presenter. Have you considered that at all?" I didn't like this one bit—I mean, technically he was right, BUT he also could have been playing a mind game with me to see if I really wanted a spot on the show, and I did. So I ignored his advice. "Yes, I've considered it and it's a risk I'm willing to take."

The auditions were over, and I was told that if I made it through to the next round I'd get a phone call telling me to meet up at a secret location. I waited for that call like I was waiting for a life-saving kidney. It happened two weeks later; I was visiting my mum in Brighton when they told me I'd got through to the next stage. I nearly peed myself, I was so happy! The plan was to meet a man with a purple umbrella at 11:00 a.m. at a location in central London. I had to go up to him and say the secret phrase, which was "Mr. Hanky Panky's lost his shoe." Next thing I knew, I was being blindfolded and bundled into a car and taken to a warehouse. It was proper MI5-type stuff and I LOVED it all!

At the warehouse I was introduced to about eight other hopefuls. We had to play the same games we'd played at the original audition, but this time, at the end of each game, we all had to vote on someone to be evicted. That person would then leave, never to be seen again. It was brutal.

These games had none of the happy vibes of the previous rounds, because now the hopefuls playing were all a bunch of real characters. You could spot them a mile away: the bitchy one, the nasty one, the loud one, the quiet but deadly one. Everyone there really wanted to be on the show and had no problem taking down whoever stood in their way. I was being my usual

charming self and trying to make the others laugh, but as the
stakes were much higher this time, the other hopefuls were not
making it easy for me.

In one of the games, we had to have a big debate about divisive subjects like abortions or political stances. I ended up getting
into a very rowdy argument with a grown man about whether we
should ban unemployment benefits. All I remember is that he
kept talking about giros. At eighteen, I had no idea what a giro
was, and to be honest, I still don't quite know what it is at thirty-
two; I think it's something to do with unemployment payment.
This set the man off on one. "You're Black, how can you not
know what a giro is!? (Racist.) Stop acting!" Shocking behavior.

Now, I've said this before and I'll say it again: I used to HATE
confrontation, so much so that if a person shouted or talked to me
in an aggressive manner, my heart would beat fast, my chest would
tighten, and my stomach would fall out of my bum. I kept insisting
that I honestly didn't know what this ignorant dude was on about,
that I was a student and that to my knowledge none of my parents
had ever had a giro, but he was not listening to me. He kept shouting over me, calling me a liar and a game planner, and made a plea
to the other hopefuls that I should be the one to be evicted next. He
was loud and proud and wrong and strong, and everyone was now
engrossed in our stupid, pointless argument. My armpits started
sweating, my chest started heaving, and then I started uncontrollably crying in front of everyone. The guy could see that I was crying, but it just made things worse. He got even louder and started
berating me about trying to get sympathy votes.

Reader, I completely lost it. I did something I had never done
before, in all the years of people being rude to me and getting

abuse from so-called friends. For some reason, right then, in my *Big Brother* audition, I decided to grow a huge vagina and stand up for myself. I literally screamed at the man with all the might my mildly asthmatic lungs could muster, like a skinny girl in a horror movie. I screamed so loud I even frightened myself. Once the screaming was done, I followed it up with "I SAID I DO NOT KNOW WHAT A FUCKING GIRO IS, SO LEAVE ME A-FUCKING-LONE! DO YOU HEAR ME!!!"

The whole room went silent. The man shut the hell up but started sniggering out of embarrassment. One of the important clipboard people approached me in a very soft and calm manner. "Hi, London, do you wanna step outside for a bit, get some fresh air?" I was clearly going through something much deeper than a debate about giros.

I don't really remember what happened for the rest of the day, but I remember feeling like I'd blown it. I couldn't believe that I had let that man get to me and ruined my one chance of being famous. I was so embarrassed by my behavior, but I couldn't deny that it actually made me feel a bit better.

At the end of the day, they said they'd call to let us know if we'd made it through that round. I didn't hold my breath, but a week later, to my surprise, a producer called me. I was through to the next round! I couldn't believe it. I just hoped and prayed that that rude man hadn't made it through as well.

After I got off the phone, I sat and thought about everything that had just gone on in the past few months. I remembered what that male voice in the dark room had said about *Big Brother* hindering my chances of being a presenter, and then went over and over giro-gate in my head. I clearly wasn't the best version of myself right now, and if I was getting upset over an audition, then maybe *Big Brother* wasn't necessarily the show for me. I also worked out that if I went into the house that year, I'd have to retake my first year of university all over again. The thought of me reliving that year was enough to make me scream again! I weighed up all my options and decided to walk away from *Big Brother* with my head held high. It wasn't the show for me. I'm happy to say that that rude giro man DID NOT make it onto the show, and in the end a man named Brian Belo from Essex won the series. I have zero regrets.

What a time. I'll never know if being on *Big Brother* could have changed my life and made me famous, but what I didn't know at the time was that the first real fame train was about to arrive. I just had to get TGI Fridays to fire me first.

Chapter 10

Thank You, TGI Fridays

Ever since my boyfriend at the time, Leon, had put the idea to try stand-up in my head, I was desperate to see some for real. I didn't really want to be a stand-up at that stage—I wanted to be on TV, either presenting an entertainment show or starring in my own sitcom, plus I didn't think stand-ups could be female, because the only stand-up comedians I'd seen were Richard Pryor, Eddie Murphy, and Lee Evans. I'd never even been to a comedy club, but my Roehampton friends had started going to the Sunday Show every week and I was dying to go with them.

The only problem was that I could never go, no matter how much I begged my boss, because I worked the late shift at TGI Fridays every weekend. I'd been working there for nearly a year, and I was over it; the hours were insane—I'd finish work at 3 a.m. some nights and be way too tired for lectures in the morning—plus I'd consumed all the Jack Daniel's sauce I could eat! I started to try to find ways to get off work early, mostly by faking asthma attacks or injuries (I once pretended I got a concussion from slipping on chocolate dessert sauce), but I'd end up sitting in my boss's office with an ice pack on my head until I was ready to work again. I knew that there was no get-out-of-work-free card that I could pull that would let me go to the Sunday Show.

After a while I accepted my fate and put the thought of seeing live stand-up to the back of my mind. That was until our original boss left and was replaced by a very strict American manager. One fateful Friday, I was running late as usual (to be honest, I was always running late, mainly because I didn't want to be there). My old boss used to scold me when I was late and make me do the washing up at the end of my shift, but this new boss was even more savage. I turned up thirteen minutes late to my shift and he fired me on the spot. That was it: one strike, I was out. I couldn't believe it. I begged him to let me have my job back, but he wasn't having it. He was actually smiling as he let me go. I rang my friends in tears, but they weren't upset at all. "Well, at least you can go to the Sunday Show now."

THE SUNDAY SHOW

Two days later, I finally went to the Sunday Show for the first time, and it completely changed my world. It was at a bar in Clerkenwell in London, a cool and trendy hub buzzing with energy, and the audience was always filled to the brim with Britain's brightest soon-to-be stars. Anyone who was anyone was there, from Ed Sheeran and Jessie J to Amy Winehouse and Daniel Kaluuya. I felt so alive just being there. I sat right at the front and was captivated by how the two hosts—their names were Jamie Howard and Little Man—every week would build the crowd up into a frenzy, and I mentally took notes. *I definitely could do this*, I thought. Just like seeing Angellica Bell on TV when I was kid, all I needed was to see people like me doing something I wasn't sure I could do. Even though they were men, culturally we were on the same level, I could relate to their jokes, we were close in age, and I knew that I could have a funny female perspective on things, too. Right after the Sunday Show, I went home and I wrote some jokes.

THE JOKES

My first-ever set was basically a seven-minute rant about how *Pro Evolution Soccer* was ruining dating. My angle was that I was fed up with men who would rather turn the PlayStation on than turn me on. Getting sacked from TGI's meant that I had all this free time to perfect my comedy skills, and so in about a week I knew the whole set by heart. I was so fucking proud of it! It absolutely killed! Well, Leon thought it did, and he was the only person that had heard it in full. As far as I was concerned, he was the only person who would ever hear it, as I had no intention of actually performing it anywhere. I saw it as more of a personal challenge, plus I couldn't perform at the Sunday Show anyway because they only booked professional comedians. All I knew was that I had written and performed a successful stand-up set, and that was enough for me.

THE TALENT SHOW

Britain's Got Talent was the hottest new thing on UK television in 2008, and universities everywhere were putting on their own versions for students. As it happened, the week after perfecting my stand-up routine, students at Roehampton University were having trouble booking their Roehampton's Got Talent show, which was happening in three days' time. Even though I didn't go to their university, I was known around Roehampton for being a bit of dancer (yep, that girl doing the splits in the middle of the dance floor again), so one of the organizers asked if I would perform a solo dance routine. Of course! But I said I'd only do it if they let me do a stand-up comedy performance in the second half. The organizer was very hesitant—"Can you even do comedy?"—to which I confidently replied yes, and that I'd been working on some new material. I don't know what possessed me to say that, but what were the chances that I'd been working on comedy material at the exact same time they were organizing a talent show? It was a sign! I had to do it!

The night before the talent show I was typing out my set so it was fresh in my mind, and I was freaking out. I couldn't just go onstage and do stand-up, could I? Who did I think I was? If this backfired it would be the worst thing to happen to my social life since Kingston Uni Uncovered! Let's face it, I'd already been laughed out of one university, so did I really need to be the talk of another? I really could just do a little dance and call it a day. But even as the doubts were swirling around my mind, I found the Sunday Show Facebook page, tracked down Jamie Howard (the host of the Sunday Show) and added him as a friend. I messaged him asking for stand-up advice, and to my total surprise he replied! Jamie was sweet and supportive, and when I told him I was performing stand-up for the first time at a talent show, he even asked if he could come. I took a chug of my Fanta Lemon, exhaled, and replied. "Of course!"

I remember that night like it was yesterday. I was pacing around backstage while others performed to an extremely packed crowd of tipsy and rowdy students. I was completely shitting it, but it was too late now, I couldn't exactly turn back! I waved at Jamie in the audience, who had come with Sunday Show co-host Little Man and some other friends. I now had two of the coolest comics from the hottest night in London watching my debut stand-up comedy performance. No pressure, hun.

The performance in the first half went seamlessly. I had come up with a genius freestyle dance routine to "Like a Boy" by Ciara. In the music video, Ciara dresses and dances "like a boy," so I started off the performance in a baggy hoody and tracksuit bottoms. I was body poppin', krumpin', and moving around like a B-boy, taking off layers of clothing as the song progressed to finally reveal a leotard and tutu underneath. I then pranced around doing ballerina pirouettes, leaps, and kicks "like a girl" and ended the performance in my signature split. It wasn't really that progressive, but I killed it. The crowd went wild! I walked offstage thinking, *You could just go home now, babes, you really could!*, but not one part of me actually wanted to. I was already itching to get back on that stage and tell those people some funnies.

The second half arrived, and the host called me back out onto the stage. "And now . . . you've seen her rippin' up the dance floor, so let's hope her jokes are as good as her moves. It's London Hughessss." I remember walking on to the stage to more cheers from the audience and thinking *fuck it. Let's roll!* I grabbed the mic, paused, and pretended to get all serious and emotional as I delivered my opening lines.

> *Students, I'm here to talk about a serious matter.* [Hand breathe]† *Ladies, I got three words for you, and I know you've heard them before because you've heard them come out of guys' mouth.* [Sigh] *These famous three words have been responsible for causing breakups in the Black community since 1998; the majority of Black males in the audience have all played a part in making these three words the most HATED words by females across the nation. These three words are . . .* PRO EVOLUTION SOCCER.

> † A hand breathe was a little flourish I did with my hand whilst exhaling to convey intense emotion. I still do hand breathes to this day!

As soon as I dropped the words *Pro Evolution Soccer*, the audience roared. It felt absolutely otherworldly. Nothing can beat the feeling of getting your first-ever laugh from a group of complete strangers. In that moment, every single doubt and insecurity I'd ever had about myself vanished and I became a whole new person. The laughter from that audience was the validation I needed. It let me know that there was nothing wrong with me—I wasn't this weird girl that everyone seemed to have a problem with—I was just ME and I was fucking funny.

I performed the hell out of my seven-minute and twenty-eight-second routine (yes, I timed it); I had the audience in the palm of my hands, and it really felt like they loved me for me. I finished my set to more roars and a standing ovation, and when

I stepped off the stage the DJ played R. Kelly's "The World's Greatest." Over the cheers I could hear R. Kelly crooning, *"I'm that star up in the sky / I'm that mountain peak up high / Hey I made it / I'm the world's greatest,"* and my whole insides burst. That was such a special and perfect moment, which I can't believe R. Kelly went on to ruin with his pedophilic ways. Now I can't enjoy that song! But for a long time, long before I knew R. Kelly was a sex offender, "The World's Greatest" was such an important and poignant song to me.

After I stepped off the stage, Jamie and Little Man greeted me with drinks and a bear hug—I think one of them even had me in a headlock! I had clearly impressed them! Little Man grabbed my face, looked me in the eyes, and said: "Do you know that you're going to be a star? Do you know how fucking famous you're going to be?" It sounds bigheaded, but in that moment I really did, and it felt incredible to finally hear somebody say it.

With all the planning and scheming I'd done in my life, trying to figure out ways to make it in show business, I'd had no idea that stand-up comedy would lead to all my dreams coming true. I had a celebratory drink with Jamie and Little Man, and the next day I planned on just getting on with uni life, but they had other ideas. Jamie and Little Man convinced their bosses to let me perform at the Sunday Show that very weekend. I did the same set and killed it in front of the cool industry crowd. The Sunday Show managers were so impressed that they offered me a regular paid gig hosting the game show segment at the club every week. Within ten days I had gone from getting fired from TGI Fridays to becoming a professional stand-up comedian! Well hun, I guess good things come to those who wait-ress.

Chapter 11

The Princess of Comedy

I absolutely loved my gig at the Sunday Show. Not only was I good at it, but I was also getting paid fifty to seventy quid a week, just to do a ten-minute game that I would have done for free. It made TGI Fridays look like slave labor. My stage name was Miss London, and every week I'd perform about five minutes of comedy and then launch into the latest fun game I'd come up with. I remember one called EXCUSE ME, which involved me acting like an angry girlfriend who hadn't heard from her boyfriend all day. I'd get three guys in the audience to calm me down by telling me where they'd been, and the guy with the best excuse won. One time, a guy said he was ignoring my calls because he was at Hatton Garden getting me something special... he then really sold it by getting down on one knee and pretending to propose!

It was a crazy time back then. I was meeting new people every week, I was starting to get fans, DJs would shout me out as soon as I entered the building. It truly felt like the high life. I honestly would have been happy being a Sunday Show game show host forever, but everything changed when I was eventually approached by a promoter. He wanted me to perform at the Hackney Empire.

The Hackney fucking Empire? I was nineteen years old and hadn't been doing stand-up for two weeks, but he wanted me to perform at the two-thousand-seat Hackney goddamn motherloving Empire?! It was a completely different world. I was so new to the whole live British comedy scene, I couldn't tell my Frank Skinners from my Eddie Izzards. The thought of me performing an actual comedy set in an actual theater was completely daunting, but of course I jumped at the chance. I wouldn't get paid for the gig and I'd get only five minutes for my set but performing at the Hackney Empire kick-started my career. I learned so much about comedy that night. That gig was eye-opening—not least because it introduced me to the Black comedy circuit.

FUNNY, BRITISH, AND BLACK

Now, some of you may not know this, but in Britain there are still two types of comedy circuits: the Black comedy circuit and the mainstream comedy circuit (which back then we called the white comedy circuit). British comedy and entertainment was—and still is—systemically racist, which basically means it was built for the white race to thrive and other races to suffer. When I was coming up, the only famous Black comic in Britain for the last thirty years had been Lenny Henry, and even though there were tons of other Black comedians who should have had their chance, they never did. It's like there was a one-in-one-out policy for Black performers in Britain, so we used to joke that we were all just waiting for Lenny Henry to die.

White comics would work their way up the circuit, gigging all over the country and then get on TV and become famous. That DID NOT happen for Black British comics; we weren't invited to perform at comedy venues like the Comedy Store and we weren't asked to join lineups with our white counterparts, so we had to invent our own circuit for our own audiences, hence the Black comedy circuit was born.

These are the biggest differences I observed:

I. The Audience

Black audiences are some of the best in the world. They're notoriously the hardest to win over, but if you make them laugh, you'll get a reaction like you've never heard before. You have to understand that Black people tend to come to comedy shows with a different agenda from white people. Generally speaking, white audiences go to a show wanting to laugh. They're perfectly happy for you to take them on a journey with the faith that it will lead to laughter. Black audiences, on the other hand, go to comedy shows thinking, "I paid my money, so you better make me laugh." They want jokes about what they know, and they want them now. The material has to be high-energy, funny, and relatable, so you can't go on that stage talking about politics or current events—that's not what they're there for. The world is hard enough for Black people as it is, they need an escape. It's all about how the comedian onstage would make you feel. It can be tough, but when you make a Black crowd laugh, it's a feeling like no other. It's loud—they laugh from their souls—and people are falling all over themselves. I once did a joke on the Black comedy circuit that went down so well, somebody threw a chair!

2. The Environment

Most shows on the mainstream comedy circuit are held at venues specifically tailored for comedy shows, namely comedy clubs. The Black community traditionally didn't have any comedy clubs, so we had to put on shows wherever we could get them. I once did stand-up in a church, at a Christian comedy night. The stage was the pulpit, and I made those grandmas laugh in the name of the Lord, the savior, and the holy ghost!

3. The Entertainment

As a lot of the promoters on the Black comedy circuit are essentially glorified hustlers looking for the best way to make money, comedy nights would be turned into variety shows and combined with fashion shows, plays, and random musical acts. Whatever they could do to get the punters in. I once did a comedy show that turned into a PSA play about diabetes in the Black community. Deffo killed the mood.

4. The Showmanship

Comedians on the Black comedy circuit are some of the best physical performers in the world. They know how to rule the stage. I would never see a Black comic just walk up onstage and take the mic—oh no. Your intro music and moves onto the stage had to be killer. My comedy style was high-energy; I was extremely animated, with facial expressions, dance moves, the lot! I would always step out to whatever Beyoncé song was hot at the time and do the full-on dance routine before I'd even told my first joke about being a badass single bitch. Nailing the "Single Ladies" routine before even saying a word meant that the whole audience would immediately be on my side. They'd be going crazy by the time I hit the *uh-oh-oh* part of the dance, so when I yelled, "Single ladies, make some noise!" the ladies would scream. It slayed every single time.

After a couple of killer performances on the Black comedy circuit, I started to get a little fan base. I was called the Princess of Comedy because I was always the youngest and usually the only girl on the lineup. There was literally no other nineteen-year-old girl like me, so I had a fresh perspective.

I started getting booked a lot. I remember the first time a promoter asked me for my fee.

"My fee?" I didn't have a fee and didn't know how I would go about setting a rate for myself, so I naively said they could just pay me what they thought I deserved. Boy, was that a mistake! I once did a gig in Manchester and absolutely destroyed the place—there were no survivors. Tickets for the night were around £15 and it was a completely sold-out three-hundred-seater. Every other male comic on the lineup got between £150 and £500. I came offstage to a standing ovation, and the promoter handed me £15.

I was underpaid or unpaid for nearly all my early years on the circuit because the promoters knew they could get away with it. Once I even got paid in chicken wings! It was a hard time, being disrespected by promoters over and over again, and it all came to a head in Ayia Napa (as most things do).

AYIA, AYIA, AYIA FUCKING NAPA!

I was working with three very dodgy promoters called Top Boyz, who to this day still owe me £1,750. They booked me for a six-week slot at a beach club in Ayia Napa. They promised me my own accommodation, but in reality it was a tiny cot bed in their huge apartment. Living arrangements aside, I sucked it up and performed three times a week to sold-out comedy nights. I was joined by fellow Black comedians Slim and Richard Blackwood, who the Top Boyz flew out, put up in five-star hotels, and paid generously.

After a while I could tell the Top Boyz didn't really like me living with them. They were always entertaining women at the house, and some nights they would lock me out and I'd have to crash at friends' hotels or on the beach. After a few weeks of this I was getting very tired of the Top Boyz—they were rude to me and always made excuses whenever I asked when I was getting paid. "You'll get the money once the six weeks are up" they'd tell me.

Five weeks into my Ayia Napa stay, I came back to the apartment to find all my belongings outside. They'd locked me out again, but this time it was for good. They told me I'd have to find my own way home and that they weren't going to pay me for any of the shows I'd done. There was nothing I could do; I had no money and I was stranded. I called Richard Blackwood in tears, and he instantly got his manager, Charlie Kenny, to send me a car and get me on the next flight home, free of charge. I was so grateful to Richard and Charlie for saving me, but I never once got an apology or payment from the Top Boyz.

After that ordeal I knew I seriously needed a change. Charlie became my manager, and things were starting to get better. I was finally getting paid for performing, but I was starting to fall out of love with stand-up. I loved performing, I loved being onstage, but I hated all the business around it and didn't trust the promoters. In a short amount of time I'd pretty much done all there was to do on the Black comedy circuit; I'd played every big theater—Stratford, Catford, Hackney, and Hammersmith— and I still couldn't see myself getting any closer to my dreams. But then the Funny Women Awards came along.

FUNNY WOMEN

(Yes, We Exist, Contrary to Popular Belief)

Okay, remember how getting fired from TGI Fridays turned out to be a blessing, because it paved the way for me to become a stand-up comedian? And I've just explained that getting stranded in Ayia Napa was ultimately a good thing, as it led me to my first comedy manager? Good things can come out of bad situations. Keep that in mind when I tell you that getting cheated on made it possible for me to win a massive comedy competition. I'll explain.

I was lying in bed with the guy in question. He is not

important, so let's just call him Tony. I was lying in bed with Tony one day, and he told me that his "friend" was helping out with something called the Funny Women Awards. It was the UK's search for the funniest woman, and she'd asked him if he knew any funny women who should audition. Well, this "friend" turned out to be the girl he was cheating on me with, but I'm so glad he did, because otherwise I would never have known about the competition. Thank you, Tony!

Tony sent me the flyer, and I applied and made my way to the heats. Before I go on, let me tell you that the Funny Women Awards was truly the whitest comedy competition I'd ever entered. It was sponsored by Nivea and the BBC, and you can't get much whiter than that! To top it off, when I turned up at the quaint hall where the heats were taking place, I was mistaken for the cleaning staff. I shit you not, one of white ladies at reception pointed me in the direction of another Black woman on cleaning duty, who was very confused but politely assured me that I wasn't supposed to be working that day. "No, I'm here for the STAND-UP COMEDY COM-PE-TI-TION!" I said to the ignorant white lady at reception. She looked mortified and eventually pointed me in the right (white) direction.

There were only eight or nine others auditioning with me in the first heat. We took turns doing five minutes of stand-up in front of a couple of judges and the rest of the female comics. I was just so happy to see people with vaginas actually doing stand-up comedy. I watched as white female comic after white female comic did their set; some of them were really funny, and some of them had no business even daring to pick up a microphone in the first place— they should've been pointed in the direction of the cleaning staff!

I was last on the lineup, so I got to study all the women that came before me. My comedy style was nothing like theirs. First of all, I was the youngest, by far. Second, I was the only person of color, and I quickly deduced that I was probably the least wealthy. Judging by what they had to joke about, they were mostly middle-class women in their thirties and posh girls in their late twenties. I studied everything: what they talked about, how they said it, whether they swore or not, what kind of language they used . . . I'll tell you one thing I didn't expect: there were A LOT of anal jokes.

Their delivery was so different from mine; there was no showmanship, no real stage presence, no energy. There was no intro music, no crowd work—they just walked up to the microphone, told some jokes, and walked off. It was so bizarre and a bit . . . boring to me. They weren't even dressed nicely! They turned up with their hair brushed back, wearing jeans and a T-shirt. They didn't even dress like they wanted to win! I, on the other hand, walked on the stage in Black stiletto boots, Primark's finest Black leather leggings, and a sequined blazer. I did not come to mess around.

I did five of my finest minutes and the judges laughed out loud for the first time that evening, and so did some of the other female comics. Not everything I said went down well, and I definitely didn't think I stormed it, but they must've thought I had potential because I got through to the semifinals. Yep, I walked through the doors a cleaner and came out a comedian!

The semifinals were a real eye-opener for me. I was the only Black female comic there out of fifty contestants, and even though we were performing in front of four hundred people at the Leicester Square Theatre, there wasn't a single Black or brown face in the crowd. My jaw dropped when I realized I was the only chocolate chip in their vanilla comedy sundae. Nowadays, I perform to predominately white audiences all the time—vanilla people love me and I love them—but back in 2009? I was scared shitless!

I was ready, though, and I felt good about my chances. I could tell the judges had liked me in the previous heat, so I just took out the part of my set that didn't kill and planned on doing more of the same. I had no idea if these people would find me funny, but I thought, fuck it! I can't turn back now, so let's just see how this goes. What's the worst that could happen? All they could do was boo me and if they do then they're racist!

I walked out onstage and told my first joke (if I recall correctly, it went something like: "Single ladies, make some noise! Yeah, I hear you . . . I'm single, too. I ain't got no love life, no sex life—I can't even get a poke on Facebook!") and got instant laughter. I told another joke, more laughter. I finished my last joke and got full-on applause. I'd smashed it. But I didn't realize it at first.

When I walked backstage, all the other comics just stared at me.

"Oh my God, you killed it!"

"Did I?" I really meant it; I didn't think I'd done all that well, as I was so used to the cackles and roars and screams from the Black comedy circuit. Yeah, sure, I'd heard laughter, but so what? I couldn't have been that good—nobody even threw a chair! It sounds like an overreaction, but I just wasn't used to the subdued sounds of white laughter and appreciation.

Long story short, I got to the finals.

Fourteen white women and I made our way to the presti-gious Comedy Store London, where the finals were taking place. Again, the other finalists were rocking their jeans-and-T-shirt vibes, whereas I was wearing a red strapless tutu-style dress, fishnet tights, and purple velvet stilettos. It was the first time I'd ever stepped foot inside the Comedy Store, and as I stared at all the amazing white comics all over the walls, I smiled when I saw Lenny Henry up there. It was a good omen.

"Single ladies, make some noise!" I bellowed as I walked out on the stage. The crowd was up for it. They laughed, whooped, and cheered in all the right places. By the time it was over, I got a huge cheer; *Job done, mate,* I thought to myself.

Whilst the judges were making their decision, the previous year's winner took to the stage and did a quick set. She was a young, beautiful comic named Katherine Ryan. Obviously, we all know Katherine as the superstar she is now, but back then she was still very new. I remember thinking she was hilarious, confident, rude—totally up my street! I could see why she'd won.

After Katherine finished her set, the judges came back onstage. I could feel my heart beating through my tits. I really wanted to win this.

Well, reader...I won! I wish there was footage of the moment they announced me as the winner, because I definitely did the whole over-the-top cry and fall to the floor thing Alexan-dra Burke did when she won *X Factor*. It was one of the happiest nights of my entire life! The judges presented me with a cute little trophy, flowers, and a goody bag filled with Nivea products (most of the makeup I had to give away because they only came in white skin tones). One of the judges, BBC comedian Stephen K. Amos, came up to me afterward and told me that he was going to work with me one day. I'd only been doing stand-up for nine months.

Winning the Funny Women Awards catapulted me straight into the mainstream comedy circuit. I was the new girl on the scene who'd come out of nowhere. I had a lot of dick jokes, but back in 2010, women doing dick jokes were seen as vulgar and crude and not iconic and feminist. I gigged to predominately white audiences all over the country. Sometimes jokes didn't always land and that was okay; I knew that if an audience didn't get me, it wasn't always necessarily to do with my material. I was a young, well-dressed, semi-attractive Black woman, so most of the time when I walked out onstage, people in the audience thought I was a singer! They would all get up whenever I came out because they thought it was the interval! I knew I didn't look like your typical British stand-up comic, and first impressions are everything, so I worked twice as hard to get the audience on my side.

After a week or so, the head of the Funny Women Awards told me she wanted me to sign with her so she could manage me. I would have been thrilled, but she tried to imply that all winners were supposed to be managed by her and I called bullshit because I knew that none of the previous comics were. I didn't really know her, and I already had a comedy manager, Charlie Kenny, my Ayia Napa hero, so I refused her proposal. Well, that made her absolutely livid, and she threatened to take back my award.

"Listen here, I made you who you are, and I can certainly take it all away!" she once said to me after a gig. I'd just won my first-ever award and here's this crazy woman trying to take it away from me! That's when I realized that there were dodgy promoters on the white comedy circuit, too. I sadly cut ties with all things Funny Women after that; 2009 me was and still is very grateful for their platform, but hun, the only people who can say they "made me" are Veronica and David Hughes.

LOOKING FOR REPRESENTATION
(Part 3)

In the end getting an agent was so easy, I couldn't believe it. All that time and hard work I'd spent researching, looking in the Yellow Pages, auditioning for *Big Brother*, and then I end up getting one, just like that. It was this easy: a friend asked me if I had one, I said no, he rang up his agency and they signed me on the spot.

My first-ever agent was a woman named Vivienne. She was a very tall, scary, fashionably fabulous older woman who made Cruella de Vil look like a vegan yoga instructor. I was petrified of Vivienne—or The Claw, as some in the industry liked to call her—but I really respected her.

The auditions came rolling in, mainly for roles in shows like *Casualty* or *Holby City* as the girlfriend of knife crime victims, but hey, a gig was a gig. I have now grown to mildly dislike auditions, but back then I LOVED them. I couldn't wait to get my hands on a script. I saw auditions as my chance to impress people, to show people what I could do, and I was just happy to be in the room.

I'll never forget the time I auditioned for Stephen K. Amos's show. He was the comic of the moment and had just been given his own stand-up and sketch show on BBC2. I remembered his words from the Funny Women finals—"Miss London, I'm going to work with you one day"—and he turned out to be a man of his word.

Vivienne called me while I was in the middle of a TV studies lecture at university—at this point I was two years into my media and television studies degree that I was caring less and less about—she told me the audition for *The Stephen K. Amos Show* was later that day. My first reaction was that I couldn't make it because I had uni! I was missing a lot of morning lectures due to coming home late after gigs, and I needed to catch up on my course or else I really wasn't going to graduate.

Vivienne had other ideas for me, though, and she delivered a line that I'll never forget, a line that made so much sense to my life that I couldn't believe I hadn't thought of it sooner. She said: "Look, London, do you want to BE on television or do you want to STUDY television?"

A light bulb went on. That was the moment I knew that university wasn't for me. It had never occurred to me before because my parents had always told me that university wasn't something I could opt out of. My mum had me saving for my student loan fees since I was five years old and whenever family members gave me pocket money, I would say, "I'm saving it for mooniversity" (I didn't even know what it was, I thought it was on the moon). All I knew about university was that I was going and it would take a lot of money to get there, probably because it was on the moon. My family was very proud when I got into Kingston, and I was proud, too, but I couldn't help shake the feeling that these lectures and courses were no longer serving me, especially when the little girl inside me still wanted to be Will Smith. So I walked out of my lecture and went home to learn my lines.

I aced the Stephen K. Amos audition and got my first-ever acting role as Stephen's sister. I walked around the BBC studios like I owned the place. I can't exactly put into words how it feels to know that you're exactly where you're supposed to be in life, but that's how I felt. Being in the studio made me feel different, more present, confident. I know it sounds wanky, but it made me feel free.

One of the other great things about being a working actor in the television industry was that I got to finally meet Sir Lenny Henry. They say never meet your heroes, and in some cases it's very true. I was once at the same after-party as Serena Williams and I plucked up the courage to go over to her and say hi. She instantly recoiled and ran off—true story. But sometimes meeting your heroes can be completely life-changing, and that's what happened when I eventually met Lenny. Lenny Henry himself probably won't even remember this but the first time I met him I had just got the part in an online comedy sketch series his production company was commissioning called *Funny Black Singles*. My manager, Charlie, got me the gig; it was me and a few other comics from the Black comedy circuit. We dressed up in wigs and improv'd some scenes about this new dating site for Black people. I don't even remember if the sketches were funny or not but I was being paid five hundred quid for my troubles and I'd do anything for Lenny.

I couldn't believe it when I saw him. There in front of me stood the man I used to write letters to as a kid, the man I had been wanting to meet and impress for as long as I can remember.

"What's your name?" he asked me.

My mouth went dry.

"It's . . . London."

"Oh, okay, London. My name's Dudley!"

I laughed so loud I snorted. I couldn't get any more words out because I was way too starstruck. I just stared at him as he went about his business and pinched myself. That day was one of the best days of my life. I couldn't believe that Lenny Henry knew my name, and I swore to myself that I would do everything I could to never let him forget it.

COLLEGE DROPOUT

My new agent Vivienne invited me to her office to talk about my ambitions. I was gigging all over the place and had done a few shows, but what did I really want? What were my dreams? At the time I had a bucket list of things I wanted to do, including being the female Fresh Prince of Bel Air and the Black Britney Spears, but I needed something more achievable. I needed a way to make money long-term. I told The Claw that I used to have an obsession with Angellica Bell, and it had been a dream of mine ever since I was a kid to present CBBC. After meeting Lenny

Henry it felt like my childhood dreams were coming true these days, so I thought I'd give it a shot. Well, it worked! After two meetings and a successful audition, another one of my childhood dreams came true: I became a CBBC presenter. When I got the call to confirm my new job, I decided to quit university on the spot.

Dropping out in my final year was a hard decision to make in principle but not in action. Sure, I'd put so much hard work and effort into it, blah blah blah, but in reality what The Claw had said was right. I wanted to try to live out my dreams and not just read about other people's. My dad was totally calm about the whole thing, but my mum wasn't so understanding. Like me, my mum is a planner, and she already had my whole life planned out for me.

My Mum's Plan for My Life:

- Be born
- Go to university
- Find a man at university
- Finish university and get married
- Have babies by twenty-five

What Actually Happened:

- I was born
- I went to university
- I fell in love with comedy at university
- I dropped out of university
- TBC

It didn't matter how funny she thought I was, she just didn't consider stand-up comedy a real job. She kept calling it a hobby! I remember the first time I told her I wanted to be a comedian, she laughed and said: "You should say that onstage, that's funny!" My mum had an old-school mentality back then; she'd moved to England from Jamaica when she was nine and had worked hard all her life to provide for my future. I don't think she'd planned on her only daughter throwing away all her hard-earned education to become a professional clown, but here we were. What we didn't know at the time is that six years after dropping out, Kingston University would invite that very same professional clown back to give a speech to its students about how to make it in the television industry. I shit you not! I had to stand there and tell a room full of students that in order to make it in television, I had to drop out of university! It went down surprisingly well; I think they admired my honesty.

Being on CBBC taught me so much about working in television, more than any degree ever could. I was live on the air every weekend, I had three cameras in my face, and I had an earpiece that was feeding me into a control room filled with directors, editors, and camera monitors. Money could not buy this type of education. I had finally become what that industry professional whose name I don't remember said I wouldn't: a professional television presenter.

I spent some of the best years of my life being a children's TV presenter. I was so proud of myself, and I loved walking into BBC TV center every day and flashing my pass at security. I would wear my pass even when I wasn't working and would make sure it was on over my coat so that everyone could see that I worked for the BBC!

In those days, kids TV was a wild place and nobody took their jobs too seriously. I mainly remember all the parties. Working at CBBC was the reason I started drinking wine! I had no choice, as there were so many work drinks! CBBC drinks, *Blue Peter* drinks, CBeebies drinks—we were always drinking! We had a thing called Wine Thursdays every week, when at around 4:00 p.m. a cart of alcohol and snacks would be delivered for all the staff, and then we'd all get together at the BBC bar after work. I loved it there; it was an old-fashioned saloon-style bar with a couple of TVs and a pool table. You never knew who you might bump into. I saw Geri Halliwell in there once and nearly lost my shit!

I couldn't believe my job involved getting drunk in green rooms and celeb spotting in the BBC bar. One night, drink in my hand as I tipsily walked to the toilets, I bumped into Alan Carr, who immediately recognized me from my six-week stint as a stand-in on his show. "Oh my God, hello, babes!" he bellowed at me and then immediately grabbed my hand. "Come with me, come and sing in the choir!" he said as he whisked me off to the studio floor. *Am I drunk or am I dreaming?* I thought to myself as Alan led me onto the Comic Relief set where the whole celebrity choir was already in place, live on air on BBC One. Gareth Malone, the choir leader, started handing out sheets of paper to me and the likes of Jimmy Carr, Dawn French, Lenny Henry, and Rick Astley, and we all drunkenly sang the words to "Never Forget" by Take That. It's truly terrible—honestly, look it up, it's on YouTube—it's some of the worst singing you'll ever hear. No choir is ever supposed to make the sounds that were coming out of our mouths. But I didn't care, I was there in the front row of this ridiculous celebrity choir, live on the BBC, loving every single minute of my life.

HOT COCOA FIASCO

The thing I loved the most about being a presenter was getting my hair and makeup done. I felt so important sitting in that chair whilst professionals worked their magic and made me look proper fit. There was a weekly rotation of about seven or eight white female makeup artists; some were better than others, and I befriended the ones that made me look the hottest. My makeup needs were simple: I always asked for glitter and lipstick and to basically look like Beyoncé in every way, shape, and form. What I never once asked for was for hot chocolate to be put on my face.

The day a makeup artist purposefully put hot chocolate on my face was another real eye-opener for me. It started out like any other day: I was sitting in my chair and drinking my tea (milk, eight sugars) when I was introduced to a makeup artist I'd never met before. She started faffing around at first, adding extra moisturizer and all that good stuff, but I assumed she knew what she was doing. Then she pulled out a clear container with a brown powdery substance inside, which she began to powder my face with. All I could smell was chocolate.

"Ooh, this smells chocolatey!" I said, to which she replied: "Well, it's called 'Cocoa.'" The cheeky bitch.

I looked like Fifty Shades of Brown. I looked terrible, like someone had colored me in.

I refused to believe that someone with her CV would be

stupid enough to make me look like I was in blackface, so once she finished my makeup, I decided to take a look through her makeup kit. There, in front of my very eyes, was a tub of Waitrose organic hot chocolate—as in the stuff that you drink before you go to bed. Well, at least it was from Waitrose and at least it was organic! I was completely shocked. I couldn't believe this woman thought it was perfectly okay to Black me up in hot chocolate!

I got my producer to ask the makeup artist about the hot cocoa and she came clean. "I'm sorry, I panicked! I just didn't have any makeup for Black skin!" she cried. I wiped the chocolate dessert drink off my face, covered my face in a bit of anti-shine, and carried on with my job. I would like to say that she got fired after this event, but Miss Sticky Fingers is still out there doing makeup to this day. Thank God she never did my makeup again, but I do worry about her getting her hands on other British Black talent. She could be out there right now putting Nutella hazelnut spread on Alison Hammond.

Hot chocolate on my face wasn't the only racially ignorant thing to happen to me once I started working in television. It's weird to say I was used to it, but going to an all-white school had prepared me for going into an all-white workplace. Remember, this is Britain, long before George Floyd died and people in the industry were nowhere near as woke. I once attended a week-long new writers' retreat at the BBC, and every day white producers would come and talk to us and give advice on our scripts. I asked one of them for advice on a storyline about my parents and she told me that I should "write about how they felt when they came here on the boat from Africa." I didn't know how to tell her that my mum came here on a plane from Jamaica and my dad's from Sussex.

As you know, I've always loved to write, and whilst living out my kids' TV dream, I put my fingers to work and started penning scripts. Real ones that looked professional and weren't about *Frasier* or The Fresh Prince. It was really important for me to write about a world I grew up in but never saw on TV. I rarely saw funny Black women on TV growing up, I rarely saw Black women who had my life or shared mine or my families' experiences. All I saw were caricatures or stereotypes. I hate Black stereotypes. I do whatever I can to push back against them or try to dispel them completely; I understand that for some people the stereotypes are true, I love chicken just as much as the next Black person. But I hated that on television, only the worst forms of Black stereotypes were prevalent. I also hated that working in television meant that people automatically saw me as a walking stereotype.

I read audition script after audition script and sometimes the depictions of Black women were laughable, they weren't fully formed humans, just stereotypical cartoons with attitude.

There were no Black comedy writers with TV shows when I started out so these depictions of Black women were almost always written by white men. That's why it was no surprise to me that in one year, every character I went up for ended in *sha*: I played a Keisha, a Tanisha, a Letisha! And an Aisha, but just once I wanted to play the part of a Lorraine or a Carol or a Jill! I wrote and I wrote, I wrote like my time was running out. I knew that someday somebody would want a Black woman to actually play a lead in a show and not just the ghetto best friend, or the baby mother, or girlfriend of a murder victim and when that time came I'd be ready. From early on I told myself that I wouldn't write shows about Black trauma. I felt like the world had had enough of watching that; I wanted to give them something different. I was a loud Black girl from South London, and everyone from producers to casting directors thought they had me sussed out from a mile away. Sadly but unsurprisingly, racism didn't show any signs of slowing down on the mainstream comedy circuit, either. I experienced my first-ever racist audience member at a white "comedy and curry night" in Hull. I should have known what to expect from the title alone, but I bundled myself into a car with the other white male comics and headed up to Hull, a place I'd only previously heard about on the news. I was on first, and the host did a great job of warming up the crowd for me. You can tell how good or bad a gig is going to go by how easily the host can make the audience laugh, and he had them in the palm of his hand. They were up for some comedy, but when I walked out onstage I could feel the crowd's energy drop. They were not expecting me.

My first joke was met with silence. That had never happened before, but I didn't let it faze me. I kept moving to my second joke. Silence and a cough. Okay, third joke. Silence and a groan. This was it; this is what it felt like to die onstage.

Every comedian talks about dying onstage, and you pray it won't happen but I knew it was bound to eventually. It sounds like the worst thing in the world, sweating your tits off as you desperately try to get laughs. I once had a literal soldier tell me that I was "brave" for doing stand-up and that he couldn't do what I do. Really? Coming from a man who gets shot at for a living?! But dying onstage didn't actually feel that bad. It actually felt kind of liberating, like the worst had happened and I was still here, thriving. Once it was clear the audience wasn't going to laugh at any of my jokes, I just started performing for me. I did my full set better than ever before; I really impressed myself! I finished and said goodnight, and the audience lightly clapped me off the stage.

I headed straight to the bar to kill time as I waited for all the other comics to perform their sets so we could hit the motorway and escape from sheer Hull. I'd just ordered a drink when a woman made a beeline for me.

"You were really funny, babes," she said like she was talking to a five-year-old after performing the role of Tree in a nativity play.

I smirked; I didn't need her pity. "Oh yeah, sure, hun. That's why nobody laughed," I replied sarcastically. Then she said something I really didn't expect anyone to ever say to my face.

"Oh, we didn't laugh 'coz you're not funny, we didn't laugh because you're Black."

I couldn't believe how racist this woman was being! But a part of me was relieved. I knew it! It wasn't because I was unfunny, it was just because I was Black! I can't help being Black, and trust me, I'd rather be Black than unfunny. I took my amaretto and cranberry and moved to the other side of the bar. I complained to the comedy promoter, but nothing happened. A few years later, Hull was declared the 2017 UK City of Culture. Great stuff.

BLACK MATERIAL

I didn't see myself as a Black comic; I saw myself as a comic. My material wasn't Black material, it was just material. Again, due to sexism, systemic racism and 'coz slavery, jokes written and performed by white men are just seen as jokes, whereas jokes told by women are female jokes and jokes told by Black people are Black jokes. I did a BBC radio gig once and one of the producers asked me not to "do any Black material tonight." I wondered what he meant by that. Jokes about my life and family aren't necessarily "Black material," they're just jokes about my life and I just happen to be Black! Imagine me saying that to Jack Whitehall—sorry, Jack, I'm sure all those anecdotes about your parents are hilarious but go easy on the white material tonight.

These microaggressions happened all the time and I got pretty used to them, but one in particular sticks out in my memory. For a very long time all I wanted was an invite to the British Comedy Awards. It seemed like such a cool and fun night, where cool and edgy British comedians were paraded around like rock stars, and I wanted to be a part of it. In hindsight, I may have been a bit overzealous in trying to become British comedy's next big star, and I should have been content with where I was. I'd been doing stand-up for over a year and had won a prestigious award, got a presenting job on Children's BBC, and was gigging all over the country, but I was hungry for more. Back then it was all about the Russells—Russell Brand, Russell Howard, and Russell Kane—and nobody was talking about London

Hughes. I was very jealous. I wanted the industry to know my name; I wanted a buzz like all the other white dudes!

I quickly realized that every comic who became a big thing went on a show called *8 out of 10 Cats*, so I decided if I was going to make my mark in comedy, I'd have to get that show's seal of approval. When I eventually got the call up, I had to go through three rounds of run-through auditions before I could even be considered, but hey, that's showbiz. I auditioned several times and every time I made it to the final round, where all finalists had to write and perform a set for the host, Jimmy Carr. Jimmy has the best laugh in the world, but I can assure you his laugh sounds ten times better when you're the cause of it. I made Jimmy laugh a lot in my *8 Out of 10 Cats* auditions—I remember once absolutely killing it to the point where two of the other comics in the run-through congratulated me: "Mate, you're definitely getting on the show!"—but I was never once asked to be on the show. The producers would say things like, "We love London, but we just don't think our audience would get her" or "If she becomes famous in her own right then we'd love to have her on the show." Week after week I'd see all the white male comics I'd auditioned with end up on the show, but I never got the call. It was starting to become very apparent to me that if I were a white man, I'd have much better luck in comedy.

It was a hard pill to swallow. The producers telling me that their audience wouldn't get me? What does that mean? Why would they not get me? Am I speaking a different language? What about me would they not understand? I knew why, it was as plain as Black and white, but I didn't want to believe it. I thought that if you worked hard enough and were a nice person then you'd achieve what you want in life. Considering how easy it had been for me to succeed so quickly in comedy, I assumed I'd be a big TV star by now, but I didn't take sexism and systemic racism into consideration.

After trying and failing to land a spot on *8 Out of 10 Cats*, the bad news continued. My agent called to tell me that CBBC was moving to Manchester and if I wanted to continue being a presenter for them I'd have to move there. It was an easy decision to make; everything for me was in London and I knew that if I moved to Manchester there was a strong chance I'd end up staying a kids' TV presenter forever. I walked away from CBBC after just over two years, and I was actually the last person to ever present CBBC from London. My family thought I was crazy! The BBC is such a big and powerful establishment that even my mum was concerned! By then she had stopped thinking my career was a just a hobby—no "hobby" pays this well, hunny, I was making funny money! But I knew I had to take a bet and invest in myself. Quitting CBBC with no other job to fall back on was scary, and it was the first of three big jumps I'd make in the early days of my career. When I did it, I was just looking forward to whatever chapter of my life was coming next.

Chapter 12

You're Really Funny, You Should Go to Edinburgh!

I completely threw myself into stand-up after I left CBBC, and after gigs people kept saying to me "You're really funny! You should go to Edinburgh!" At first, I wasn't quite sure why that many people were recommending Scotland to me. I mean, I knew it was pretty but I also knew it was cold, the food was probably bad, and there weren't many Black people there. Let's just say it was not my number one holiday destination. It turns out that Edinburgh hosts the world's biggest comedy festival and up until that moment I'd never even heard of it. I thought I'd give it a visit and see what all the fuss was about. To say it completely blew my mind would be an understatement. For the entire month of August, the whole town shuts down and becomes a stage for comedy. You can literally see comedy anywhere; on the street, in a café, in a church, in a gym, on a crosstown bus, in an old HR office! You can see comedy at any second of the day, at midnight or before your first cup of coffee; and the types of comedy you can see are vast—stand-up comedy, alternative comedy, improv, mime, naked comedy (it's real, just trust me), musical comedy, anything you want is waiting for you at the Edinburgh Comedy Festival. I stepped off that four-hour train ride from Euston to Edinburgh Waverley and everything I thought I knew about being a comedian was completely turned on its head. This was about more than just making people laugh, it was an art form.

My first-ever Edinburgh show was called "Funny Miss London" and I performed it in the cinema room of a bar called the Banshee Labyrinth on Niddry Street. "Funny Miss London" was an hour of stand-up material all about my life that I may or may not have written entirely on that train to Edinburgh. I talked about being bullied, trying to fall in love, my white grandparents—come to think of it, it was a lot like this book, actually! I performed the show for free, every day for a month, and hardly anyone saw it. I think the most audience members I ever had in on one night was thirteen (okay, I know that's true, I wasn't above counting), but that honestly didn't matter to me. It just felt good being onstage doing my art. I went to see a lot of other comedians' shows that month, and I became an even bigger fan of the scene. That month I realized that not only is comedy truly subjective, it's also an art form.

I liked to see what all the other comics were speaking about, and also what was missing. In 2011, when I was first at the festival, the one thing I noticed missing were females. No matter what dusty basement or abandoned train station or decommissioned nuclear power plant I went to, I only saw men performing. The likes of Kevin Bridges, Jason Manford, and Michael McIntyre were absolutely dominating the city with sold-out shows left, right, and center, but no female comic even came close. And don't get me started on diversity—there was none. I'd seen more Black people at a Trump rally! There are thousands of shows on at the festival, and at the end of the month, eight or nine of them get nominated for best show, and the winner gets a cash prize. Nobody really cared about the cash prize, though, because the award itself is so prestigious that just being nominated could put you on the fast track to British comedy legend status. "Funny Miss London" didn't get nominated. It didn't get reviewed. In fact, the show wasn't even listed in the Edinburgh Comedy Festival brochure. But again, truly, it didn't matter to me. I was there to be a student, and I spent a lot of time just letting other comics show me how it was done. I took notes! It was different from gigging at local comedy clubs. Watching a comedian's show was like getting a glimpse of their world. You were literally spending thirty minutes to an hour inside another comic's mind. I learned so much from my first time at the festival and knew that one day I would be back. After the month was over I left Scotland with a newfound confidence and . . . my first-ever, official boyfriend.

BOYFRIEND NUMBER 1

I only consider someone a boyfriend if they've met my parents, and Charlie, an alternative stand-up comic, was the first real-life boy I ever brought home. I've had a few imaginary boyfriends like Tony Blair, Marcell, and Fabio, the imaginary mixed-raced scuba diver, but of course, they didn't count. As you can imagine, my mum was so ecstatic that I was finally back on track to being pregnant by twenty-five, she practically started picking out her wedding hat. Charlie and I met on day twenty-two of the Edinburgh Comedy Festival. When he approached me at one of the comedians-only bars, I was definitely drunk, but I remember thinking he was witty, cute, and very much a gentleman. Charlie was also white, and not only was he white, he also was the first white guy I'd ever dated, and I was the first Black girl he'd dated. The culture clash took some getting used to, but I can highly recommend dating outside your race, some of the best people were made that way! Look at Zendaya! But if you're a white guy dating a Black girl, you NEED to be sensitive. I've dated a few white guys who have said the wrong thing . . . racially speaking. Here's a few tips, so that ebony and ivory can live together in perfect harmony:

Three Little Rules to Dating a Black Girl

1. **DON'T CALL YOUR BLACK GIRLFRIEND A NUBIAN QUEEN**

   I know it seems like a compliment, but it's not. Women of color are not your Nubian queens or your Latina princesses or Geisha girls; they're just normal human women with a different color skin hue than yours, okay, my Caucasian king?

2. **DON'T MAKE A BIG DEAL ABOUT HER HAIR**

   A British Black woman's hair is very confusing, even for them! I'm thirty-two and still don't know how to properly do my hair myself. I've worn wigs, weaves, and braids, and had it natural, but my hair is still a mystery to me! Due to immigration and slavery, Black

British women have found themselves in a country that doesn't respect their natural hair. The harsh British wind and freezing cold rain breaks, dries, and frizzes out their locks, and then Western society tells them that their natural hair isn't acceptable—it's deemed unprofessional—and that, in turn, breaks their spirits. And trust me, things are no better in America. So in some cases, Black women have no choice but to switch it up with wigs and weaves so they can fit into modern-day Western society. Don't question it, hun, just accept that you might not ever see your Black girlfriend's real scalp.

3. **DO EDUCATE YOURSELF ON HER CULTURE BUT DON'T GO OVERBOARD!**

This is a BIG ONE, and I'm talking from experience here. Yes, celebrating your partner's culture is important, but going too far just makes it seem like you're not comfortable around Black people. I'm aware of and can appreciate British culture without singing "God Save the Queen" whenever my white boyfriend enters the room. No need to overcompensate by learning Bob Marley songs by heart, or Martin Luther King Jr. quotes. You don't need to be able to cook rice and peas, and stop saying "Wa Gwarn" to her uncles! It's not necessary, just chill and don't overthink it.

Charlie, my first white boyfriend, was an overthinker and I didn't realize this until it was too late. I thought my little sister Maya's tenth birthday party would be the perfect opportunity to introduce him to my dad, my stepmum, and my brother and sisters. He had already met my mum and was a huge hit, mainly because he was polite and had a penis, but my dad was a lot harder to please, especially as I'm his eldest and truly most magnificent daughter.

I briefed Charlie beforehand: "Just be yourself and don't swear!" Swearing in front of my dad is a big no-no; none of us kids have ever sworn in his presence, and the harshest expletive I've ever heard come from his mouth is the phrase "sugar plum fairies," uttered when he stubbed his toe or dropped his keys. NOBODY swears in the Hughes household, it's crass and it's fuckin' disrespectful! Charlie wasn't a huge swearer anyway, so a part of me thought I didn't need to bring it up—just in case he panicked, started overthinking and ended up swearing by default—but I thought I should mention it as he was anxious to make the best first impression ever.

Now as I told you before, the Hughes family are a bunch of jokers, and since Charlie's a comedian, I told him they might end up roasting him and that he had to be ready to roll with the punches. He said he was ready, and oh, how I believed him. Maya's party was at a bowling alley. We arrived and I introduced him. He was polite, we bowled a bit, there were a bunch of tiny screaming children around—it was cute, no issues. The drama started when we got back to my dad's house.

Four ten-year-old partygoers, my little sister Maya, my older little sister Sakilé, my big brother Joel, my dad, my stepmum Harlene, Charlie, and I were all in the living room playing a game called *Dance Central* on the Xbox. *Dance Central* is a virtual game that comes with an electronic dance mat; you step on the arrows on the mat in time with the player on the screen to get points. I don't mean to brag, but the Hughes family is very good at *Dance Central*; in fact, we're all pretty good dancers, full stop (well, except for my sister Sakilé—all moves, no rhythm, bless her). We all love to dance, and not because we're Black but because we're awesome. What I didn't realize was how much Charlie loved to dance, too. Charlie had all the confidence of an extra in *Fame*, but all the technical dance ability of a drunk dad on a night out. I stepped onto the dance mat, aced it, showed 'em how it's done! Halfway through the dance routine there's a part in the game where the player on-screen stops dancing and leaves you to freestyle in real time. The freestyle section isn't worth any extra points; I'm sure most people just use it as their time to rest, and I usually keep it simple, a little light footwork, nothing too crazy. Once I finish my performance, my little sister Maya steps on the mat. She aces it, perfect score. Next up, it's my brother Joel's turn. He shows off, flawless performance. Then it was Charlie's turn. Charlie stepped onto the dance mat. It was his first time playing *Dance Central*, but like I said he had all the confidence of a professional dancer. In his mind I knew he thought he was going to smash it. The music starts, and he's off beat from the onset, missing counts and missing steps, but my family are encouraging him. "Come on Charlie! That's it!" As he gets comfortable with the moves, he starts to really hit his stride, words like "perfect" and "great" and "100%" are appearing on the screen. Go on Charlie, yes! *That's my boyfriend,* I think to myself, but that feeling is short-lived as he enters the freestyle section. As we all previously demonstrated, the freestyle section wasn't a moment to go too crazy, but Charlie wanted to impress this Black family. He wanted to show off, so he did something that no other heterosexual white male has done in the history of humankind.

Charlie dutty wined.

The dutty wine is a Jamaican dancehall and bashment dance move predominantly done by Jamaican women in the mid-2000s. It's taken from the song "Dutty Wine" by reggae and dancehall artist Tony Matterhorn. It's a complicated dance—when the song comes on, women are supposed to bend their knees, bend forward, and sexually gyrate their hips whilst spinning their heads around like a propeller. It was huge when I was a teenager, all the girls did it! Not to brag, but I was actually awarded Miss Dutty Wine champion whilst on holiday in Jamaica in 2006. But this was 2013, I hadn't dutty wined in years and besides, this was a sexual dance made for, and I repeat, JAMAICAN WOMEN. So I had no idea why my white boyfriend was performing it in front of my family at my ten-year-old sister's birthday party!

My brother cracked up first. Not a burst-out-loud laugh, but a silently awkward what-is-he-doing laugh. My brother looked at me, I looked at my dad, who was NOT IMPRESSED. My dad would never raise his voice, but if he didn't like something or deemed it inappropriate, he would get this look on his face that simply said, "I'm disappointed and this needs to stop." I knew my dad was seconds away from pulling that face, and I couldn't take it anymore. The freestyle section had only about ten seconds left, but I had to put a stop to the dutty-wining madness! "Err, Charlie, what are you doing?" The tone of my voice was jokey, so it wouldn't hurt his feelings, but assertive enough for him to get the hint and stop it right now! But then Charlie clapped back, bold, wrong, and strong; he confidently replied,

"What? White man can't dutty wine?" and kept on going.

All the air got sucked out of the room. I think I died for a few seconds because my spirit definitely left my body. My dad was now doing THAT face. Charlie had committed some of the biggest faux pas.

1. He assumed that an old, blatantly sexual Jamaican dance would be an appropriate thing for a stranger to do at a family gathering for a ten-year-old, a dance my dad has personally never seen me do, a dance that nobody except Black women with very strong knees should even attempt!

2. It was obvious to the Hugheses that Charlie wouldn't have attempted that dance move if we were a white family. He wouldn't be gyrating around like a horny drunk dancehall queen if we were the Clarks from Cornwall! He stereotyped us, and tried to impress us, but it came across as ignorant. Why would that impress us? My dad's never even been to Jamaica!

3. When he didn't get the reaction he expected, he brought race into it. "What? White man can't dutty wine?" Who says that?! I still don't know why he said that?! What did the fact that he was white have to do with anything? Why was his whiteness on his mind? The tension in the room was palpable and Charlie could feel it, because after the freestyle dutty wine from hell, he did the ONE

THING I told him not to do. He missed the final steps of the dance routine and said a very loud and audible "OH SHIT!" and then once he realized he wasn't supposed to swear, he said, "Oh shit! Sorry!" My dad's face looked like someone had just come into his home and pissed on his carpet. "Umm, Daddy, he said a swear word," Maya chimed in. Charlie went bright red. I didn't go red because I'm Black but if I could, I would have. Charlie finished the game and sat down. The only word circling in my head was "WHY?" Charlie wasn't ever invited back to my dad's house again, and we broke up a few months later. It was a sore subject back then, but to this day my family still teases me about it. We'll be happily watching a film as a family and my brother Joel will, out of the blue, say, "Remember the time London's boyfriend dutty wined for no reason and then swore in front of dad?" They won't ever let me forget it.

MY FIRST OFFICIAL BREAKUP

My breakup with Charlie was so drama-free that it was weird. I guess we both knew our relationship was coming to an end because it happened so casually. I was at his house and we got into an argument over something stupid. I walked away thinking he would come running after me, but he didn't, so I just carried on walking all the way home. That was it, over! I never cried over him. Friendship breakups were the only relationships that turned me into a blubbering mess, but for some reason romantic relationships rarely do. There were many reasons why Charlie didn't get my breakup tears, but I think the main one was because I knew (and this is gonna sound harsh) that he was my filler boyfriend.

ALL girls have had a filler boyfriend, whether we want to admit it or not—a boyfriend we know we're not going to be with in the long run but someone that was nice enough to do for now. In my twenties, every single guy I dated was a filler boyfriend! I knew this going in, mainly because I knew I wanted to be a famous megastar, and none of the guys I dated would be able to handle that. I envisioned myself on red carpets and getting snapped by paparazzi, and I knew that Tony from marketing or Dan the computer technician was NOT going to be the beau on my arm at the Oscars. Sounds harsh but it was true, hun. We all have our calling and purpose in life. I found mine early on, and I knew that if you wanted to get with me, you needed to have similar aspirations. Charlie DID have potential though, but his dreams were all over the place—he was a stand-up comic/dancer (see: mortifying birthday part, above)/journalist and between you and me, he wasn't really that focused on any of it. I heard he makes organic beard wax now. He was also my first-ever stand-up comic boyfriend and I couldn't just place all my eggs in his chuckle basket! There were so many other stand-up comics out there to sample, and trust me, I pretty much sampled them all. Stand-up comics, improv comedians, alternative comics, comedy writers, all of them! Throughout my career I dated and slept with some of the funniest white men in British comedy (okay, not all of them were THAT funny). But I worked up a good roster of top-tier totty. However, dating comedians isn't something I'd usually recommend unless you're actually a comic yourself. You need to really trust your comedian partner and understand the lifestyle, because if I'm honest, comedians like to have sex with each other . . . A LOT! Hey, it's a lonely job gigging around the country! You've got a gig in Halifax, they've got a gig in Halifax, you both perform, drinks at the bar, then it's "Fancy coming back to my hotel room?" normal stuff; it's not a crazy statement to suggest that in the tiny world of British comedy, everyone's pretty much hooked up with everyone else, sometimes regardless of if those people are in a relationship or not. I've definitely had a few women's comedy husbands try to hook up with me, but I never sleep with married men! I let them go down on me because I'm a feminist. My comedy sex roster looks like an all-star episode of *Mock the Week*, but it was just a bit of fun—I didn't love any of them. I don't think I've ever actually been in love, just in lust, lots and lots of lust.

WHAT'S LOVE GOT TO DO WITH IT?

Beyoncé has a lyric that goes *I'd rather die young than live my life without you* that to me is L-O-V-E. Beyoncé Knowles-Carter has been dangerously in love, crazy in love, and drunk in love with Jay-Z and to be honest, love, I really can't relate. I think one of the reasons is because I've been so focused on my career that I didn't really take falling in love into consideration; it was always something I'd do once I reached my goal. There was no guy on Earth that I cared about more than becoming Britain's answer to Whoopi Goldberg and because of that, men became a bit of a distraction to me. A fun distraction that would often take me to nice restaurants and make me come several times, but a distraction, nevertheless.

Speaking of orgasming several times, now's a lovely time to let you know I didn't have my first orgasm until I was twenty-three! With Charlie, my dutty-wining boyfriend! I know! Crazy! But he really did put some of those dancehall moves to good use. I finally became one of those women in a Channel 5 blue movie that said words like "Oh God, yes!!" and "Right there! Please don't stop!" Sex was definitely worth the hype and I am so glad I eventually discovered orgasms because I had no idea what I was doing all those years beforehand! Once I figured out that men could give me mind-blowing vaj fireworks (sometimes) my thirst for the D grew much stronger.

I had just been through my first official breakup and I was on the rebound. It was no surprise that I became a bit of a sex savage. I was dating A LOT and having casual sex A LOT, I'd mastered the art of sleeping with guys with no strings attached. I know some girls who can only get with guys they love or have a very strong connection with, but with me, it basically helped if I didn't. The less I cared about the dude, the better the sex was. I wasn't worried about whether he would call me in the morning, or if he thought I was good or bad in bed. If I was attracted to him, he had good energy, and didn't say anything stupid, there was a strong chance I was smashing him. It felt liberating, and I think me acting that way made men want me even more. "You're just like a guy" they would say to me, which is ridiculous. I don't understand why men don't think women enjoy casual sex just as much as they do. News flash, we do!

My mum once looked me in my eye and said, "When you get older, the sex stops, and nobody tells you that . . . so have as much sex as you can while you're young . . . I wish I did." Well, I'm doing it for you, Mum! Dating in London before dating apps was great; guys actually approached you and asked you for your number. No one does that anymore, now you just order it online and get dick delivered to your doorstep like Uber Eats! I used to get most of my dick from bars and nightclubs, in the good old days when a guy would see you and approach you with a cheesy chat-up line. Mine were usually based around my name. Here are some of my favorites.

"Hey London, what's your last name? England?"
"Oh well, I'd LOVE to spend one night in London."
"London? Well, let me see your Shepherd's Bush!" (That dude definitely got a hand blow for originality!)

I like chat-up lines with a bit of creativity, not the usual "You come here often?", which only ever works on white women in movies. Honorable mention to the guy who walked up to me at the bar, started smashing up some ice with his fists, turned to me, and said, "Hey, so now that the ice is broken, can I buy you a drink?"

THE WHORE-RING TWENTIES

By my midtwenties my career had stalled, but my hoe phase was in full swing. I was having a good time, safely, no pregnancies, no STDs, but I had one crazy night that made me slow down my hoe train just a little bit. I was at a club dancing, living my best life, and this cute guy caught my eye. He was bustin' out some serious moves in the middle of the dance floor, but in a sexy, cool, confident way, not a *Saturday Night Fever*, I'll-break-into-the-worm kind of way. I was impressed, I was aroused, I wanted to smash. His eyes met mine and he smiled at me, then gestured that I should come at him. He wanted a dance-off and you know I never back down from a dance-off. I spun myself over to him, started twirling around, and then hit him with a little salsa move (it usually throws 'em off their rhythm), but he caught it, and me, and we started salsa dancing. He spun me around and dipped me, and I fell in love on the dance floor. A circle started to form around us, but it felt like we were the only people in the club. I smiled at him. "Do you wanna go someplace a bit more . . . horizontal?" He grabbed my face and kissed me. It was a good kiss, the type of kiss that makes your knees go weak and your vaj do backflips. I took that as a yes! We go to his house, it was huge! A four-bedroom town house in northwest London!

He could only have been around twenty-two or twenty-three, how could he afford it?! I'd hit the dick jackpot! He shut the front door quietly, as if not to wake anyone, and my heart sank a little. Ah, okay, he's got roommates. I walked past a family photo on the mantelpiece. Oh no, much worse . . . he still lives with his parents! My vaj got drier than a digestive biscuit. I wasn't sure how I felt about getting jiggy with a dude while his rents were asleep upstairs, this wasn't 2007! I made an executive decision that sex was off the table, but I would still let him go down on me for my troubles.

"I just need to go and tidy my room, be right back."

He bounded up the stairs, and my sex drive went with him. Tidying his room? What was he, twelve?!! Why did he have to spoil it all by saying something stupid! What had started off so sexually promising had gone downhill fast, and I was thinking of an exit strategy. It was only midnight; I could essentially make a run for it, go back to the club, and the night wouldn't be a complete disaster. I made for the front door and then paused. The door seemed familiar. I turned around and walked back into the living room. In fact, the whole house had a familiar vibe to it. I thought it must've been the layout—a lot of London houses have the same layout—it probably just reminded me of my grandma's house, or my cousins' house. I kept walking around looking for clues. I didn't recognize the art on the walls or anyone in the family photos, either. Interesting. I then came across a bookcase. I'm a bit of a book snob, I judge a book by its cover, and I judge a person by their books. I was having a little look through the books on his shelf—mainly car magazines and business management books—and I wasn't impressed, until I noticed a book I had. A book by comedian Tina Fey called *Bossypants*. Now this was a very niche book to find on a guy's shelf. It was relatively new and the only people I knew who owned it at the time were female comics. It was basically our Bible, we all had that book, I had that book. "HAD" being the operative word in the sentence because at that moment, for the life of me, I couldn't remember the last time I had seen my copy. As I tried to recall, I absentmindedly picked up *Bossypants* and started thumbing through it. I was impressed that he had this book, too. *We're book twins*, I thought to myself. As I flipped to the last page, I stopped in complete shock. I instantly remembered where I'd left my book, because I looked down and there were my initials, L. H., written in the corner of Tina Fey's *Bossypants*. The book I was holding was mine. I'd left it at his house, and his house was so familiar because I had been there before. I was about to double-fuck him!

I was MORTIFIED! I couldn't believe I was about to sleep with the same guy twice! My hoe phase was so prolific that I had clearly slept with all the men in London and now I was doubling up! I was getting so much dick I'd started lapping them! But then the embarrassment started to fade and turned to annoyance. I can't believe he didn't remember?! How dare he not remember that he'd already slept with me!! I tried to make a run for it again just as he walked down the stairs and asked, "Hey! Where are you going?" Now, the old me wouldn't have said anything, she hated confrontation, but the new confident comedian me had matured, ready to face her challenges head-on . . . And was also a little drunk.

"This is my book!" I said, as if I was a detective who'd just found their leading bit of evidence.

"Oh, cool, you found it!" he said to me a little too casually.

"Yes, I found it! Because I've been here before, I left it here!! We slept together! How dare you not remember me!!?" I was going in on him, clearly angry but mainly to cover up my embarrassment.

He gave me a funny look and said, "What?! Of course I remember you, London! Why do you think I kissed you and brought you back to my place!" The penny dropped as I went through the night in my head. He saw me at the club, we danced for about five minutes, he kissed me like a pro, and then we went home with each other. He took me home because he knew me, but I thought it was just because I was incredibly alluring! He continued, "I thought it was weird when you asked me what my name was, but I thought you were just playing hard to get, doing a sexy role-play thing, pretending we were strangers, of course I remembered you!" My embarrassment circle grew ten times wider and swallowed me whole. "You do remember me, right, London?" But I didn't, I had no clue, I remembered the inside of his home before I remembered him, what a disaster! I was truly the whore that forgot! Tina Fey saved me that night. I took my copy of *Bossypants*, made my excuses, and left. I never saw him again. (I don't think.)

After sleeping with pretty much all the eligible men in London, I decided to slow the hoe life down a bit, to see if I could find a meaningful connection, or at least a quarter of whatever Beyoncé was talking about in her songs. I was all rebounded out, bored of casual dating, and I decided I wanted a guy in my life who 1) I actually remembered and 2) I could bring home to meet my parents. I started dating a guy named Daniel, who was a few years older than me and really had his shit together. We met at a club in East London. His energy attracted me. It wasn't his looks—he wasn't the most attractive flower in the garden—but he was a smart and witty rose, and I loved making him laugh. He'd bought his own flat in Camberwell, worked a proper nine-to-five in the city, and cooked dinner for me like a Michelin Star chef. We went on a few dates and after a while I was staying over at his house every other night. Daniel was a man, whereas all the guys I'd dated before were definitely leaning more toward childish boys. I was so done with dating boys that after my last breakup, I'd made some important rules that my new potential boy (man) friend had to adhere to.

1. **HE CAN'T HAVE A SINGLE BED**
   You'd be surprised at the number of men in their early to midtwenties who still have single beds! Having sex in one feels like camping! I don't think anyone over the age of seventeen should sleep in a bed where they can't do a starfish. It's not normal.

2. **HE CAN'T LIVE WITH HIS PARENTS**
   Again, another one you would think goes without saying, but it was slim pickings out there. There are men in their thirties and forties who still live with mum and dad and it's not sexy! Ever tried to whisper an orgasm? It feels like holding in a sexual sneeze. Pass.

3. **HE HAS TO HAVE FREE PARKING OUTSIDE HIS HOUSE**
   This rule is arguably the most important. I cannot tell you the number of parking tickets dating has cost me. Nothing kills postcoital bliss like waking up at 6:00 a.m. to get out of his bed and move your car!

I drove a black-and-pink brand-new Mini Cooper— her name was Courtney. Courtney would always find herself outside some dude's house first thing in the morning with a bright yellow ticket on her windshield. I couldn't live that life anymore. Whoever I fell in love with now needed to have a private garage or a council-approved visitor's parking permit.

It was really difficult to find a guy that fit my new criteria. They would have free parking but still live with their parents, or lived in a house share, but had a single bed. I was over the moon to find that Daniel ticked all three of my boyfriend boxes. He had the potential to be more than my next filler boyfriend! Daniel introduced me to all the finer things in life. Before dating him I was shopping in Primark, eating McDonald's, and going to nightclubs for fun. He took me to high-end restaurants and jazz bars. We had brunch in art museums and went shopping on Carnaby Street. Daniel made way more money than I did, and at times that made me feel insecure. It was the first time a guy had ever made me feel that way. The guys I'd dated before didn't really have their life together, and to be honest, neither did I, BUT I was a comedian, and I was on the telly, so by comparison, I was really going places. But after leaving CBBC, my career had stalled, and so had my funds. I wasn't going anyplace fast—well, except to McDonald's to get a chicken nugget meal. I'd moved back in with my mum and stepdad, who by now had sold the hotel, retired, and bought a big house in Brighton. My mum couldn't wait to have me back home. Thank God I had a double bed and a two-car garage, but I wasn't even meeting my own dating criteria at this point! I was in a transitional period in my life, and Daniel came around at the right time.

After a while I'd met all Daniel's friends, even his mum! I assumed I had entered early girlfriend territory; he was the only guy I was dating, and I was at his house all the time. I'd even drop him off at work in the morning and stay in his flat when he wasn't there. This went on for a few months, and eventually I got bored of packing a bag every time I came to see him and decided to leave some stuff at his. Harmless, I thought. Oh no, big mistake, HUGE.

I'd had a shower and I left a plastic shower cap in his bathroom. When he came home from work, he said, "What's this?" He looked extremely annoyed. "You can't be leaving your things in MY house, London!" I was so confused!

"What's wrong, it's just a shower cap!?" I was upset that it was such a big deal to him, total red flag! Like I said, he cooked for me every night, I'd met all his friends and family, I was driving him to work in the mornings, why couldn't I leave a measly shower cap at his house? He could sense I was upset and tried to calm me down. We had never officially had "the talk" to decide what exactly our status was, but I assumed we were heading to Couple Avenue. But that reaction made it pretty clear I was still in Side-Chick Alley.

"I like you soo much, I'm just not ready for a relationship yet." What a phrase. Guys say the "I'm not ready for a relationship" line a lot, and I find it funny that most of them say it without realizing that they're already in a relationship. Whether Daniel wanted to admit it or not, if it walks like a girlfriend and quacks like a girlfriend then it's a girlfriend. In hindsight, that should have been enough to walk away. The non-relationship (according to him) was doomed. But Daniel was so good with words, he always had a way to bring me round to his way of thinking. He once used this dating analogy where he compared me to a house.

"You're like an amazing Victorian town house that needs renovations. Obviously it's an amazing house and I've bought it, but I need to get the builders in to do some work on it before

I move in." And can you believe I took that as a compliment?!? I remember telling my dad about him a few weeks later, but David Hughes was not impressed with the house analogy AT ALL.

"He's never going to ask you to be his girlfriend. He is not serious about you...listen to me, I'm a man, we know these things." My dad was right, but I didn't want to hear it. Apart from the shower cap thing, Daniel had let me into his life in so many ways, I knew it would only be a matter of time before he fell head over heels for me. And luckily for me, Valentine's Day was coming up.

MY UNFUNNY VALENTINE

Most people view Valentine's Day as a way to SHOW your love for the person in your life. I view it as a way to TEST the love of the person in your life. If Daniel and I had a future, Valentine's Day would show me. So I went shopping! I scraped together all my money and got Daniel an expensive Barbour coat I knew he wanted. It was the first designer thing I'd ever bought and it wasn't even for me! I also got him a Gucci watch he had his eye on, and then I went to Build-A-Bear Workshop and made him a fluffy toy Labrador. He'd always wanted a real Labrador, and we'd talked and joked about getting one together. I thought a toy one would be cute. When you squeezed it, a recording of my voice played saying how much I appreciated him. All in all, it was the most money I'd ever spent on any guy, ever. Now, I don't give to receive. I actually enjoy buying people presents, and I couldn't wait to give Daniel his, and see his face light up.

But there was still a part of me that couldn't help but wonder what he'd got me.

Well, I didn't have to wonder long because Daniel didn't get me anything for Valentine's Day. I gave him his gifts; he was happy about the coat and the watch but looked uncomfortable and embarrassed by the toy dog. He put it away in his closet and I never saw it again. I think at one point he even suggested I take it home. I don't know what upset me more, that he didn't seem to appreciate the presents I gave him, or that he forgot to get something for me.

"Don't worry, babes, I've been busy with work. I'll get you something nice for V-Day, I promise." I believed him. I was hopeful that he saw the care and effort I'd put into his V-Day gifts and he would reciprocate. A week later Daniel gave me my Valentine's Day present. It was a cheap unwrapped notepad, a pen, and some pink Post-it Notes. "For you to write your jokes in, innit!"

That's when I knew it was over between us. He didn't directly say it, but his actions showed it—he was never going to move into this unrenovated Victorian town house. Who buys the girl in your life, someone you're repeatedly having intimate moments with, a notepad for Valentine's Day?!! I ended things with him, but it broke me, mainly because I couldn't understand why I wasn't good enough for him. I cried, but I wasn't really crying about him, I was crying about me. It felt like I was in school again, not good enough for the popular boy. I drove the hour and twenty minutes from Camberwell back to Brighton a complete sobbing mess. As I hit the motorway a beautiful song by Laura Mvula called "Sing to the Moon" played on the radio. I looked up at the moon and it was full . . . I started to sing along. *"Hey there you, shattered in a thousand pieces / Weeping in the darkest nights."* The song perfectly summed up my raw emotions and so I sung, I sang to that bloody moon. All that was going through my mind was, why? Why was I not good enough? What was wrong with me? Why didn't he want me? Why did I choose to believe this man's opinion of me was the gospel truth, why did I seek validation from the Book of Daniel? Why was I a Victorian town house that needed renovations?! I saw Daniel at a New Year's Eve party a few years later, and I asked him why it never worked out between us. He revealed that he had actually been cheating on me with another girl the whole time we were together. I wasn't even surprised! That was all I needed to hear. All that time spent thinking I wasn't good enough when in truth, he was the problem, not me! And, in fact, no one woman was good enough for that cheating little prick! No wonder he got so annoyed when I left my things at his house! After Daniel, I pledged to never let a guy make me feel that low about myself. I would never again give a man the power to make me feel like I wasn't worthy—like I needed fixing up or changing. I don't need men to validate me! I hear Daniel's married now. I guess he found a town house he actually deemed worthy enough to move into. I hope it gets repossessed.

Chapter 13

Funny and Failing

By the age of twenty-four, I considered myself a failure. I was back living with my parents, single, a university dropout, and my job as a kids' TV presenter was over, my first Edinburgh Comedy Festival attempt had been a bust, and I'd had EVERY SINGLE TV show I pitched rejected. I was feeling very unmotivated, to say the least. Time to pay a visit to my agent, Vivienne.

Vivienne had assured me that not moving to Manchester with CBBC had been the right decision, and I believed her. I knew that I was talented enough to get work in London and I'd been wanting a get-out-of-kids-TV-free card. Now don't get me wrong, there was and still is nothing wrong with being a kids' TV presenter, but it just wasn't reflecting my current life. The job had been paying my bills but hindering my long-term goals. It was a filler, the "Charlie" of jobs! After a while, I'd even stopped doing stand-up because it felt weird when parents came up to me after I'd just been onstage telling dick jokes for twenty minutes, asking, "Can I get a pic please, my daughter loved you on CBBC?" I was both proud of my job and growing slightly embarrassed by it. People stopped seeing me as the little miss dynamite of comedy; I was just the girl who introduced Tracy Beaker and Scooby-Doo. Walking away from it gave me the opportunity for a fresh start. *I'll be fine,* I thought to myself, *the offers will come rolling in.* I didn't take into consideration one small thing. I'm a Black woman, trying to be a famous comedian, in Britain. Let's just say the phone wasn't exactly ringing off the hook.

"Black people just aren't in this year"—was the *exact* response I got from my co-agent David Lazenby after asking why I hadn't had many auditions. As if Black people were a pair of high-waisted jeans. It was 2013. I knew I had to leave my agent if I was going to get any further in my comedy career. By now, some of my white male friends had become household names and I seemed to be going backward! My mum didn't understand. She'd see a comic I knew on the TV and say, "Isn't that Russell Howard? How come he has a show and you don't have a show? You've been doing comedy longer than he has!" or "What do you mean you haven't heard back from that audition? It's been a month now; don't they have someone at HR you can speak to?" My career was getting so bad my mum asked me if I would consider signing on and getting benefits. She knew I wouldn't be able to get a proper job, as the last one I'd had was six years ago at TGI Fridays! I was broke, but my pride wouldn't let me sign on. "I'll sort it, Mum," I said, and promptly started looking for new representation.

I got a meeting with an entertainment agency called Avalon and I was excited because they represented all the huge white dudes in comedy. Unfortunately, it went horribly. "What happened to you?" the agent asked me.

"Excuse me?" I said, trying to decipher what this man was referring to.

"You won the funny woman competition and you were everywhere, and then you just disappeared. What happened?" I didn't know that was how people perceived me. Disappeared? "Just to clarify, I don't wanna sign you, I just wanted to know what happened." Wow ... okay, sir, thanks for nothing.

I left that meeting feeling even worse about my comedy career. Apparently I was already a has-been. Then to really sink the ship, the next day I got an email from Vivienne. Somebody had informed her that I'd had a meeting with Avalon, and she dropped me on the spot, just like that, via email. So cold. After three solid years with an agent, I was now unemployed and unrepresented. It felt like someone had pushed me off a cliff with no bungee cord. *What am I supposed to do now?!* I thought to myself! Was it all worth it? I could have had a degree in television, a nine-to-five job, and a normal stress-free life, maybe I'd have a decent flat by now, even a dog! But instead, I took a huge gamble, followed my dreams, and it led me right back to my parents' house in Brighton.

I turned to self-help books and autobiographies during those times. I needed something to give me hope. I knew every secret *The Secret* had to offer. I was doing daily affirmations and getting diddly squat. This couldn't be how it ended for me! I read about how Richard Branson moved back in with his parents at my age and couldn't even afford the five-pound cab journey back home, how Oprah Winfrey had been fired from her job as a broad-caster in her thirties, how Simon Cowell was broke and trying to make it in the music industry in his twenties. If they could all turn things around, so could I! I started to develop a tough skin. I'd say to myself: when your life goes to shit, just scream "plot twist" and remember that it'll be a great chapter for your autobiography one day.

I may have been down, but I refused to be out.

PLOT TWIST!

Within a month, I bumped into a friend of mine who recom-mended his agent; her name was Tiffany Agbeko. She was a badass, and after one meeting she signed me on the spot! Tif-fany worked for a company called John Noel Management. JNM used to look after Russell Brand, and at the time he was a complete rock star, everything I wanted to be in comedy. He was in movies, had taken America by storm, and even managed to marry popstar Katy Perry for God's sake! He was my com-edy idol and whatever his management did to get him there, I wanted them to do the exact same thing for me. JNM signing me built my confidence right back up, my new plan was now total world domination! I wanted to be Comedy Beyoncé. I was going to act, write, do stand-up, be a presenter—I could do it all, and I wanted it all! So, so badly.

I worked like my life depended on it, writing TV show after TV show ideas, scripts upon scripts, auditioned my arse off, taking meetings with anyone who would see me. I networked. I socialized. I went to the opening of an envelope! I still lived in Brighton, so I would wake up at 6:00 a.m., drive two or three hours through London traffic, park my car, get on a train and then a tube into central London, just to do a ten-minute audition, and then I would turn around and go all the way back again. I spent a lot of time on the road, but I loved driving. Some people had a cigarette or a drink when they needed a break from life; I had a nice long drive. I would hop in Courtney the Mini Cooper and hit the M23, blasting Two Door Cinema Club; Beyoncé; or Tyler, the Creator, all the way. I'd have my two hands on the wheel and eyes on the road whilst my brain would be elsewhere imagining my future. Every time I thought about future me, she was in America sipping champagne on a balcony overlooking Beverly Hills or getting papped on a red carpet.

My new agent worked her arse off for me. Within a month or so, Tiffany had helped land me my first lead role, on a prime-time TV prank show called *Bad Bridesmaid!* See? I knew all I needed to do was stick it out. I'd been through the shit and now it was time for my sunshine. I was convinced that this was the job that would change everything and make me famous!

BAD BRIDESMAID

A bride-to-be on a hen do (that's a bachelorette party, for you US folks) has to fool her bridesmaids into thinking a comedy impostor (me) is also a bridesmaid and a part of her wedding. Over the course of the weekend, the comedy impostor sets crazy demands and challenges for the bride to follow. If she completes them without her real bridesmaids suspecting a thing, she wins a honeymoon to the Maldives. It was a fucking mental idea.

Six female comedians were chosen for the show, and we each had our own one-hour episode with different brides and bridal parties. I was the token Black comic on the show. My bride was Black, all her bridesmaids were Black, and our episode was responsible for all the diversity in the entire series. No pressure then. I had to go undercover, on a hen do, for three days with a bunch of girls I didn't know and intentionally piss them off. We had a camera crew following us, and all the girls except the bride thought they were merely filming a fly-on-the wall documentary about hen parties. My job was to cause absolute chaos and sabotage the weekend as much as possible without raising the suspicions of the other bridesmaids and causing them to find out that they were actually on a prank show.

My character was a total diva, a delusional TV presenter who brought attention to herself by any means necessary. I was pranking a group of girls from Hackney, East London, all around my age, with very strong personalities. They were the bride's older cousins, sisters, and best friends and were SUPER protective of her. I had to rile them up, ruin the hen do, and make it as difficult as possible for the bride to win the honeymoon, all without the bridesmaids suspecting a thing.

"What do I do if one of the bridesmaids hits me?" I asked the producers. It was a genuine question. I'd been hit by girls for less!

"Oh, don't be silly, they won't hit you!" the producers replied. Famous last words.

After three days of big pranks I was doing really well. The girls had no clue I was an impostor and I was seriously proud of my acting skills! So far I'd managed to: Ruin their game of bowling by refusing to play because it was "beneath me" and "celebrities don't bowl." I then jumped on the mic at the bowling alley to announce to all the customers that a celebrity was in the building and I'd be available to sign autographs; ruin a game of polo by freaking out and having a nervous breakdown because I thought I saw paparazzi in the bushes trying to snap a pic of me; get the bride to give me an intense shoulder massage in front of everyone to calm my "anxiety"; ruin a peaceful life-drawing class by standing next to the nude male model and insisting everyone draw me instead. In between these big pranks, I had to stick to my backstory. My *Bad Bridesmaid* character was a famous TV presenter who was dating the groom's best friend, a shallow, narcissistic fame whore who happened to be "close personal friends" with every single celebrity the girls mentioned.

Oh, and I also didn't eat food because I was on the "air diet." Every lunch break, whilst the bridesmaids were chowing down on burgers and fries, I would sip water and suck in air like a goldfish, declaring that "It fills up my lungs and tricks my body into thinking I'm full."

I was the perfect Bad Bridesmaid, and all the other women despised me.

It was the final day of filming, and my last piece of sabotage was based around a beautiful photo shoot with a top-notch photographer. All the bridesmaids had the same dress, but in different colors, and the bride had two unique white wedding dresses to choose from. I remember the girls were all getting their pictures taken, the bride dressed lovely in white and her bridesmaids were rocking the hell out of their yellow, orange, green, and blue maxi dresses. While they were occupied, I slipped out of my bridesmaid dress and into the wedding dress the bride hadn't chosen; every part of my body was telling me not to do it. These girls hadn't been shy about voicing their disdain for me. They were rude to me on and off camera, talked over me, laughed in my face, gave me evil looks, and made sly and cutting remarks. Coming out in a wedding dress was, quite possibly, a tiny step too far. I felt so sorry for the bride, who was completely stressed out. "London, you're killing me! I can't take anymore!" she would whisper to me in between the challenges. Her little sister was giving her a hard time for putting up with me, but the bride had to go along with it or else she wasn't going to win that honeymoon.

The wedding dress on, I composed myself and walked out of the bathroom and straight onto the set of the photo shoot. Wanting to make a grand entrance, I started humming the wedding march, "Dum dum de dummm, dumm dum de dumm...! What do you guys think?" All the bridesmaids' faces dropped, the bride looked constipated, and her little sister was beyond seething. They screamed things like, "What the fuck do you think you're wearing?" and "Where's your bridesmaid dress?!" but I calmly ignored them.

"I didn't want to wear a bridesmaid dress, I want to wear this," I said with all the poise and grace of a pageant girl. I smiled at the bride. "Can I wear this dress for the photo shoot please?" All the girls stared at her, the tension so thick you could cut it with a sword. The bride paused, her eye twitched, she exhaled slowly, and said,

"Yeah . . . sure you can."

"What the fuck!!" her sister yelled. "Why are you letting this bitch control you?!" Her cousins all screamed at me, and the bride tried to get her sister to calm down. I ignored it all, twirling around in the dress and posing for the photos. The photographer (also not in on it) found the whole ordeal highly entertaining. The bride eventually placated the group and we all fake smiled for the group shot, and I put my arm around the bride and did a big cheesy grin.

"We look like twins!" I said, whilst the girls all muttered expletives under their breath.

The photo shoot was over, and I felt the bride breathe a sigh of relief. But she still had one more challenge to overcome. That instant, I turned to the bride, looked her dead in the eye, and asked if she'd let me wear this beautiful white wedding dress to her wedding. All the girls burst out laughing! "This bitch can't be serious." But I was dead serious (well, not really, the producers made me do it). I looked the bride right in her face and asked her again, slowly. One of the cousins snapped first, screaming, "You are not wearing that fucking dress to my cousin's wedding!" She kept repeating this statement to me, getting more and more frustrated with every syllable.

"Okay, but I didn't ask you," I replied sweetly. The tension level was World War III at this point. "Can I wear it, hun?" I asked one more time, and the bride gulped, looked down at her feet, and then said, "Yeah...sure why not." At that point, all hell broke loose! Everyone was shouting, and the bride's little sister yelled,

"Who the fuck do you think you are?! I've had enough of you now!" She drew back her fist and punched me right in the face. I was shocked, but I didn't drop character for a second. I grabbed my face and asked, "Why did you hit me? Are you upset about something?"

"GET THE FUCK AWAY FROM MEEEE!!!" she screamed and ran away, followed by the bride, now crying, chased by all the cousins. I'm still twirling around in my wedding dress, the cameras are rolling, and all I'm trying to convince myself is "This is going to be GREAT television!"

The next morning, the producer comes into my hotel room. "We're at the homestretch now, we're doing the big reveal in an hour, you've been fucking great!" I was just relieved that it was finally over, since doing the show had started to test my mental health. I knew I was acting, and it was a prank show, but sometimes I felt like I was back at university again with the mean girls. My character felt very real to me because I was essentially playing a heightened version of myself; my character was even called London Hughes and she *was* a children's TV presenter. All the bad bridesmaids on the other episodes got to change their names and identities, but I couldn't for fear the girls may recognize me from my time on CBBC. Whenever the girls were being rude, or insulting my bad bridesmaid character, it felt like they were actually insulting ME.

"I told you the girls would punch me!" I said.

"I know; that was so crazy, but you were so good!" the

producer replied, no apology. She went straight back to the task at hand, the big reveal. The plan was to have a last lunch with all the girls on camera where we'd all talk about our highlights of the weekend. I would stand up and make a speech, revealing that I'm a comedy actress, and that they'd actually been on the ITV 2 show *Bad Bridesmaid*, and putting up with my antics for three days had just won the bride a beautiful honeymoon!

I was going over my lines when there was a knock at the door. It was one of the bridesmaids. FUCK! The producer quickly fled to her adjoining room, whilst I tried to hide my notebook, the papers of research I had on the bridesmaids, and the leftover burger I had from lunch. We'd come way too far for them to see I'd broken my important "air diet" and discover it was all a prank! When I let the bridesmaid in, I could see she was literally seething with anger.

"I've got a lot to say to you, so you need to just listen." I sat on the bed as she continued. "You are literally the worst person I've ever met! You have completely ruined this whole weekend for me and I'm usually opposed to violence, but I'm soo glad you got what you deserved at that photo shoot!" She then starts laying into me about everything from my looks to my talent. It also didn't help that I had a giant picture of myself in my hotel room, just in case any of the girls ended back here one night. She spots it. "I mean, what the fuck is this?! You think you're so amazing, but you're nothing but a bitch that's going NOWHERE in her life! You say you're apparently a children's TV presenter, but I would never let my child watch you on TV, you think you're this famous celebrity but you're not and never fucking will be! London Hughes? I've never even fucking heard of you! And I'm glad I haven't! If you ever came on my TV I would throw it out the window. You're just a fucking nobody who thinks she's something special!"

Now, the real London Hughes wanted to say so much to shut this woman's mouth. The cameras weren't rolling, this wasn't "good content," this was just me in my hotel room getting accosted by a woman who doesn't realize she's on a prank show; but I had to stay in character. So I took the abuse and when she'd finished her hate-filled rant, I politely showed her the door. I paused for a moment and took stock of the whole weekend. I was getting paid 5K total to be on the show, at the time the most I'd ever been paid for one project, but somehow it still didn't seem like enough. The producer burst through the adjoining room door and said, "I heard the whole thing! Oh my God, are you okay?" I thought I was, but I wasn't, I was the opposite of okay. I burst into tears, right in the producer's arms. She hugged me. "Just keep it together, there's only an hour to go to the reveal, you can do it."

The reveal took place in the library of the hotel we were all staying in. I walked in and smiled at the girls, and every single one of them gave me the death stare. I also sensed a little attitude from the bride; even she had enough at this point. The girls all stood up one by one and said what they loved about the weekend. None of them could hide their anger, and each used their moment to make little digs at me, saying things like, "This weekend would have been perfect if SOME PEOPLE had stayed at home."

I let the girls speak, and then it was my turn. "I'd like to say something if I may."

"Please don't," the bride's little sister barked back.

As I stood up to talk, the girls rolled their eyes and snapped at me to sit down, but I ignored them. I had a little black book with my speech written in it, and I opened it and started. "This hen weekend has brought with it highs and lows, ups and downs, and lots of twists and turns." I then went on to speak about the bridesmaids individually, saying all the things I admired about them, and even apologizing for all my drama and attention seeking. But the girls weren't buying it. None of them softened; their death stares were screwed on tight. I complimented them all some more, calling the sister who hit me "wise beyond her years and a truly wonderful lady" and the cousin who had shouted at me an hour ago in my hotel room "a wonder woman with a kickass body." They didn't budge, but it was okay because I was about to bring it home.

"You think I'm a spoiled attention-seeking diva, and you'd be right, but only for this weekend. Because there's something I have to confess to you all . . . I am a kids' TV presenter and 'London Hughes,' BUT I'm also an actress . . . until this weekend I'd never even met the bride. This weekend we joined forces to bring mischief and mayhem, but for a good cause, because by putting up with me, you've won a honeymoon for the bride and a spa break for yourselves! This isn't a documentary about hen dos, you're actually on the new ITV 2 prank show *Bad Bridesmaid!*"

Silence. And then the sister pipes up, "Stop fucking acting. Oh God, this girl's delusional!"

"No seriously, guys," the bride chimes in, "this is a prank show; she's been acting this whole time!"

"Wait, so she's not coming to your wedding?!!" It finally

sinks in—the producers come out of hiding, their hands filled with flowers and gift baskets for the girls.

"CONGRATULATIONS! You guys all did so well!"

I left the room and watched the girls' expressions on the camera monitors—the bride's sister looked ecstatic, but the bridesmaid who was just in my room calling me an untalented bitch looked mortified. I looked like I needed a stiff drink! I was reunited with the girls for lunch, and they were all shocked to actually see me eat something for the first time. None of them apologized for how they treated me, but I could tell some of them felt a bit embarrassed. I didn't need their apologies though; I was just so glad it was over and done with. I just wanted to go home.

"When does this air again?" I asked the producer.

I couldn't wait until the show was on TV. I was counting down the days! I'd arranged a little viewing party at my mum's house in Brighton, with all the Brighton girls coming over to watch my acting debut. I'd planned the perfect night. What I didn't plan for was my grandfather on my mum's side passing away, and his funeral landing the morning after my episode of *Bad Bridesmaid* aired. The viewing party turned into more of a small gathering, and I tried my best to enjoy the show now and deal with my wonderful granddad Zack's funeral tomorrow. My mum really tried to enjoy the show, too, bless her, but she couldn't, her head was elsewhere.

Watching it, I felt like a serious actress. It finally got to the photo shoot scene, and I couldn't wait. This was it! The whole of the UK is going to see this woman punch me in the face and it'll go viral! Let's face it, none of the other bad bridesmaids on the other episodes pissed their marks off so much that they twatted them in the nose! Oscar-worthy shit, mate! I knew that once people saw this scene... I WAS ABOUT TO BE SO GOD-DAMN FAMOUS... WHAT? THEY CUT IT OUT!!????

The producers thought that showing the punch would ruin the lighthearted feel of the show, so they edited it out. I got punched in the face for nothing, and I was livid. I hated the edit of the show—not only had they left out the punch, they'd also left out a lot of other funny things I'd said and done. I guess I gave them way too much content for an hour episode! The episode finished, and my only thought was, "Why did I put myself through that?!" The show was a hit, though, with Twitter and Instagram popping off.

My friends disagreed with my assessment. "You were amazing!" "You killed it!" "You should be so proud!" And that was it, the show was literally over, and I had to go to my beloved granddad's funeral and be strong for my mum. All my family and friends were there, and even though I knew they'd probably watched *Bad Bridesmaid* the night before, of course I didn't expect anyone to even mention it to me. I was there to support my mum, my grandma Myrtle, and pay respects to my grandad... but as soon as I entered the church, Grandma Myrtle bellowed, "There she is, my little *Bad Bridesmaid* superstar!" I hugged her so hard. Here I was at her husband's funeral, and she's escorting me around the church like she was my agent at a networking event. "Yes, this is my granddaughter! Did you see her on ITV 2 last night?!! Wasn't she wonderful!" It was a very surreal day, to say the least. My granddad Zack had a beautiful and touching send-off, and I was finally famous... in my family's eyes.

Bad Bridesmaid had given me back some confidence, but it didn't change my life. In reality I didn't become famous overnight. The phone didn't ring any more than it had before, but I was proud of what I'd achieved. I also had proof of what I was capable of! I wasn't just good at acting, I was punch-you-in-the-face-on-prime-time-TV good at acting, and not even ITV's editing skills could stop people from seeing that!

CBBC VS. CITV: THE BLOODS VS. THE CRIPS OF KIDS' TV

The next job opportunity that presented itself was a weekend morning children's show called *Scrambled!* on CITV. I know, I know, you thought I was through with children's television, and I was! But I was also very broke. Tiffany said it would be "a great chance to earn some bread-and-butter money" and she was right—I'd already spent the *Bad Bridesmaid* money and my overdraft was starting to give me evil looks. Plus, it was the kind of show I would have given my left tit to be a part of as a kid, so I had to at least consider it as an adult. They were looking for four presenters to host a two-hour kids' show on Saturday and Sunday mornings. We'd be introducing the shows and doing games and sketches—right up my street! *Oh, this job is completely mine*, I thought to myself as I entered the day-long audition process, and it was. Just like that, I was back to being a children's TV presenter.

I want to thank kids' TV for keeping me employed over the years. I think I'm the only TV presenter in Britain who has worked for both CBBC and CITV. The BBC and ITV are massive rivals, so that's literally like saying I've been in the Bloods AND the Crips! Comedy and entertainment shows always seemed to overlook me, but kids' TV welcomed me with sticky open arms. I presented *Scrambled!* for five series, and thanks to it, I became an ambassador for Barnardo's children's charity, visiting kids all over the country; got four Guinness World Records under my belt (the most bangles put on a wrist in one minute; the fastest time making a ham, cheese, and tomato sandwich blindfolded; the tallest number of paper cups built in one minute; the tallest tower of hats worn by one person at any time, SINCE YOU ASKED); became a regular feature on a gunge (that's slime in the US) fetish website; and met my second-ever boyfriend . . . Matthew.

Now, I'm sure many people can relate to the weird workings of the universe: Whenever you really want something, it doesn't happen, but the moment you stop caring, that's when it's yours. You always see outfits you really want to buy when you're broke, but the moment you have money, there's nothing in Topshop that suits you! This happens to me with men. I always end up getting a boyfriend when I'm not looking for one.

I met boyfriend number two through my new bestie and *Scrambled!* co-presenter Arielle Free. She invited me to an event at the British Film Institute in London; the only problem being I was at home at my mum's two hours away in Brighton.

"You should come! It'll be a free bar."

I was there quicker than you could say porn star martini. London Hughes don't refuse a free bar, mate. It was some independent film event where we had to watch a bunch of short films and were then rewarded with free drinks afterward. I was the first one at the bar when Arielle introduced me to her friend Matthew. He was around my age and seemed really smart, so we chatted and shared a couple laughs. I had no interest whatsoever in dating; I felt like I'd had enough dick to last the end of my twenties . . . but there was something special about this dude. He had a nice energy and made me feel good.

Well, it wasn't long before the free drinks started to dry up. I was very tipsy and trying to sober up with some hors d'oeuvres, when Matthew did something very cheeky. He apparently took my phone out of my hand whilst I was having a conversation with him. I say "apparently" because I didn't see him do it. I carried on chatting with him as normal and then all of a sudden, my heart panged with fear.

"Where's my phone? Shit! Matthew, have you seen it?"

"No, when was the last time you had it?"

Now before you label him as a common thief, Matthew was playing a prank on me. My phone was literally in his hand the whole time he was talking to me. In fact, he was waving it in my face, but I was too tipsy to notice.

"Not sure where your phone is. Want me to help you look for it?"

"Yes, please," I said calmly, trying not to lose my shit. So Matthew starts up the hunt, and he's really going for it, confidently suggesting places for me to look, helping me search under tables. He was proper going for it! I was just so flattered that a guy I literally just met hours before cared so much about me finding my phone. What a gentleman!

"Could you ring it for me!?" I say, completely out of hope at this point.

"Sure," he says. "Take my phone and call it." And he gently pops my iPhone into my hands. I'm so confused.

"Wait? This is my phone, did you . . . ?" A considerably more sober penny drops. "Oh my God, you had it the whole time!!! I'm such an idiot!"

"I was literally waving it in your face, London! How did you not realize!?" He laughs. I unlocked my phone and my heart skipped a beat. There was something about his confidence. Who has the balls to do that!? Also, you know I'm a sucker for a creative chat-up line. This blew "now that the ice is broken" guy out of the water. I checked to see if he'd put his number in my phone. When I saw he hadn't, I was kind of disappointed.

"Did you put your number in it?" I ask, knowing the answer.

"No I didn't . . ."

"Well, you should . . . I'll text you."

And that was that, pretty simple. I don't know how I knew, but I left that BFI event thinking, *yep, that kleptomaniac is going to be my next boyfriend.*

A month later and we were a couple. I was obsessed! He was smart, kind, funny, handsome, and had a pretty decent peen! The only problem was my boyfriend rules . . . he failed them all.

1. HE CAN'T HAVE A SINGLE BED

Matthew had a single bed.

2. HE CAN'T LIVE WITH HIS PARENTS

In his parents' flat . . .

3. HE HAS TO HAVE FREE PARKING OUTSIDE HIS HOUSE

In a £5.80 an hour pay-and-display parking only residence.

I couldn't believe my bad luck. But I must've really liked him because despite all of the above, we stayed together for two years! I adjusted my rules. Instead of sleeping in his single bed, we slept on the sofa bed in the living room. I couldn't be mad at him for still living with his parents because hey, I now lived with my mum. And I sucked it up and paid for...A LOT of parking tickets.

LAMBETH COUNCIL PARKING AND TRANSPORT SERVICES...

London Hughes ✓
@TheLondonHughes

In my future autobiography I'm going to dedicate a whole chapter to my hatred of Lambeth council parking, transport and street services.

12:40 PM • May 17, 2016 • Twitter for iPhone

...did NOT respect my love life or my driver's license. They penalized me for having the audacity to have a boyfriend who lived in Zone 2. I got the most parking tickets of my life in the two years that I was dating Matthew. They handed them out like Oprah giving out free cars! *You* get a parking ticket, and *you* get a parking ticket! You could only park for free outside Matthew's house from 9:00 p.m. to 7:30 a.m., which meant that I could only go to his house at night. What kind of evil, cold-hearted corporation would do that to a brand-new couple?

They literally turned us into nocturnal animals! And even if I decided to cough up and pay for a couple of extra hours parking so I could hang out with my boyfriend, they'd just give me a ticket anyway! I got a ticket because my right wheel wasn't in the parking bay properly, because I didn't fully scratch off the year on my visitors parking permit, whenever the parking attendant misread my license plate, for paying at the wrong pay-and-display machine, and once because the pay-and-display sign was hidden by a tree! It didn't matter what I did, Lambeth council would find me and fine me. Sixty quid every single time. One hundred twenty if I took too long to pay it. I would always try to fight the ticket, but they never let me off, even when it was obvious they were in the wrong. I spent thousands of pounds on parking tickets, and I was livid. Lambeth council parking and transport services didn't want Matthew and me to be happy. They don't know the meaning of happiness! They were clearly jealous of our relationship and jealous of my car. They probably wanted us to be pen friends or pedestrians or something. To this day, I blame them for being the reason we broke up. Okay, that's a lie, our breakup had nothing to do with parking tickets, but it was the reason I couldn't afford to buy a Louis Vuitton handbag until I was twenty-eight years old, and for that I'll never forgive them!

NO CHILDREN NO CRY

I always say you can have it all, but you can't have it all at once and that's how I felt. I had a boyfriend my parents approved of (he didn't try to dutty wine at my little sister's birthday), but career-wise I was a kids' TV presenter again. It didn't exactly feel like I was sliding backward, but it didn't feel like forward movement, either. Also, by now I was twenty-six years old, past my twenty-five goal age. I wasn't famous, I wasn't living in Miami, and I definitely wasn't married to Tinie Tempah. And in terms of societal goals, I was extremely lacking. My brother was married, my cousin was married with a child, and I...had just successfully got out of my overdraft. My mum was now getting broody on my behalf. Now that I had a boyfriend, she was of course expecting kids to follow.

"The happiest day of my life will be when you give birth," she told me one day for no reason.

That was A LOT of pressure, and I didn't have the heart to tell her that that day will probably never come, because I, London Hughes, cannot stand the thought of having kids. I hate children. Not individually, but the concept of them as a whole: human puppy dogs that society tells us we have to give birth to and raise until the age of eighteen, or else we're somehow less than a woman. I don't adhere to the notion that motherhood is something you should aspire to, in the same way I don't believe that marriage is, either. Motherhood, like marriage, is a beautiful thing that happens if a woman wants it to, but if she doesn't, she shouldn't be disparaged. I hate that from the moment we're born, women spend their whole lives preparing for motherhood. We're even given toy babies to play with, WHILST we're still babies! Tiny four-year-old girls pushing around toy baby strollers with plastic fetuses inside! Doesn't anyone else think that's weird? All the life skills we're supposed to acquire are solely to benefit our future children. Women need to learn how to cook . . . so that eventually they can get a husband, have kids, and cook for their family. Why is having a family the only end goal for us? Women need to find a man . . . so that you can eventually settle down, get married, and have a family.

Cinderella only lived happily ever after BECAUSE she found her prince, who I assume she would then settle down with and have kids with. Why did Cinders need all that to be happy? Why couldn't she have found a top-tier job in finance and a solid friendship circle instead? Women should be allowed to not want children as their end goal. I don't see myself at age seventy with grandkids. I see myself at age seventy getting gently dicked down by my life partner, whilst occasionally jetting off to fabulous dinner parties all over the world. Which, FYI, I can afford to do, because I didn't spend my life savings on having children! I look at people who have children and I truly respect them, but I don't envy them. Raising a human is very hard work, and clearly not everyone's good at doing it and that's why there are so many mass murderers and Instagram influencers in the world.

I'm a proud aunty, and as much as I'm completely obsessed with the children in my life, I know that I'd never become the superstar comedy legend I want to be if I also added motherhood to my plate. Now don't get me wrong, I think you can be a successful career woman AND a great mother, but you can't do them both at the same time. At some point one or the other will suffer. Even childless billionaire Oprah Winfrey said she wouldn't be Oprah Winfrey if she had also been a mother . . . and if I have to choose between being a mother or being Oprah, hun, I choose Oprah! I'll be so rich, if I ever get lonely I'll just

buy a robot child! Without the thought of future babies cloud-
ing my judgment, I could focus entirely on the things that made
me happy: men and fame! Now I'd got the man, but I was still
clearly working on the elusive fame part. So close, but yet, still
so far.

SILVER-SCREEN DREAMER

I booked a role in the latest installment of the Bridget Jones franchise, *Bridget Jones's Baby*! See? Even fictional characters were
having kids now! Finally, the chance to appear in my first-ever
movie. My character was named Woman in Shop and she was
only in one scene, but she had a full-on conversation with Renée
Zellweger! I say "full-on conversation" when it was about three
lines total, but it was only Renée and me in the scene. I'd be acting alongside an A-list movie star!

We filmed our scene in an enormous Sainsbury's in Woolwich, South London. It was a huge production with massive
cameras on cranes and tons of extras, but the interesting thing
was the shop was still very much open to the public. Our scene
took place in the biscuit aisle, where we had to have a conversation whilst standing in a queue (filled with extras). But because
the extras looked just like normal people, and the store was still
open, real customers kept walking into the queue and messing
up the shot. It was going to be a LONG day, but it didn't bother
me; I loved it all. I could live on set forever.

When a movie is high profile, it's usually shot under a pseu-
donym so details and scripts don't get leaked to the press. This

film had a silly fake name like *Ladies of London*, even though it was pretty obvious it was actually Bridget Jones since Renée Zellweger was starring in it with a very noticeable British accent. But Renée had recently come under massive public scrutiny for looking different than she had when she burst onto the scene years ago. Her face had, for lack of a better word, changed, and nobody recognized her now; that led to some confusion.

"What film is this?" one of the extras asked me between takes.

"It's the third Bridget Jones movie."

"What? No it's not, where's Renée Zellweger!?"

"Right there, mate, standing by the custard creams!"

"THAT'S RENÉE ZELLWEGER?!"

Now, Renée Zellweger is and always has been gorgeous, but I found it crazy that people didn't recognize Bridget Jones on the set of a Bridget Jones movie. We'd been filming all day, I'd been nailing my three lines over and over again, and before long, early morning flew into late afternoon. An influx of teenage school kids started coming into Sainsbury's. They would notice the giant movie set on aisle seven and watch in excitement. It started to cause a bit of a distraction. We were halfway through a take and a kid yelled out:

"OH MY FUCKING GOD!"

It was very loud, and immediately Renée graciously blushed and lowered her head at clearly being spotted by a very excitable fan. I looked up to see where the yell came from, and in front of me were three hyperventilating schoolgirls.

"LONDONNNNN!!!! THAT'S LONDON FROM CBBC!!!"

I couldn't believe it. Here I was on set standing next to an actual movie star, and I was the one getting noticed! I waved at the girls, and they squealed and waved back. I felt amazing! I swear to God, if I had a dick it would have grown ten sizes in that very moment. Renée was so charming. She had been professional and sweet to me all morning, but after the schoolgirls' reactions, she perked up and said (still in her Bridget Jones Voice):

"What is it you do again, London?"

I smiled proudly and said, "I'm a stand-up comedian."

"Well, you must be an awfully good one!"

The rest of the day went by perfectly. The schoolgirls waited for my scene to wrap and we took selfies. I felt like such a bad bitch. I drove back to my mum's house a winner.

Fast forward a year or so and *Bridget Jones's Baby* was finally coming out in cinemas! I'd told everyone I knew about filming my scene in Woolwich Sainsbury's with Renée Zellweger, and I just couldn't wait to see myself on the silver screen. I wouldn't shut up about it—slipping it into every and any conversation. Even though my part was small, it was mighty, and in my mind I knew that once people saw it, they would say, "Sure, the movie was great, but did you see that Woman in the Shop? She's going places!" I was so convinced my three lines were going to change my life that I hired a publicist to help promote me and get the word out about my big break! Looking back on it I was pretty delusional. The role was tiny, but nothing this big had ever happened to me before.

I got an email from the producers about the fancy screening for all the cast and crew at the Odeon in the West End. *This is it,*

I thought to myself, *THIS IS WHEN THE MAGIC STARTS!!* I took my whole family with me. I dressed up really smart but not too smart—I wanted people to think I went to fancy film screenings all the time. This was nothing but a normal night out for London Hughes.

The cinema was packed, the atmosphere was buzzing! The director came out and thanked us for all our hard work and then Renée Zellweger came out and thanked us, too! It was weird hearing her speak in her natural American accent, since the whole time we were on set together, she didn't slip out of a British accent once. What a professional. Hun was seriously Method! I still don't know if I actually met Bridget Jones or Renée Zellweger that day. The movie started and I yelped, yes YELPED with glee; my insides felt like an overexcited mush of fireworks, sparkles, glitter, sweet and salty popcorn, and the green tea and banana I'd had for breakfast.

I couldn't tell you if *Bridget Jones's Baby* was a good film or not. I wasn't paying attention at all, I was just holding my breath and counting down the minutes until I saw my face. About three-quarters of the way into the film, it finally came to my scene.

Bridget opens her fridge, she looks inside, and realizes all she has left is half a pint of milk.

"Oop, better pop to the shops," she says (I'm paraphrasing, but it was something like that).

My bum clenched. I knew that if she was going to the shops, she'd be going to Sainsbury's, and that's where she'd bump into Woman in Shop. This was it, you couldn't get any more big time than this. I was about to debut in my first-ever Hollywood movie. I couldn't breathe. I leaned into my family and whispered (okay,

I shouted), "This is it, guys! This is it! I'm coming up next!" I watched as Bridget Jones grabs her keys, puts on her coat, and heads to the shops . . . and I kept watching the very next scene as Bridget Jones walks down a London street carrying two huge Sainsbury's shopping bags.

Yep. My scene had been cut from the film.

I couldn't believe it. I felt the pricks of tears sting the backs of my eyes. I was so embarrassed. It took my family a second to clock what had happened.

"So! Where are you then?!"

"My . . . my scene got cut," I say, still in complete shock.

"Aww, never mind darling, I'm sure you were great!"

I wanted to get up and run out of the cinema, but that would have been ungracious. I sat through the rest of the movie, feeling completely humiliated. My mind went through all the people that I told about the movie. Why couldn't I have kept my mouth shut? I waited until the end credits and then made a swift run for the exit. The tears didn't actually roll down my face until I was safely out of view of anyone associated with the film. My big Hollywood break that never happened—how was I supposed to live this one down? Matthew did his best to cheer me up, but I felt like a fraud. I know it's stupid, but at the time I truly believed I was cut from the film because I was a terrible actor. The reality is that movies run long and people get cut all the time, but I was adamant that my omittance from the film was because my three lines clearly ruined it.

I was low for about a month, but, all was not lost, because a few months later *Bridget Jones's Baby* got released on DVD. There, in the DVD extras, was deleted scene number 3, featuring

Woman in Shop! I studied the short scene over and over again, and I was pretty good! I looked cute, my acting was on point, I was funny, I was really making the most of those three lines! I was really proud of myself. Sure, it wasn't the same as being on the big screen, it was the fifty-inch screen in my mum's living room, but here it was, proof of my achievement. It was real, it existed, it actually happened. I had acted alongside a Hollywood movie star, even if nobody actually saw it. Not bad for a washed-up children's TV presenter.

Chapter 14

Fake It 'til You Make It

I'm a strong believer in faking it 'til you make it, even if the only person you're trying to fool is yourself. If deep down you don't have the confidence to do something, just keep telling yourself that you do. Eventually you'll make it happen. Hey, it's what men do! Men have been faking it for centuries, fooling themselves and sometimes even the world into thinking they actually know what they're doing. Even my babes Michelle Obama said, "I have been at probably every powerful table that you can think of, I have worked at non-profits, I have been at foundations, I have worked in corporations, served on corporate boards, I have been at G-summits, I have sat in at the UN; they are not that smart." Faking it is crucial, but for me, I was only half faking it. I believed that all the things I was saying out loud would happen to me eventually, they just hadn't happened quite yet. They say you should prepare for the job you want, and not the job you have, and so I decided that if I was going to be a famous comedy star, I needed to start acting like a famous comedy star.

And what do famous comedy stars have (apart from drinking problems)? Publicists.

My agent, Tiffany, thought a publicist was a waste of money at the time, and looking back on it, she was right. But I was just frustrated with my lack of forward movement. I was failing a lot more than I was winning. I'd take a tiny step forward, then have a massive fail, repeat, repeat, repeat. It felt like my career wasn't really going anywhere and needed a kick-start. I read somewhere that investing in yourself is the best investment you could ever make, so I spent my kids' TV money on a very expensive, boutique publicist. I just wanted to get my name out there a bit and be invited to all the swanky events. I wanted to be the "IT" girl people were talking about. That's how I got my first-ever invite to London Fashion Week.

MAJOR FASHION WEEK FAIL

London Fashion Week has always been on my fame bucket list. To me, it was synonymous with chic celebrity high society. Anyone who's anyone got invited and I was currently a no one who wanted to be a someone! I put on a cute outfit and carried myself with all the confidence and bravado of a mediocre white man, even though inside I was totally out of my comfort zone! I kept telling myself that if I acted like I belonged, people would think I belonged. I sat front row at the Paul Costelloe fashion show. Even though everyone in the audience was supposed to be focusing on the models, it became pretty clear to me that people who

sat front row at LFW also wanted all eyes on them. I was literally sitting next to a man dressed up as a pink latex Barbie doll.
The event was in an old warehouse decorated in mid-century
gothic chic and the models looked like skinny zombie goddesses.
It felt good to rub (and sometimes squeak) shoulders with fashion's coolest movers and shakers for a while, and after a champagne or four I was starting to feel like I actually *did* belong.

"You coming to the after-party, hun?" my new front row
friend asked me. I most definitely was attending. Parties are
my thing. I'm a self-confessed party gal. I love dancing, I love
making new friends, and I'm used to all eyes (naturally) being
on me when I'm in party mode. To quote noughties popstar
Kesha, *"The party don't start 'til I walk in,"* and I could feel it in
my Marks and Spencer's Spanx that the after-party at London
Fashion Week would be my moment to shine. I saw it perfectly
in my head: the DJ playing a Beyoncé song, me perfectly execut-
ing the routine to "Single Ladies" full out as the crowd cheers.
London Fashion Week? Pah! It'll be London's fashion week
once I'm through with it! The party was in a cool renovated shop
on Oxford Street. It was packed with insanely fabulous people,
decked out in designer duds from head to toe. I was doing my
best trying-not-to-try-too-hard impression in some Doc Mar-
tens, old Primark jeans, a sparkly boob tube, and my mum's
vintage cardigan. I walked through security, got stamped, and
then I saw it: the illustrious red carpet.

I'd never done a red carpet before. I don't think you'll be
surprised to learn that the closest I've ever come to walking a red
carpet was when I once walked on a carpet that was red.

My heart started beating in my throat. I watched as celebrity after celebrity stepped up, and about twelve paparazzi flashed their cameras; the loud clicks were intoxicating and the bright flashes eclipsed the room. I wanted to be on the other end of those camera lenses. I watched how the girls posed, what directions they were looking in. I was transfixed, studying every move, wondering if I'd be able to pull it off with as much poise and grace. There was a queue forming for the carpet, and I joined it; Cara Delevingne and a few other hot model/influencer types were in front of me all looking like they'd stepped right out of the oven: flawless skin, freshly made. They *looked* like they were queuing for a red carpet. I looked like I was queuing for the toilets. I asked myself what I thought I was doing. I didn't NEED to get my picture taken. I could easily just ignore the red carpet, grab a canapé, and start living my best life on the dance floor, but a voice in my head wouldn't let me leave. "You belong here, you were invited, this is what you came for, go and do the carpet!" Then another voice in my head said, "Are you sure you want to do this, what if the paparazzi don't know who you are, hun?" I panicked and texted my publicist, and she confirmed that my name was down to do the carpet. I had nothing to lose, so I quickly practiced smizing (where you smile with your eyes), downed a glass of champagne, and said, "Let's do fashion week baby, yeah!"—in my head, obviously.

I walked up to the red carpet, and stood confidently in front of all the paparazzi, all scruffily dressed middle-aged white dudes. It was now or never. I stood up straight, put my hand on my hip, outstretched my left leg, sucked in my gut, smized, and then flashed them my biggest smile...and nothing. The paparazzi just stared, all of them looking at me like I'd just farted. None of them lifted up their cameras, they all just seemed to mutter among themselves. My heart started racing. I looked to the left and the right, but there was no one else on the carpet but me. Maybe they were on a break? I continued posing.

The paparazzi all started to avoid eye contact with me. They checked their phones, looked at pictures on their cameras. I couldn't take much more of it. "Excuse me," I said in my quietest voice, because I wasn't quite brave enough to use my normal voice. They all heard but continued to ignore me. Now I don't know what to do, my brain is literally yelling, "Run away! Run off the red carpet!" But I'd been standing there for too long now, everyone else was looking at me. I had to commit, since walking off the carpet would be even more embarrassing than staying put. I'm here, I've posed, I have to get a picture! "Err, excuse me . . . guys?!" I say again, this time a little bit louder. One of the paparazzi dudes seems to take pity on me. He leans in and speaks to a woman with a clipboard. I have no idea what her job was, but she looked very important. The woman with the clipboard comes over to me.

"Oh, I'm sorry . . . did you want a picture?!" she asks.

"Yes, please!" Finally! This was all just a big misunderstanding, and this nice clipboard lady is going to tell these men to take my picture, because I'm London Hughes and I'm meant to be here! I readjust my stance and flick my hair behind my ear, ready for the onslaught of flashing lights. I exhale, ready . . . and . . .

"Okay . . . give me your phone, then," clipboard woman says.

"Huh?"

"Give me your phone and I'll take the pic for you."

My heart sinks all the way into my arsehole, and all the paparazzi guys start to look away as not to make this any more embarrassing for me. "I'm here, I've posed, I have to get a picture," I say to myself as I reluctantly reach into my handbag and give clipboard lady my iPhone 5. She then stands in front of the paparazzi and takes three terrible pictures of me. I pose as if this was the endgame I wanted all along! My pride wouldn't let me show weakness. After what feels like several hundred years, clipboard lady finally gives my phone back. I say thank you to her and for some reason I also say thank you to the paparazzi, and then I slowly strut off the red carpet and into a gaping hole in the center of the Earth that has conveniently opened up, ready to swallow me whole.

I stayed at the party and tried to enjoy the rest of my night, but it was ruined. I was ruined with embarrassment! Most people in showbiz will tell you they've all had a fear of stepping on a red carpet and nobody knowing who they are. Well, I got a chance to live that fear! I wanted to erase the night, so I drowned my sorrows with all the free champagne I could find, and a couple dozen beef sliders. I never got to become the life and soul of the LFW party. I got so drunk I could barely do the macarena, let alone the full routine to "Single Ladies"! The night ended with Matthew coming to pick me up; I was far too paralytic to get the tube home. I woke up the next morning terribly hungover, but unfortunately I remembered everything! I was giving myself extreme secondhand embarrassment, playing flashbacks in my head of posing for a smartphone on the red carpet. But then, just like that, my inner winner voice chimed up. I love her. Whenever I feel absolutely rock-bottom shit about myself, she appears. That morning, she said: *This was just a moment in time. There will come a day when you step on the red carpet and not only will paparazzi take your picture, they will also shout your name.* God, she was right. I had to start somewhere, and I couldn't exactly get any lower than I felt right then, so the only way is up.

There's a saying that I absolutely adore about getting what you want out of life. When a man tries to catch a butterfly with a net, he'll swing and miss several times, tire himself out, and the butterfly will fly away. But if the man stays still and patiently waits, the butterfly will eventually land on his nose. I felt like the man with the net, attempting all these ways to be seen and become a famous social butterfly, thinking time after time that *this* will be my big break, no *this* will be my big break! I was trying so hard to make it work, swinging and missing, swinging and missing! Surely by now something had to give! I just didn't know how to make it happen for myself.

Now, I'm no stranger to hard work. A part of me always felt like my dream career wouldn't happen unless I did *something*, because hard work beats talent when talent doesn't work hard. But I was working so hard, and I was so bloody tired. In that moment, I just decided to give in and accept that this was my life now. I wasn't a movie star, or a comedy queen. I was a children's television presenter, and maybe that's all I was ever supposed to be. It's something to be proud of! I was already living someone's dream life, maybe it was time I learned to be grateful. My go-to saying was and always is "Don't force it." I'm an "If it's meant to be, it'll be" person. Everything I was doing up until that point felt like I was desperately forcing a piece into a puzzle that clearly didn't want to fit. So, I decided to let it go, but deep down I just wanted a butterfly, any butterfly, to come and land perfectly on my nose.

Little did I know, Phoebe Waller-Bridge would be that butterfly.

SEX SHOP WORKER

Tiffany emailed me one morning to say I had a job come through—a small role (only a day's filming), but for a BBC Three show called *Fleabag*. *Fleabag*? The name sounded familiar, and then I remembered it had been a one-woman show at the Edinburgh Comedy Festival, although I never got the chance to see it. Phoebe Waller-Bridge was the creator. She also wrote a show called *Crashing* that I'd auditioned for but hadn't landed. I told Tiffany I'd be thrilled to audition.

"No, it's not an audition. She's giving you the part, filming's in a couple weeks."

Now, let me stress that people don't just *give* you parts on TV shows or films, everyone has to audition. I had to go through three rounds of auditions just to play Woman in Shop, which ultimately got cut from *Bridget Jones's Baby*! You were only *given* parts if you know the director or creator, or if you're Idris Elba or something. Here I was, being given a part in a TV show, just like that, and I had never even met Phoebe Waller-Bridge.

I walk onto set and sit in hair and makeup. It's a lovely day and I'm in good spirits as I go over my scene. I'm playing a sex shop worker. It's a small part but I'm thrilled for the work! I'm still racking my brain trying to think why I was chosen for the role when PWB herself walks in.

"London Hughes, thank you so much for doing this! I'm so sorry the role is so small!"

I hug her and thank her for the part, and she tells me she's a huge fan and thinks I'm hilarious! Apparently, she'd seen my audition tape for a role in *Crashing*, and even though I didn't get that part, she enjoyed my tape and decided to put me in her next show. I couldn't believe that failing an audition actually led to getting a job! I was over the moon! We chatted it up some more like we'd been friends for years. She was inquisitive and kind, and I could instantly feel how warm and genuine she was.

I filmed my scene with Phoebe in a very tiny, sweaty, sex shop in Kent. We had a great time, and I remember thinking she was such a natural to work with, making me feel so calm and appreciated. At lunch, Phoebe and I chat it up, and she tells me all about the show and I'm just sitting there soaking it all in. She also tells me she just signed with a big fancy agency in Beverly Hills called United Talent Agency. I'd never heard of UTA, but they represented all the big names in Hollywood. I listened intently as Phoebe opened up about her life and career and I instantly got goose bumps. There were so many amazing things about to happen for her, and I felt so excited just to be a tiny part of it. I left the set feeling inspired and ready to take on the world again. Phoebe was going places, and she saw something in me. I was more than just a kids' TV presenter to her! This amazing little genius butterfly had landed right on my nose and I didn't want to let her down.

Life ticked on, and Matthew and I celebrated a one-year

anniversary, beating out the nine months with Charlie as my longest relationship to date. Before them, my longest relationship was with Marcell the sex teddy bear and my Caffè Nero loyalty card. This was progress! He took me to Paris for the first time to celebrate. When I got back, I received an email from the producers of *Fleabag* about a little wrap party. Now, yes, we know I love a party, but after London's fashion week fiasco I decided to approach this one a bit differently. I had zero expectations, and really just wanted to see Phoebe again.

The wrap party was in a private bowling alley on Brick Lane, East London. I laughed and drank with the rest of the cast and crew, and then it was time for an all-important karaoke session. "What song are you gonna do, London?!" Phoebe asked. I know it sounds silly, but at that moment I made a decision that would be one small step on the path that led me to where I am today. One tiny, insignificant song choice helped change everything—Britney Spears's "Oops! I Did it Again." I grabbed a straw and positioned it in my hair to look like a head mic, and then performed full out, with the dance routine and everything. Countless hours of popstar training in my parents' living room was gonna finally pay off! The whole cast cheered, and at the end of my performance, Phoebe grabbed me. "London, you're a-fucking-mazing! You killed that! I didn't know you could do all that! Why the fuck are you just sitting on all of this talent?"

It was such an honest and direct question, but I truly couldn't answer her, because I didn't feel like I had just been sitting on my talent. I'd been trying for several chapters now to be a star! "Have you ever done the Edinburgh Comedy Festival?" she asked.

"Yeah, but not properly. It didn't go so great the first time."
To be honest, after my underwhelming performance at the festival in 2012, I had no intentions of ever returning unless it was
to get drunk and/or sleep with cute comics.

"You NEED to do a one-woman show at Edinburgh! People
need to see that! You're fucking amazing; promise me you'll go
back to that festival!" I smiled. I'd never met someone so passionate about the career of a person she'd just met. It was electrifying being around her. It was like she really saw me, and
saw *in* me what, during the best of times, I also saw in myself.
She made me feel like I wasn't crazy. If you want to work in
entertainment, you need to get used to failure. And I'd been
failing a lot lately. I'd written several scripts and TV show ideas
that had all been rejected, I wasn't landing auditions, and I was
creatively and financially spent. Hearing her words, at that particular moment, reignited something in me. I promised Phoebe
I would go back to do Edinburgh. I was buzzing when I left the
wrap party, mentally preparing my next one-woman show.

Later that year, my episode of *Fleabag* aired. The show was an
instant hit, and I must admit out of all the random TV shows
I thought would give me my big break, I had no idea that *Fleabag* would be the one to do it. I got more attention for being the
sex shop worker in episode 3 than anything I'd ever done in my
life, and that includes two years on CBBC and an appearance in
a widely distributed Kia car advert! When the show was at its
height, people would literally stop me in public and ask, "Excuse
me, were you in *Fleabag*?"

"Yes! Yes, I was! I was the sex shop worker in episode 3!" I was so proud of myself, I was so proud of Phoebe. What a feeling to be part of a show that the whole world enjoyed.

LENNY HENRY KNOWS WHO I AM!

Comic Relief was putting on a little comedy tour to highlight the next generation of up-and-coming stand-up comics, with Lenny Henry hosting one of the nights, and they asked me to perform. It had been seventeen years since I wrote my first letter to Lenny Henry asking to be on his TV show and seven years since I'd been in an online comedy series his company produced. I remember doubting that he'd even remember me.

The show was packed and for a great cause, and reader, your girl absolutely slayed it. I had no choice but to! Sir Lenny Henry was watching me! We spoke backstage, I introduced myself again, but this time I didn't need to. "Of course I know who you are, London Hughes! Great set tonight!" I couldn't believe it, the guy I used to write letters to, begging him to notice me, finally noticed me! It felt like a full circle moment. We spent the whole night laughing and joking backstage. It felt like I'd made a new friend, but I was still way too embarrassed to let him know that I used to write letters to him when I was ten.

After that night I went home and just stared into space for a while, saying to myself, "Hun, you shared a stage with one of your comedy heroes tonight. Never forget this feeling." Whenever a life-changing night happens to you, no matter how big or small it is, it's so important to take stock of it. I call them "What is my life?" moments—moments where you have to pinch yourself to remember it's actually happening to you. If ten-year-old me knew that seventeen years later she'd be sharing a comedy stage with the guy she wrote letters to, she wouldn't believe it! Well actually, that's a lie. Ten-year-old me was a total badass and she would've totally believed it.

Another "What is my life?" night happened a few weeks later at the Comic Relief main event. It was a great night and raised millions for charity, but the personal highlight for me was bumping into my babes Phoebe Waller-Bridge. It was the first time I'd seen her post-*Fleabag* and fame really looked good on her! We caught up and had a great night out, and she introduced me to model Cara Delevingne. It didn't seem like she remembered me from Red Carpet Gate, which was certainly this comic's relief. (Sorry I had to do it!) It just goes to show that embarrassing moments are just that—moments. A seemingly cataclysmic event for you is just someone else's Thursday night. "What is your life, mate!" I said to Phoebe.

"London, it'll be your life soon, trust me," she replied. After the event was over, Cara invited Phoebe and me for drinks at the very swanky celebrity hotspot the Chiltern Firehouse. We hopped out of our black cabs and were instantly blinded by a wall of paparazzi cameras. I won't lie, it did feel good to be on the other side of the lens, but honestly that light is goddamn blinding! I truly don't know how celebrities manage to walk in a straight line, in heels, whilst looking cute, as fifty paparazzi shoot tiny balls of lightning into their face! I think we need to give the Kardashians a bit more credit guys, it truly is a skill. Cara was used to it; a pro, she kept her head up and strutted through the back door of the Chiltern Firehouse. Phoebe and I weren't used to all the fanfare. She giggled as I covered my face in a true celebrity-that-doesn't-want-to-be-seen style and said, "No pictures! No pictures!" I knew the paps weren't for me, but I couldn't help it. When would something like this ever happen again?

Cara bought everyone at the bar a whiskey sour, such a classy move. We partied the night away and all I remember is waking up the next morning in Cara's hotel suite whilst her beautiful husky dog licked my face. It was an insane night. I got the feeling that it was just another normal night out for Cara and Phoebe, but for London Hughes it was EVERYTHING!

CHICKEN MERRY, HAWK DI NEAR

There's an old Jamaican saying that I loathe, which goes "Chicken merry! Hawk di near!" Loosely translated, it means the chickens are happy, but the hawk is around the corner. The saying basically means you should never get too excited about anything, because you never know what's round the corner. You could lose it all or a hawk could eat you. I strive not to live my life that way. I try my best to be a merry little chicken at all times and celebrate things that make me feel good. I'm not giving that hawk my energy, hun! Well, even though I despise the saying, it didn't stop that hawk from coming to bite me in the arse.

After riding my Comic Relief high, everything soon came crashing back down to earth. I got an email from Comedy Central UK explaining that they had rejected my TV sitcom pilot *28 Dates Later*; it was about two girls who work in a cinema and love romantic comedies. I'd spent years on it and Comedy Central was my last hope. They seemed keen, but after working on edits for several months, their response was: "Sorry, we're not looking for any female lead content right now."

Can you believe that was their actual response?!? I counted my failures: eight TV shows rejected in six years. To put it mildly, I was pissed. But I also knew that no other Black female comedians were getting their own TV shows, either. In fact, female comedians in general were missing from mainstream British television back then. Throughout most of my life, I consistently saw the same (extremely few) female comics on TV: white ones. Absolute legends like Jo Brand, Jennifer Saunders, Dawn French, and Ruby Wax were now all in their late forties or fifties, but there didn't seem to be a new fresh batch of female comics coming up to join them. Yet every other week it seemed like a new white male comic popped up on the BBC as a "new face to watch." It was becoming pretty clear to me that I wasn't exactly the problem.

Comedy Central's rejection had a way of making me work harder. It's what I've always done whenever anyone doubted me: I'd get angry, cry a bit, and double down. This particular rejection set off a chain reaction in me, and I wrote like a mad woman, creativity falling out of every crevice. I wrote twenty-five sketches in one week. Collectively, they were called *NO FIL-TER: 25 sketches based on the hilarious but somewhat delusional life of London Hughes*. I churned out page after page, sometimes waking up in the middle of the night to write. It sounds pretty morbid to say this, but all the while, I just kept thinking to myself, "If anything happens to me, and I die before I get to make my comedy dreams come true, this will be proof that I was funny, this is the proof that I was a good comedy writer, and all I needed was a chance." Once the sketches were all finished, I clicked save, exhaled, and turned on my TV...

...And immediately saw an advert for a show called *Chewing Gum*, a comedy series starring a Black actress named Michaela Coel. At the time, I'd never heard of Michaela—she wasn't a stand-up comedian, we'd never crossed paths, but she'd managed to get her own comedy show on E4. "How the fuck did she do it?!" I'd been trying to do it for the last six years! Let me be clear, I was *ecstatic* for her, and for what it said about our slowly progressing culture, but I was also sad for myself. I knew in my bones that the very fact of her existence in that space would hinder mine. I was all too familiar with the ridiculous way the industry worked when it came to Black talent. One in one out, it was the Lenny Henry theory all over again. Now that Britain *finally* had a Black female sitcom, the chances of getting another one made were slim to none. This merry little chicken had nowhere to go! (Sidenote: I was totally right in my thinking—to this day Michaela Coel is still the only British Black woman to ever have her own sitcom.)

Chewing Gum meant that I had to change up my career plan. I couldn't just focus on trying to make it big in Britain anymore, I had to see the bigger picture. There were now only three things on my to-do list:

1. Film my *No Filter* sketches for YouTube.

2. Come up with solid plan to make it big in America.

3. Do a hit show at the Edinburgh Comedy Festival.

I might be paraphrasing but someone once said something along the lines of, "Insanity is doing the same thing but expecting different results," so here I was, changing it up, hun! Task one on that list had been pretty simple to achieve; my boyfriend Matthew was a cinematographer and had all the equipment and know-how to help make *No Filter* happen! I asked Matthew if he could help me film some of the sketches for YouTube, and within a month we'd filmed fifteen hilarious (if I do say so myself) sketches starring me and all my favorite talented comedy friends! There were sketches like "One of the Lads London," a mockumentary-style sketch where I try to join an all-male football team just to hook up with the men, or "The Seagull," a fun sketch about the time a dude tried to make me get on a bus after a date. I don't do public transport, hun. Making these videos took over my life; I'd produce them, act in them, direct them, and then put them up every week on my brand-new YouTube channel. Now, the sketches didn't exactly take the comedy world by storm. In fact, it was the complete opposite—the videos were averaging only a hundred or so views each, but it didn't matter to me. My work was finally out there, my WORTH was FINALLY out there! If anyone wanted proof of my talent, all they had to do was type my name into YouTube. It was a tiny win.

Next I had to figure out my America plan! Sure, America had always been the end goal, but now I began actively making plans on how to get there; letters to Will Smith weren't going to cut it this time! I googled comedy schools and acting classes in LA, thinking maybe I could audition and get some sort of scholarship. I spoke with my parents about my plans for really making a go of it in the States. I assumed they'd be excited, but unfortunately, they also lived via the "Chicken merry, hawk di near" complex. My dad would sometimes quote the saying to me and say, "Okay but, don't get too excited, don't get your hopes up too much," and my mum would always worry about my career as if at any moment I'd be back working at TGI Fridays. I didn't blame them for feeling jaded about my career goals, I'd been jaded at one point myself, but my parents weren't like me. My dad was a realist, and my mum was an immigrant Black woman. They didn't spend a lot of time living in the land of wish and hope. I was different, though. I loved a wish and a hope, a dream and a plan.

I pride myself on being an optimist, and even when life seemed to serve up some serious shit sandwiches, I always try to look on the bright side. I think that's how I managed to maneuver the crazy world of British comedy and entertainment, and part of the reason I'm here writing this book today. A realist would say the chances of me becoming a Hollywood comedy star were very slim, an optimist would say go for it, you never know what could happen, and a pessimist would say don't give up your day job.

My agent, Tiffany, was a realist.

"Hun, you're not going to make it in America when you haven't even made it in Britain yet!"

Brutal. It really stung, but in her defense, she was sort of right. A plan like that had never worked in the comedy world before. No other British comics had made a splash in America before cracking the UK first. Her company JNM represented Russell Brand. He was HUGE in the UK and then went to the States and did the hit film *Forgetting Sarah Marshall* and became a literal movie star! Whereas I would be the girl trying to make it in America who couldn't even make it on an episode of *8 Out of 10 Cats*! Actually, at that point, I couldn't even get on *Big Brother's Bit on the Side*! This became a huge point of contention between Tiffany and me. She certainly believed in me, but she saw the entertainment industry differently than I saw it. I saw it through the eyes of a Black woman. I saw my Black peers go from doing nothing in the UK to getting hit shows and movies in the States.

Idris Elba was on a terrible Channel 5 soap called *Family Affairs* before he moved to the US, slept in his car, and landed *The Wire*. My mate Nathalie Emmanuel had a tiny part on the E4 soap *Hollyoaks* before she headed stateside and landed a major role in the Fast and Furious movie franchise. And don't even get me started on Daniel Kaluuya: before *Get Out*, he was known for being in one episode of *Black Mirror* and playing Posh Kenneth, the token Black guy with one line in every other episode of *Skins*. Making it big in America first may seem unconventional for white British talent, but for Black British talent, sometimes it was our only option. It's one of the reasons comedian Gina Yashere moved to America, and now she has her own show on CBS, and why actress Cynthia Erivo headed stateside and now she has an Emmy, a Grammy, a Tony, two Oscar nominations, but somehow *zero* BAFTA nominations. The UK likes to pretend it doesn't see us. It's hard if you're Black, it's harder if you're a Black woman, and it's even harder if you're a Black woman in comedy.

I wanted to be a British Comedy Beyoncé, a force of nature

that could do it all! But how could I be Comedy Beyoncé when Britain doesn't even have a Beyoncé! The biggest soul singer in the UK is a white woman! (No shade to Adele, though, she is truly amazing.) Britain doesn't have an Oprah, a Whoopi Goldberg, a Tiffany Haddish, a Halle Berry, a Viola Davis, a Regina King, an Ava DuVernay, a Shonda Rhimes, or a Serena Williams. When it comes to world-famous Black British women, all we have are Naomi Campbell and Scary Spice. Now, I refuse to believe that's because Black British women aren't as talented as their American counterparts. The talent is there, but the opportunity and support are not. Special mention to Michaela Coel for forging her own path, but even though she has broken barriers with the success she's achieved, it feels like she is the exception that proves the rule. The British entertainment industry all too often seems to chew up and spit out talented Black women, and I refused to let them do it to me. Google "British comedians" right now, all you'll see is a sea of white dudes . . . and that, in a nutshell, is why I wanted to go to America.

HI, LOS ANGELES? YEP. IT'S LONDON CALLING

"How do you know you wanna move to LA if you've never even been!?" is what my friend Amy said to me ten minutes before I spent the last £1000 in my account on a flight to LAX. She was right of course. I'd been talking about my "American dream" for years, and it was time for some action. Even though I'd thoroughly done my research, everything I thought I knew about

Hollywood I'd learned from movies, songs, and US sitcoms. The closest I'd actually ever been to Los Angeles, California, was a trip to Disney World in Florida. I thought all Black people played basketball, and all white people lived in Beverly Hills. If I was going to stick to my Hollywood plan, I needed to give LA a trial run, a chemistry read. I needed to see if we really clicked with each other.

After a ten-hour flight, I landed in LAX already smitten. The fucking sun was shining! I don't think you understand how important it is to see sunshine. I'd spent my whole life on this Earth only seeing the sun on occasion, and even if I saw it, it was still bloody cold. But here it was beaming consistently, almost showing off, and it was December! In the Uber to my hotel, I rolled down the window on the freeway and stuck my head out, literally like a dog, just taking it all in. The palm trees, the insane houses, the Hollywood sign! It looked even *better* than in the movies. It made me catch my breath. Hun, I was home.

LA had ten days to show me a good time, and I had a feeling it wouldn't disappoint. But after checking into a cheap hotel on the Sunset Strip, I realized I wasn't entirely sure what to do next. I had no friends, no plans, nowhere to be. So I looked on the Soho House app. Soho House is a worldwide members club chain that caters to creatives, and I practically lived at the one in London. They always put on cool events for their members—seminars, comedy shows, screenings, the works. I decided to check the LA one out.

Black and in Hollywood—A Discussion was the event being held that very night, my first night in LA! What are the chances? It was a panel hosted by actors/writers/comedians the Wayans brothers, and in the audience were a bunch of Black Hollywood creatives, from TV directors to writers, comedians to actors. I asked questions, I networked my arse off, I got a selfie with Shawn Wayans! I had the best night and made a ton of connections. When I got back to my hotel, about forty business cards fell out of my bra.

Over the next few days, I went to the Soho House every day and sat at the bar drinking cocktails, writing, and reading *The Celestine Prophecy* (the number one book for dreamers). The celebrity spotting at Soho House was insane. People always say that you bump into celebs in Los Angeles, but I didn't really realize how true it was. In just a few days I'd seen J. Lo and A-Rod on a date, Idris Elba in a business meeting, and Bianca from *EastEnders* having a coffee. It felt so exciting just being in the city, like anything could happen at any moment.

Two days later, a new friend that I'd met offered me a tour of Paramount Studios. He was a writer and worked on the lot. I was so happy I forgot to breathe. I'd wanted to visit one ever since I saw the behind-the-scenes episode of *The Fresh Prince of Bel Air*! When I pulled up, I spied the beautiful water fountain and the giant arches with "Paramount Pictures" and those gates opened to let me inside, I actually got a tad emotional. I was in the place I'd always dreamed I'd be. As my new friend casually showed me around, I just let it all sink in, eyes wide with excitement. I sat on the "life is like a box of chocolates" bench from *Forrest Gump*, saw a giant water tank they used to film water stunts, and I visited the insanely accurate streets of a New York set. I drove little golf buggies around massive soundstages and had lunch in the actual restaurant that all the movie stars have lunch in! It became very clear to me that this was where I was meant to be. Who turns up in LA and within a few days has a personal tour of a famous Hollywood studio lot? London Hughes does, that's who! LA was calling my name, hun, but it didn't stop there.

My friend was being the perfect tour guide and showing me everything he had access to, even the writers' kitchen where they keep all their snacks. He finally took me around a corner where lots of cameras were set up, and a few actors' trailers were parked. "This is where they film the Netflix comedy series *Love*."

"Oh my God, I LOVE that show!" *Love* was a show by Judd Apatow, and I was a HUGE fan of his movies *Knocked Up*, *The 40-Year-Old Virgin*, and *Trainwreck*, which was a hit breakout film for Amy Schumer, one of my new favorite comedy baes. I was desperate to be the first Black girl in a Judd Apatow anything, which I promptly told my friend.

"Oh, really? His offices are right over there," he replied, way too calmly.

Okay, wow. I digested the information as best as I could, but my intestines felt like they were cartwheeling. Again, I had been in LA only a few days and had already somehow managed to get myself into a position where I was literally standing outside the office door of one of my favorite filmmakers. "I actually know him; shall we see if he's in, go say hi?"

WHAT!? Now, I need to stress that this was a new friend, a kind American man I'd met for the first time that day. We met through a mutual friend, and he didn't owe me anything. He barely knew me, and yet here he was, this magical studio lot genie, just making all my Hollywood wishes come true. As if he hadn't already done enough for me, now he wanted me to casually walk up and say hi to a famous Hollywood producer. It was only a Tuesday! What was my life, mate?

The words "Yes, please!" couldn't have left my mouth sooner.

I prepared myself for what I was going to say to Judd Apatow. Would I try to make a joke? Should I fangirl? Or act cool and aloof, like I go for meetings with Hollywood execs every Tuesday? What was the play here!? Everything felt so surreal. I believe in fate, kismet, manifestation, the universe, all that good stuff, and I just knew all of it had to have been in play here, because everything was happening so effortlessly, so easy. I got my meeting with my first-ever Hollywood exec. Unfortunately, Judd Apatow wasn't in that day, but we met with his colleague Brent Forrester, the showrunner on *Love*, who also worked on *The Office*. We ate lunch with Brent. I couldn't believe that this man decided to spend his lunch break talking to a little Black female comic from the UK. I told Brent my story, and showed him *No Filter*, my comedy sketch on YouTube. He said he loved my energy and ambition, and actually called me a unicorn. But what he did next blew my tiny British mind.

Without saying a word, he took out his phone and emailed top US talent agency William Morris Endeavor and told them to take a meeting with me. Yes, that's right, WME, one of the big three talent agencies! The people who look after some of the biggest movie stars on the planet, yeah them. They replied to him instantly and agreed to see me. The next day, I had a meeting with Melissa Myers, who was in charge of the international comedy department. I need to stress to you again that this was not normal. People don't just take a tour of Disneyland and end up sitting down with Walt. It was all too easy.

I don't know anyone who's gone to Los Angeles on holiday and nabbed a meeting with a top Hollywood agent! I'd only heard stories about young hopefuls leaving their hometowns with aspirations of making it big in Hollywood, only to end up with their dreams completely squashed. It happened every day in LA and had even happened to someone I knew. A colleague at CBBC quit and moved to Los Angeles to follow her dreams of being a famous Hollywood actor, and five years later she currently worked in Hollywood as a waitress at a pirate-themed restaurant. It happened all the time to amazingly talented people. Hollywood chews up dreamers and spits them out, and to be honest, until I'd visited LA for myself, I had no idea if I'd be any different. Let's be honest, this "life-changing" trip could have been a complete disaster. It could have popped my delusional comedy bubble and caused me to wake up and smell the English breakfast, but it did the exact opposite. It made me dream even harder, and it made me realize that what I wanted wasn't completely out of reach. I'd only been in LA for five days and I was effortlessly making these kinds of career moves. Imagine what I could get done if I lived there!

The meeting with WME went really well. Melissa loved my *No Filter* sketches and although she didn't sign me on the spot, she wanted to see me perform live. I told her my plans for a big show at the Edinburgh Comedy Festival next year, and she promised to come. I was buzzing and called Tiffany with the news. She had managed to get me a meeting with another huge talent agency, ICM. Unfortunately, they didn't sign me, either, but it didn't matter. I was moving forward, making connections, networking in Hollywood!

LA showed me the best time. I spent the rest of my vacation making new friends, drinking cocktails, and flirting with hot American boys. I did so much with my ten days in Tinseltown that on the last day, just like God, I rested. I spent my last night in my cheap LA hotel room thinking about what was left of my old life in London. Now that I'd been here and tasted the sweetness of the American dream for myself, I knew I just had to devour it all. Everything made sense to me in Los Angeles. In England, it always felt like my dreams were too big, but here it felt like anything and everything could happen. It was all here, waiting for me! I just had to grab it. I left LA with so much hope and headed back to Britain with my head held high. I just knew one day LA would want me back. I also knew there was something that I didn't want back. My boyfriend, Matthew.

Chapter 15

Superstar! (It's Just Nobody's Realized It)

Coming back to rainy, cold London from gorgeous, hot, sexy LA was pretty sobering. I didn't even want the plane to land at Heathrow Airport! I couldn't help but worry about what that said about my relationship. Things weren't looking good for Matthew and me. Our relationship wasn't necessarily in a bad place, but there was a part of me that started to see him as more than just a filler boyfriend. Matthew was kind, caring, creative, had a company filming music videos and online content, and he once brought a packed lunch to work every day for a month, just so he could afford to buy me a Louis Vuitton handbag! He was a great guy! But after my life-changing trip, all my priorities changed. I could clearly see myself living in America, and try as I might, I just couldn't see myself doing it with him.

"Would you ever move to America with me?" I randomly asked Matthew one day.

"Move to America? Babe, I don't see myself moving out of South London!"

That's all I needed to hear. I knew it was over. The problem was, I couldn't exactly break up with him. He'd done nothing wrong, and I really cared about him. What sane person breaks up with their boyfriend because they think they're going to move to Los Angeles, even though they've only been there once on holiday! Reader, I know it seems crazy, but I think you can probably tell by now that I'm a little bit crazy. It wasn't fair to lead Matthew on when I knew where I was going to end up. I had a vision for my life, and as sad as it was, I just didn't see him being part of it anymore. In less than six months after my return from LA, I was a single woman again, Matthew and I were over, and I was back living with my mum in Brighton.

Matthew took the breakup hard; he called me every day in tears. I didn't cry, even though I felt like it, because even though I knew I was making the right decision, part of me was afraid I'd go back on it. To combat the pain of my obliterated love life, I focused on the last thing on my to-do list:

DO A KILLER EDINBURGH SHOW

Given that my previous Edinburgh attempt had been a bit of a failure, there was nowhere to go but up. I decided to call the show *LONDON HUGHES: Superstar (It's Just Nobody's Realized It)*. Again, it sounds bigheaded, but I'm sure you know me well enough by now to know that I was being completely serious. That's exactly how I saw myself. My LA trip had given me this new sense of pride; I was even more confident in my starlike abilities! Just because I wasn't a household name right now, didn't mean that I was never going to be one. I used to believe that the people in charge of entertainment knew what they were doing. I called them the gatekeepers—the commissioners and heads of channels who decide which TV shows get made, and which comedians become the next big thing. I soon realized that when it came down to it, those gatekeepers just didn't know everything. They weren't some all-seeing, all-knowing comedy geniuses, they were just humans, most of whom couldn't perform stand-up comedy if they had a gun to their heads. It wasn't my fault those gatekeepers couldn't see my magic. Brent Forrester saw it just by having lunch with me, Phoebe Waller-Bridge saw it after one audition, and Alan Carr saw it when I was in university. Just because they didn't see it, didn't mean it wasn't there.

This new take on my career changed everything and I threw all my energy (and all my money) into my 2017 Edinburgh show. It was a high-energy, all singing, all dancing performance with many, many, many props. I'm a go hard or go home type of gal, so I went full out and got a director, a lighting guy, and a very talented friend to do live voice-over. I even hired back the expensive boutique publicist to do all the press and asked a famous comedy pal for a quote that I could put on all the flyers, which read:

"London Hughes is funny, vivacious and has Beyoncé's moves on speed dial! Watch her go!"—Sir Lenny Henry

I wanted this show to set the comedy world alight! They would soon know the name LONDON HUGHES!

The show was about a young Black girl from South London

who dreamed of being Britain's answer to Whoopi Goldberg. (Oh, I wonder who that could be?) I told the story of my career to date through the medium of iconic British television shows. It starts in my childhood bedroom with me dancing to Britney Spears. I then turn on the TV set and physically try to get inside. Once I'm in, I realize that nobody on TV looks like me. "They're all old white dudes." I decide I want to be the face I never saw on TV growing up, so I use British TV shows to help me (and the audience) try to figure out where I fit in in. There's a *Supermarket Sweep* section, where I run around the stage with a shopping cart and the audience has to find the inflatable clues that help me with my career and throw them inside. There's a *Wheel of Fortune* section where a random audience member spins a cheaply made wheel, which had all the ways I attempted to be famous on it, and then I got the audience member to reenact whichever scenario it landed on. There was a *Who Wants to Be a Millionaire* segment, in which the audience has to help me answer questions on how to improve my love life.

The show ends with me realizing that I was never going to be a household comedy name in Britain, because British television doesn't have any Black female comedy household names. Right at the end of the show, I decide to focus my attention on moving to America, and it ends with a giant spotlight on me as a Hollywood-style voice-over says, "Will London Hughes make it in America?! Will she get a star on the Hollywood Walk of Fame? Will she ever get a Hollywood agent?"

I say, "Of course she will" and then Bruno Mars sings, *"Don't believe me just watch!"* and the lights go black. All in all, that one-woman show cost me over 15,000 English pounds. I got a one-hundred-seat venue, put posters up all over town, paid thousands on marketing yet . . . still . . . nobody came.

Well, I say nobody, but some of my mates came and filled up seats. On average, I was performing in a one-hundred-seat theater to between four to seven people a night. I was absolutely devastated. There were so many variables that went into why that show was a huge flop, but the main one was my venue. The Edinburgh Comedy Festival is all about getting the right venue. There are shit-hot venues and there are not-so-shit-hot venues, and then there was my venue, in the arse end of Edinburgh. Initially I wanted to perform at a top venue called the Pleasance, where all the big-name comedians performed. I'd emailed Ryan, the Pleasance venue coordinator, telling him all about myself and the show, but he didn't even reply. Actually, none of the top comedy venues replied to me. I wasn't important enough, I wasn't a well-known name, I guess I wasn't worth replying to.

The other thing that hindered my show was that my expensive boutique publicist was a tad bit out of her depth. Most comics were promoting their Edinburgh shows by doing bits on massive comedy variety shows. My publicist had me showcasing my comedic talents at retirement homes. I shit you not. I performed a special preview of *Superstar (It's Just Nobody's Realized It)*, to a room full of Scottish old-age pensioners, two of which fell asleep mid-performance, and half of whom had no idea why I was there.

Despite everything going against me I still gave a hell of a performance. I went out every night for a month and performed to those four to seven (sometimes ten) people like I was performing for tens of thousands! I literally left the stage dripping with sweat and by the end of the one-month run I'd lost ten pounds. All I wanted was a good review. A good review would make people want to come and see the show. A good review can change everything.

Eventually my first review came in: three out of five stars.

It opened with "Somewhere along the road to Edinburgh, London Hughes has been poorly advised..." I felt like I'd been punched in the vagina. The review said that although I showed some superstar potential, the venue was terrible, and the running time was way too long. I was inconsolable. To the average eye, the review wasn't that bad, but I'd set such high standards for myself, I always have. I'm not sure why I've always been so competitive with myself. I'm sure a therapist would tell me it's because I'm the middle child, or because growing up I always felt that I was in my brother Joel's shadow, or because I still carry some trauma from being bullied. All I know is, for as long as I can remember, I have aimed for the bloody stars, and anything short of that was a failure to me. I knew the kind of Edinburgh festival experience I wanted to have, the one I felt I deserved, and this wasn't it.

I hung around some of my peers who'd had hit shows that year. The hype around them was insane. If you had a hit show, the comedy fans stopped you for selfies, the gatekeepers and comedy execs cooed over you at industry parties, other comics respected you and then badmouthed you behind your back, plus you got to do so much press. Then you'd have important meetings every day, comedy execs were taking you out to dinner, and you were having brunch with the bigwigs! A hit show at the festival could truly change your whole life. I wanted that, I expected that! But my show was doing so poorly that by now,

I'd have settled for my name appearing on the SOLD-OUT SHOWS board just once. It never happened.

I didn't have an amazing Edinburgh, I didn't have a good Edinburgh, by my standards, I had a considerably bad Edinburgh. I would stay in bed and cry all day, and then at 9:00 p.m., it was showtime, then back to crying. But although I was down, I distinctly remember trying not to feel sorry for myself. Some nights I would cry until I started laughing at the fact that I was crying my eyes out because I didn't get a five-star review at a fancy arts festival! People were literally dying of hunger or in wars all over the globe, and I was weeping over a lack of metaphorical stars.

I was holding out hope that Melissa Myers, the agent at WME in LA, would keep her promise to see my show. It didn't matter to me if there were eight people in the audience or eight thousand, if she was there, I'd give her a show to remember! We emailed back and forth, and she said she was coming. I gave it my all every single night, and I even started to lose my voice. I had to give it my all, you never know who could be in the audience! But by the end of the long and grueling month, eight comedians were chosen by a panel of top industry critics and nominated for best show. I was not one of them. That same week, I got an email from Melissa Myers. She was finally in town for the festival, but sadly she wouldn't be able to see my show, as she was busy with one of her clients who *had* been nominated for best show.

That was it, all my hopes were dust. After my final show, I had dinner with Tiffany. We ate pizza, and I was officially defeated. I cried. I cried harder than I had at my Pizza Hut birthday party. I had given the festival everything. So much money, so much sweat, so much hard work went into that show. Oh well, at least my mum really liked it! She came up to Edinburgh with my stepdad to visit me and saw it five times, and even though there were only six to ten people in the audience, Mumsie was always the one laughing and clapping the loudest.

Tiffany told me not to beat myself up about Melissa not coming; she knew it had always been a long shot. American agents are very busy people and the chances of an American talent agency signing a comic like me, who had hardly any profile in the UK, was very slim. "You just need to be more famous here first, then they'll come running, I promise," she told me. I told Tiffany that I was angry. I was angry because I knew that I had it in me to take this arts festival by storm. I'd seen all the shows that had hype that year—mainly performed by posh white dudes talking about their middle-class lives, or edgy white dudes doing experimental comedy—and I was "the urban comic," competing with thousands, to make noise at a very white arts festival. I finished my pizza, and Tiff and I hugged it out. I could see in her face that she felt sorry for me, and part of me felt like I'd let her down. I picked myself up (again) and told myself I'd never feel this way again. One day I'd be back at this festival, and I'll be doing sold-out shows to critical acclaim. The Edinburgh Comedy Festival will know my name. I'm London Hughes, Superstar and one day, Edinburgh would realize it.

HEAD UP QUEEN, YOUR CROWN'S SLIPPING.

There's something about falling flat on your face that gives you no choice but to pick your head up and look to the sky. I thought I'd been at rock bottom before, but I now realized that that hadn't been rock bottom, that had been the crystal middle. NOW I was at rock bottom! Whew! During that long and painful six-hour train ride from Edinburgh back to Brighton I thought of all the things I could have spent that £15K on as salty tears of embarrassment trailed down my face. I thought about how I was expected back on set to film *Scrambled!* the very next day, entertaining the children of the nation and inspiring them all to go and follow their dreams after I'd just spectacularly failed at mine.

There was something strangely cathartic about giving something your all and having nothing left to show for it. Just to keep you up to speed on my current failures:

- Dropped out of university
- Sacked from Babestation
- Sacked from TGI Fridays
- Moved back in with my parents
- Cut from a blockbuster movie franchise
- Had every single TV show I'd ever written rejected
- Had two failed attempts at the Edinburgh Comedy Festival
- Produced a less-than-popular YouTube channel
- Had no boyfriend or potential love interests
- And I was now about fifteen grand in debt

I pulled into the *Scrambled!* set and went into hair and makeup. I was filming a recurring sketch where I dressed up as an inflatable duck. God, I hated that sketch, but hey, it paid the bills. As I got changed into the oversized fluorescent yellow duck costume, I had no idea that moments later, another career butterfly would land on my nose. Out of the blue, my *Scrambled!* co-presenter Luke Franks got an email from his agent, which he shared with everyone in the room. His agent said they wanted him to audition for *Celebs Go Dating*. *Celebs Go Dating* was a popular reality TV show where celebrities (and I use that term very loosely) went on dates with members of the public for audience entertainment. The show had run for a few seasons and was a ratings hit. To be honest, most reality TV shows were ratings hits, because Britain has an almost embarrassing obsession with reality TV.

SUPERSTAR TO REALITY TV STAR

It was 2017, and reality TV stars had become the new YouTubers. Instant stars, overnight sensations. Reality TV shows attracted big audiences and their cast members amassed huge online followings, so entertainment execs started using them on every single show. Untalented popular people flooded every TV station and late-night entertainment slot across the UK. They were presenting TV shows, were guests on panel shows, they even had their own entertainment shows made for them! The public loved them and the press adored them, so every few months TV channels would churn out more and more of these talentless Barbies. Being a reality TV star was a lucrative talent factory. They all looked the same, they all did the same things, they all went on the same TV shows, they all had a fashion line or a book deal, they were in every single TV advert, and they were all absolutely cleaning up! TV producers didn't look for people with skill, talent, or experience anymore, it was all about their social media following, which made life as an up-and-coming talented person with two thousand followers under her belt very challenging. Now I was being overlooked for jobs for the girl from *Gogglebox*, or the girl from *The Only Way Is Essex*, or the girl from *Geordie Shore*, or the girl from *Made in Chelsea*! The networks were raking it in, so they just kept making more reality shows. *Celebs Go Dating, Celebrity Coach Trip, Celebs on the Farm, I'm a Celebrity... Get Me Out of Here!, Celebrity First Dates, Celebrity Ghost Hunt*! I couldn't get booked on any of these entertainment shows because I wasn't famous enough and nobody was willing to give me a chance. It was becoming pretty clear to me that TV execs would rather hire a female reality TV star with zero talent and a huge following over a female comic with tons of talent and a small following. I knew that for people in Britain to take me seriously as a comedian, first I'd have to get them to notice me. By becoming a reality TV star.

I sent an email to Tiffany asking her to get me an audition for *Celebs Go Dating*. I knew that if they were considering meeting my *Scrambled!* co-star Luke, then they'd probably be up for meeting with me, too. All I needed was an in, a chance to get in the room with the producers, and I'd make sure that that job was mine. I was going to be on a reality TV show about dating. Wow, what a perfect time to be newly single.

Tiffany didn't share my vision at first. She really cared about talent, which is why we got along so well. None of her other clients were reality TV stars; she had no use for what's-her-face from

Ex on the Beach or that dude from *Celebrity Come Dine with Me*. Tiffany was worried about my brand. She knew I wanted to be taken seriously as a comedian and wasn't sure that going on a reality show was the way to do it. I told her to trust me.

I walked into my *Celebs Go Dating* audition with no doubt in my mind that I would end up on the show. I was very familiar with the show's casting process. They would hire between six to eight celebs to star in the series, most of them white, but there would always be one token Black celeb. Entertainment shows in Britain ALWAYS had one token person of color. And I knew that the majority of the celebrities picked for the show would be well-known reality TV stars because they had huge followings and would bring in big ratings. What weirdly worked in my favor was that pretty much every famous British reality TV star was white (yep, there were zero non-white famous reality TV stars in Britain in 2017). So even though I didn't have a big following, and I was nowhere near as "famous" as the other "celebs" on the show, I had no real competition getting on it because they needed their token and there simply weren't any reality TV stars of color around to take that spot. Thanks, British systemic racism! All I really had to do was impress the producers, charm them, make them laugh a bit, and the job would most likely be mine.

The audition process was simple. I sat down with the producers for a chat. They wanted to know why I'd be right for the show. It was like the *Big Brother* auditions all over again, but now I was ready and prepared. I wowed them with funny stories about my disastrous dating life, told them all about my rules for a boyfriend, my breakup with Matthew, the Tina Fey book story, Daniel's Victorian town house analogy, and getting Post-it Notes for Valentine's Day! But what truly sealed the *Celebs Go Dating* deal was my Las Vegas story.

WHAT HAPPENS IN VEGAS, GETS YOU BANNED FROM THE PLANET HOLLYWOOD CASINO IN VEGAS

It was my first time in Las Vegas, and I had already decided that it was going to be a fucking movie. I had planned to do it all, see it all, and sleep with it all. I was primed and I was ready, bring on the debauchery! The only problem I didn't foresee was that the girls I decided to go with weren't exactly the debauchery type. FYI ladies, don't be like me, DO NOT go on holiday with your brother's ex-girlfriend and her mates. It won't end well for you.

We had a suite at Planet Hollywood and I was so ready to live my best life. The girls I was staying with, however, were not. I wanted to enjoy the nightlife, they wanted to stay in and watch *Keeping Up with the Kardashians*. I decided to go it alone and pop my Vegas cherry solo. My first night I ended up meeting some random American girls in the lobby and tagging along with them to a nightclub. It was packed, but their friend had a table. I was drinking Cristal champagne and making all the guys fall in love with my cute British accent. We partied and partied until after a while your girl was D-R-U-N-K...the type of drunk where at any point you could fall asleep into an ice bucket. I decided to make my excuses, head back to the hotel, try to find some food, and sober up. I had no idea what time it was. To be honest, the rest of the story is a little patchy because I don't remember how I got back to my hotel, but I do remember walking along the Vegas Strip for a bit, at some point taking off my shoes. I was a complete mess, hun. I made my way into the Planet Hollywood Casino. Things were dying down a bit but I spotted a guy playing roulette.

Now, I am not the gambling type, I love money way too much to waste it on chance. I had no interest in actually doing any gambling, but I was drunk, and I talk A LOT of shit when I'm drunk. I go up to this guy who turned out to be an Australian named Striker and drunkenly say, "Put it on twenty-four black, babes!" Reader, the only reason I said this was because 1) I was twenty-four years old at the time and 2) I am Black. I have no idea how the roulette wheel works, never played the game in my life, wasn't even sure there was a twenty-four black, I just knew they said stuff like that in the movies. I chuckled at my own statement and continued through the casino, but before I could reach the slot machines, Striker the stranger caught up with me.

"I did what you said, you just won me three hundred dollars!" he shouted. He'd clearly had a bit to drink, too. "How can I repay you?!" he said. Then I replied, without missing a beat, "You can let me sit on your face!!" I loved that phrase, "sitting on face"; it was poetry to me. I used to say it all the time, for no reason. I'd see someone cute on TV and I'd be like, "Yep, I'd sit on his face." It always threw men off their guard and made Prudy Judys squirm. I loved the effect saying a sentence like that so casually had on people. I laughed at my own statement again. I was on fire, mate! I carried on walking to my hotel room, not expecting what happened next. Striker said, "Okay, come and sit on my face." I stopped in my tracks. Was he serious? He looked serious. "Where do you wanna do it? Oh, and my name's Striker by the way, what's yours?" I couldn't believe it, here I was in Las Vegas, Sin City, for barely twenty-four hours and a man I did not know was casually offering to eat me out. I was extremely flattered! Now, there is a version of me that said, "I was joking sir, don't be silly" and quietly headed off to her room, but she must have called in sick that day because Drunk Las Vegas London thought it would be a great idea to let this Australian man go down on me. We found a secluded area behind a poker table, Striker lay on his back, and I gracefully perched over his face. It was very convenient that I was wearing a dress that was too small for me, so I'd gone out for the night sans underwear. I didn't even have to lift up my dress, and soon I was perched and perfectly bouncing on this man's face without a care in the world. Eyes closed, living my best life, hun. All of a sudden, I felt two pairs of arms grab my shoulders and hoist me up in the air. I got lifted off Striker's face by two angry-looking security guards.

"We don't do this type of thing here, ma'am, this is the Planet Hollywood!"

I was so fucking startled, and Striker, who was being pinned to the ground by another set of casino security, was confused, too. I started panicking.

"I'm so sorry . . . I didn't mean to . . . but . . . this is Vegas??!!" I was slightly unimpressed. I thought this was the city of sin where anything goes. I had no idea they would look so harshly on a little bit of casino cunnilingus! They separated Striker and me and I never saw him again. They took me through a secret door at the back of the casino and put me in a jail cell. I was terrified.

"Do you know that what you did tonight was a felony, miss?!" a scary-looking man with a badge asked me. I actually didn't, I had no idea what I did was a crime, but there was no way in hell I was being arrested for sitting on a man's face, my parents would absolutely kill me! So, I turned on the charm, and turned up the British accent.

"I'm so sorry, sir, I'd had a bit to drink. It's my first time in Vegas, I just assumed that anything goes. It'll never happen again, I promise. I am so so soooo sorry, Officers." I wanted to cry, but the ordeal sobered me up so quickly it had drained all the moisture out of my body. I literally started dry wailing. All that was going through my mind was, *Does this mean I have a criminal record now? Do I get a phone call?! Who was my lawyer?* I'd clearly seen way too many episodes of *Banged Up Abroad*, but I knew this wasn't going to end well for me. I was way too cute to go to prison! God, I'd give anything to be in a hotel room watching the Kardashians right now! I sat quietly in my cell for a while, absolutely and utterly hopeless. "Do . . . I get a phone call?!" I asked one of the guards. He could see the fear written all over my face, and he looked me dead in the eye and started laughing.

"No, this isn't a real jail."

"What?" I said, trying to catch my breath.

"Nah, this is casino jail—we just put you in here so you can sober up."

"Oh . . . so I haven't been arrested?"

"Do you see any police officers around here?" he replied, then carried on eating his sandwich. I eventually got released from casino jail with a bottle of water. I'd been in there for twenty minutes total. God, it felt so good to be out. I got unofficially banned from the Planet Hollywood Casino (I say "unofficially" because I've definitely been back there since), and I told myself I would never sit on an Australian stranger's face ever again. The end.

The producers salivated over that story and a week later I got the call. I was starring in the new series of *Celebs Go Dating*.

LONDON GOES DATING

Being on a reality TV show was an absolute whirlwind that I did NOT prepare myself for. It was a lot, almost too much, and that was by my standards! They kicked off the show with a huge launch night at a fancy club in the West End. I got my hair and makeup done, was picked up in a swanky car, and dropped off at the top of a glitzy red carpet. I got out of the car and a million flashes went off in my face. "Over here, London, over here, please! Here!" I was ready! I did the same pose I'd perfected at that fashion week party, got my angles, I was smizing—it felt amazing! Gone were the days of me stepping onto a red carpet and nobody knowing who I was. I had arrived, huns!

The show filmed for three of the most full-on months of my life. We had to date various members of the public, captured by camera crews, and then go to the celebrity dating agency and talk on camera about our feelings and experiences. After we'd been on ten dates, we'd choose one lucky civilian to take to the finale in Cape Verde, West Africa! They paid me £30,000 to do the show, the most money I'd ever been paid to do anything at the time! To be honest, I would have done it for free. They were literally paying me to go on dates with cute guys and eat free food at swanky restaurants.

The first time I met the rest of my *Celebs Go Dating* castmates was at a fancy star-studded mixer, all filmed for the show. I was joined by Gemma Collins, a reality TV star famous for her time on one of the OG reality shows, *The Only Way Is Essex*. Gemma Collins, or The GC as she liked to be known, was reality TV royalty and boy didn't she know it, and in fact she would make sure you knew it, too. I couldn't stand her, to be honest. To put it in the nicest way I can, she was a complete and absolute dick turd. She was rude to the crew, her castmates, anyone and everyone. She shouted at producers, she walked off set, showed up hours late for filming, threw fits, and repeatedly let us all know that we were "nobodies" and "lucky to be on the show with her." I tried to avoid her drama as much as possible. The rest of the cast were angels by comparison. There was Sam Thompson, from a reality show called *Made in Chelsea*, Ollie Locke, also from *Made in Chelsea*, the late great "Muggy Mike" from *Love Island*, a socialite named Talia Storm, an Olympic taekwondo fighter named Jade Jones, and me, good old London Hughes, the comedian and token Black girl.

The *Celebs Go Dating* mixer was the first time I realized that my Blackness would come into play on national television. It's a common fact that Black women are the least swiped right on

Tinder. There are a lot of men on this earth who simply don't find Black women desirable and as the only Black woman on the show, it crossed my mind that there may be some men reluctant to date me. The rest of the girls on the show were all blondes, and everyone loves blondes, don't they? Let's just say I wouldn't have been surprised if a few of the men thought that I wasn't exactly "their type on paper." It honestly annoyed me, but hey, this is the world we live in. The producers filled the mixer with tons of available and eligible bachelors, men of all races, ages, and sizes. Black guys, white guys, Asian guys, old guys, young guys, short guys, and tall guys, a smorgasbord of potential dick! A camera crew followed us around as we made small talk with each of these men. I spotted a couple of cute ones, and even though I was genuinely open to meeting someone new, that was not the point. This was work for me. I turned on the funnies and played it all up for the camera. It was going great, I was in top form. At the end of the mixer, we were told by the dating agents that we had to choose a guy from the party to go on a date with. I had my heart set on a few of them, but at the last minute, purely for entertainment purposes, the producers flipped the script on us. They made all the female celebs stand in a line opposite all the eligible bachelors.

"Okay, eligible men, you've spent the evening getting to know our gorgeous celebs, but what you didn't know is, now it's time for YOU to decide who to date...So, step forward if you want to date...Talia Storm." Of the about three hundred men in the room, fifty of them stepped forward for Talia. Almost all of them stepped forward to date Jade Jones, and even a few stepped forward to date The GC. But no one stepped forward for me. None of the Black guys moved a muscle. I was shocked, but I wasn't surprised.

Dating in London as a Black girl, more often than not, you'll come across Black men who don't date Black women. It's a phenomenon to me, something to do with their own internalized racism. Honestly, I'll bet Black women are the only race of women in the world who'll meet another guy from their own race and have to think, "But does he even date Black women?" It's draining! I've had that thought on many occasions, especially in the circles I've moved in. Why do you think most of my boyfriends have been white men!? Personally, I don't really have a type, huns, London is open! But the majority of the Black men I came across in my career fields exclusively dated white women.

It was embarrassing to think that I wasn't desirable enough to even land a date on a reality dating show. My inner hype woman kicked in: "I don't know what those guys are thinking, I look drop-dead gorgeous!" I told myself. I had on a sparkly gold dress, a pair of Topshop heels, my wig had been laid and straightened to perfection, and my face was beat to the gods, darling! I looked and felt like an absolute bad bitch; it wasn't my fault they couldn't see how cute I was. I tried not to let the rejection faze me, and I kept reminding myself that it didn't matter because I was at work, but, in all honesty, my ego was a little crushed. Eventually one of the guys took pity on me and reluctantly stepped forward. His name was Tino and he was my first official date on the show.

THE FAME GAME

Celebs Go Dating came on every night at 9:00 p.m. on E4 and after my date with Tino aired, the followers came flooding in! I was a hit, huns! I'd made the executive decision to just be myself on my dates—funny, entertaining, witty, and honest. I clowned around, I talked with my mouth full, I burped, I was awkward, I enjoyed my food, I did anything to stay memorable whilst remaining true to who I was. The clips of me on various dates went viral, and I became a fan favorite on the show. My Instagram followers went from three thousand to forty-five thousand in a week or so. I was now what they call "an influencer."

Reality TV fame was wild and it was stupid, and I definitely got caught up. When I looked at the life of a reality TV star from the outside in, I couldn't stand the thought of them. I assumed they were all just untalented money-grabbing chancers trying to stretch out their fifteen minutes of fame. But then I became a reality TV star myself and everything changed. I was in all the papers! All those thousands of pounds wasted on my boutique publicist, when all I had to do was get a gig on *Celebs Go Dating*. I was enthralled by the glitz and glamour of it all, and I learned so much. For one, I had no idea that people actually called the paparazzi on themselves. Sure I'd heard it mentioned in songs, but I didn't know that people actually did it. Reality TV stars do it ALL THE TIME. The producers even made us do it, so whenever we left a building and got into a car there'd be conveniently placed paps outside. For the finale in Cape Verde, we all had individual paparazzi sessions. We'd have to frolic about and laugh on a sandy beach and pretend not to notice the paparazzi photographer taking pics of us. Sometimes they would even direct us, make us stand a certain way or walk toward the camera, just so they could get a perfect shot. The next day those shots would be all over the *Daily Mail*, made to look as if we had no idea that someone was standing right there snapping pics of us. I found it all so fake, but so bloody fabulous. I'd go to premieres, shop openings, fashion launches, galas, brunches, and got snapped by paparazzi everywhere I went. If I was having a girls' night out with one of my reality TV star friends, by the end of the night someone would message a pap, then boom, flashing lights and the next day it's: *"Celebs Go Dating* star London Hughes spotted leaving restaurant with mysterious hunk." I loved the attention! I rang Tiffany to tell her all about it. I wanted her to start getting me invited to more events and calling paparazzi for me all the time.

"London you are NOT a reality TV star, stop this! You have talent! Remember, you don't want to just attend the premiere, you want to be IN the movie!" She was totally right. To quote a famous *Love Island*er, "I'd completely lost my head." I was so caught up with keeping up with the Kardashians that I totally forgot what separated me from them. We were not the same. Reality TV stars HAVE to call paparazzi on themselves because they are their only currency. They're not celebrated for a skill, they're celebrated for being themselves, which means the moment the public stops caring about who they are, they become irrelevant. They had to be seen at this event, wearing that outfit, dating that guy because if they weren't, they'd be considered old news. I had forgotten, for the moment, that I had talent. What

I didn't know was that someone across the pond had noticed it and was desperately trying to get in touch with me.

A GIFT SENT FROM HAVEN

I remember exactly where I was when Tiffany rang me to tell me that a talent agency in the US wanted to sign me. I was in West London, stuck in traffic. It was the end of 2017—I was still filming *Celebs Go Dating* and on my way to set. "Mate, you'll never guess what! I've been contacted by a talent management company from the US, they found your *No Filter* YouTube sketches online, and they want to sign you. They're based in Los Angeles, and I've done my research, they're the real deal! Congratulations!"

It was the news I'd been waiting to hear my whole life. I'd dreamed about this moment so many times, envisioned how it would all go down, and now it was finally happening right there during rush hour, in the back of a Mercedes Benz C-Class. I was finally getting the call that would change everything. I hung up the phone, looked out of my car window, exhaled, and slowly gave myself a pat on the back. This was it, I could feel it in the bottom of my vagina. It was finally MY time, everything was starting to happen for me. The company about to make my US dreams come true was called Haven Entertainment, and they represented a lot of writer-comedians and produced movies and TV shows. Haven's newest manager, Chanell Hardy, had been stuck in a YouTube rabbit hole one day and stumbled across my *No Filter* sketches. Again, I need to stress to you guys that these sketches had gone nowhere near viral, my *Celebs Go Dating* stint hadn't even aired yet, and I was sitting on about two hundred plus YouTube subscribers. The chances of her randomly finding my sketches among the sea of viral cat videos, unboxing videos, and makeup tutorials were nonexistent!

The next day I had a Skype call with my new potential US managers, Chanell, Amy, and Jesse from Haven. I told them the whole London Hughes story, basically a condensed version of everything in this book so far. They listened and laughed and when I finished, they said the words I've been wanting to hear a Hollywood manager say ever since ten-year-old me called up Foxtons Estate agents looking for "representation." They said: "London Hughes, we think you're going to be a massive star, we want to sign you," and then, reader, I cried like a little bitch.

But things were only set to get even more crazy because by spring 2018, I was packed up and on a plane back to that beautiful sunshine city, Los Angeles! I knew I'd be back in LA one day but I had no idea it would be so soon. I reflected on who I had been the first time I'd visited: a dreamer using the last bit of money she had to buy a plane ticket, not knowing anyone or anywhere to go, staying at the Ramada Plaza because that's all she could afford. I was so proud of that girl, she manifested all of this.

I met with my new US managers and signed all the contracts, then they took me out to dinner. I got on really well with my new manager, Chanell Hardy, a cute Black girl only two years older than me. I was really impressed by her. Chanell and I had so much in common and became instant besties. I felt safe with her, and was eager to kick-start my comedy career in the US. She pictured me starring in hit movies, Emmy-winning

TV shows, and on giant billboards taking over the whole town! Oh, how I loved the sound of billboards! I couldn't wait to get started! But it wasn't that simple. In order to work in America, I needed to get something called an O-1 Visa, an expensive permit that allows international talent to work and live in the US. O-1 Visas are awarded to non-Americans with unique abilities, the official term for them is "individuals with extraordinary talent."

To apply for an O-1 Visa, you have to prove to the American government that you're better qualified and more suited in your chosen field than an American, and that you'd be an asset to the US industry. To prove this, you needed about six grand, lots and lots of press, proof of work, and letters of recommendation from prominent people in your chosen industry. So close and yet so far! I had some serious work to do. Meanwhile, back in the UK, Tiffany was fighting off entertainment producers left right and center, because after *Celebs Go Dating*, everyone started wanting a piece of the London Hughes pie.

FINALLY SEMI-FAMOUS

The same producers who wouldn't answer Tiffany's calls a few months ago, the ones who said, "We love London, but we're not quite sure our audience would get her," were now the ones begging for me to come on their shows! Shows like *Mock the Week*, a staple for any British comic. Going on it was like telling the world, "Why yes, I am a professional and famous comedian." It was a rite of passage, a very white rite of passage. *Mock the Week* only ever hired one female comic per show, if at all, and 99 percent of the time they were white. They couldn't even do us the decency of having a token person of color in every episode! In seventeen series, there'd only ever been four Black female comedians on the show. I was the fourth and the youngest to debut on the show. It was truly groundbreaking shit. I was slowly starting to make my mark in the entertainment business and having so much fun doing it.

My new success meant that I could finally move out of my mum's house. I moved to a posh members-only house share in southwest London, and to live there you had to make a certain amount of money each year and prove you were a professional creative. I felt good about myself, huns, I was a professional creative! Moving back to London at the height of my reality TV fame was absolutely insane for my social life, and I won't lie, it also did wonders for my ego. Let's just say there were plenty of new dudes in my DMs! I got stopped in the street by fans every day asking for selfies. It was just so nice to feel appreciated. I'd spent so much of my career fighting to be seen, trying to prove myself. I was so used to highlighting the injustices against female comics or speaking up against the injustices against Black British talent, trying everything I could to break the bloody British door down! And now I could... just exhale. I'd done it, huns. I was so extremely well versed in struggle and failure that I'd forgotten what it felt like to actually win, and God, it felt so good!

I decided to celebrate myself more, every win, no matter how big or small. I started treating myself and spoiling the people around me. I went to Harrods for the first time ever and bought my first Gucci bag. I bought Tiffany and me matching Givenchy jackets, took Mumsie out to countless fancy dinners, got my dad a brand-new telly, took myself on mini spa breaks, got massages every Tuesday, and took my family and friends on luxury holidays! I was living my life so well, I became my own sugar daddy!

BE YOUR OWN SUGAR DADDY

I have never dated a rich man. Don't get me wrong, I've always wanted to! I wanted to be that girl that guys send their credit card details to and say, "Go on, treat yourself" or the girl that gets flown out on getaway trips to Dubai "just because." I never got those guys. The closest I'd been to bagging a rich guy was dating Daniel and HE got me Post-it Notes for Valentine's Day! It had always been this romantic dream of mine for the man in my life to take me on a dinner date to Paris. One pretty normal evening he would surprise me out of the blue with dinner reservations, and we'd hop on the Eurostar and then we're there, eating frogs' legs with a gorgeous view of the Eiffel Tower! So extravagant, so romantic, so joie de vivre! Well, I waited, and waited and that day never came. So one day I just thought: *Fuck it! I'll take myself for dinner in Paris!* I hopped on the Eurostar and by 7:00 p.m. I was seated at a swanky bar near the Champs-Élysées, having just ordered a steak (medium rare of course) whilst a beautiful woman onstage sang some sweet, sweet French jazz. I had no idea what she was singing about (all I can fluently say in French is je m'appelle est la piscine, which loosely translated to "my name is the pool") but in my head, whatever the jazz lady was singing was French for "Hey, London Hughes, you're a bad bitch!" I felt so awesome sitting at that bar alone, sipping fancy expensive-arse champagne I couldn't even pronounce. I'd have lit a smooth cigarette if it wasn't for my terrible asthma.

Sitting at that bar, I thought about my lack of love life. Now well into my late twenties, I had two ex-boyfriends under my belt. Never been married, no kids, just comedy career and chill. I wondered what was next for me. With hard work and determination, it felt like I was finally on track to the exact career I'd dreamed of, yet I still had trouble getting the men right. But I decided at this point it didn't matter. Some people considered marriage or kids major life goals, but for me, sitting at a bar in Paris was just as an important life goal as any of them. It felt like a tangible step toward success, something I achieved on my own, without the help of a man. I didn't actually NEED a man, for anything, in my life. Deep down, I knew that now that my life was starting to go the way I wanted it to, I'd have to start taking the men in my life more seriously. No more filler boy-friends. But in the meantime, I felt perfectly fine dating myself. I left Paris a whole new woman, evolved, like a Black girl Poké-mon and I wanted that feeling to last forever.

TELL THE KIDS I SAID GOODBYE

I had now completed my fifth series of *Scrambled!*, over two hundred episodes in the can, officially the longest job I'd ever had. The producers told me that ITV had just commissioned two more series and they wanted me to be a part of them. I'd just spent a boatload of money in Paris so my wallet said, "Yes please" but my heart said, "Err, think carefully about this, hun."

Now that things were finally starting to happen for me, and I
was actually allowed on comedy shows in the UK, it felt like a
natural time to finally say goodbye to kids' TV.

My producer didn't understand my decision. "But you don't
have another job to go to; why would you turn down work without something else to fall back on?" He was right, even though I
was getting spots on entertainment shows, I didn't have a solid TV
series I was a part of. Maybe I was being premature, and I should
do a couple more seasons? I was taking a huge risk walking away
from guaranteed work. The last time I walked away from kids' TV,
I ended up broke and back at my mum's house. In the end it all
came down to a stupid analogy that made so much sense to me. I
looked at my hands. I'd done five series of *Scrambled!* I lifted five
fingers, my whole left hand, and told myself I shouldn't lift another
finger unless I wanted to do my whole right hand, too. And I didn't.
I was officially hanging up my inflatable duck suit. Goodbye, children's television, I'll miss you; thank you for all the memories.

Things I Learned from All My Years in Children's Television

-
-
-
-
-
-
-

Puppeteers are *really* good at fingering.

Chapter 16

Don't Hate the Playaz!

"It's a hip-hop comedy panel show," my mate Jolyon explained to me whilst we were having lunch at Shoreditch House one day. He showed me the treatment for the show, and there was a picture of me underneath the words TEAM CAPTAIN. "ITV 2 is interested, it's gonna be huge, and obviously you know I have to have you on board as a team captain!" I adored Jolyon's passion for the show, and it sounded epic—two teams of comedians and rappers going head-to-head and battling it out each week for bragging rights, with challenges like "The Great British Break Off" (you have to battle an actual break-dancer) or "Come Rhyme with Me" (making an improv comedy rap on the spot about hilarious items). It sounded like a great idea at the time, and I wanted the chance to feature in a series, any series, that wasn't aimed at six-to-ten-year-olds. I told him if the show got greenlit, I'd be in. But honestly, I was dubious about the show actually getting picked up. ITV was one of the whitest terrestrial channels on TV. They once had a giant billboard that read ITV, WHERE ALL THE ENTERTAINERS ARE with all their top presenters standing in a line, and that line was whiter than Boris Johnson's friendship circle.

A few months later I got a call from Tiffany. "So there's this new show called *Don't Hate the Playaz* that wants you as a guest..." He did it! I was so happy for Jolyon! And I was about to be a team captain on an entertainment series! Finally, somewhere I could really show off my comedic talents and...wait. "What do you mean they only want me on as a guest?" Apparently, when ITV green-lit the show, they decided that I "wasn't team captain material." They didn't think I'd be right for the show and suggested I only be on as a guest instead. Instead of the full series, I'd appear in only one episode. I was fucking livid.

I naively thought that after *Celebs Go Dating*, I was done having to prove myself, but nope.

TV execs were STILL struggling to see my value. Jolyon, bless him, was so apologetic. "Mate, I tried. I'm sorry, I thought you were perfect for it but they said no!" I wasn't angry at him of course, I was angry at the ITV execs, and what have we all learned by now, huns? When London gets angry, she works harder.

I was hired to be a guest in the first episode of *Don't Hate the Playaz*, and on my way to the set I vowed to myself that I would give such an amazingly entertaining performance that every other show without me would be dull in comparison. I wanted the producers to see how truly huge of a mistake it was to recast me. I ate it all up and left no crumbs. I gave them ENERGY. I danced, I rapped, I sang, I used my presenting skills and my stand-up comedy skills. I had killer one-liners and set the other comics up with jokes. I was witty and outrageous, and the studio audience loved me. I was so in my element, at one point I even did the splits! Jolyon was right, the show was epic, and I had so much fun being a part of it! It was a perfect showcase for my talent, and I was truly gutted that for whatever reason, the producers couldn't see that.

In the car on the way home from set I got emotional again. I had no idea why the UK entertainment industry had SUCH a hard time trusting me. I could see the careers that my friends had. Now, I know everybody has their own journeys and we all work hard, but it truly felt like I had permanent shit on my face at all times! What was wrong with me? Why was I just okay, but never good enough? Why is it that some people got to where they were based on potential alone, but everywhere London Hughes went, she had to bloody do backflips to prove herself again and again and again! (Sorry, I refer to myself in the third person when I'm frustrated.) It was just a TV show, but it felt like a metaphor for my whole life. Then came the doubts. Maybe I shouldn't have quit children's television (again)? Maybe I should have just stuck to reality TV? They seemed to be the only genres that didn't view me as such a risk. I was embarrassed, I was angry, I was devastated. I called up Tiffany (bless her) with tears of frustration, and the next day she rang me back crying with tears of laughter.

"You did it, babes! After your performance last night, ITV admitted that they couldn't do the show without you. They want you for the FULL SERIES...AND I've made them pay you double!" I joined the cast of *Don't Hate the Playaz* and had the time of my life. Series one was a huge success, and I'm pleased to say that by the end of series two, I had won the show its first and only Royal Television Society Award.

**Best Entertainment Performance—
London Hughes, for her work on
Don't Hate the Playaz**

And all that, from the girl they didn't initially want on the show! At this point, I'm going to say something wanky and inspirational. Don't let anyone put you in a box, don't let anyone tell you who you can or can't be, just believe in yourself and they'll soon see.

YOU GOTTA HAVE FAITH, HUN

Confession: I'm a terrible Christian. Sorry, honestly I'm just plain awful. I used to be proper God squad as a kid; I bloody loved God! The church always seemed so cool to me. Any place that served free bread and wine on Sundays was I place I needed to be! I even went to Bible study during the school holidays. Whilst my friends were in the park, putting buttercups under their chins and playing with Pogs (if you don't know, ask your parents), I was in a hot, musty church learning about the trials and tribulations of Shadrack, Meshach, and Abednego (if you don't know, ask your pastor)! At thirteen, I knew all the books of the Bible and could recite them by heart, but by eighteen I was so not down with G.O.D. Christianity actually started to annoy me. I had all these unanswered questions: If God is supposed to love everyone, how come he hates my mate Gay Steven? How can God let people die? And why hasn't God stopped my mum from buying me knickers for Christmas? Things got worse when I eventually had to stop going to church because I couldn't afford it. My pastor and his wife were always running off to Barbados to "spread the word," and guess who had to pay for the flights and accommodation in Jesus's name? Not to mention the constant pressure to put money in the collection plate, the offering plate, and the donation plate. They even made the congregation give 15 percent of our wages to the church every Sunday. It's called giving a tithe—apparently it's in the Bible, but at the time I was a student and a waitress at TGI Fridays, and I'm pretty sure God didn't want me to be broke! So I decided to quit Christianity altogether and felt that it was more beneficial (and cheaper) to just be spiritual. Being spiritual's great. There's less guilt and paperwork and fewer rules about sodomy.

I now believe in the universe, and that the universe is probably just another word for God, or Buddha, or Allah, or Oprah. I also believe that we're all made up of cute little different energies that we can feel and draw from and, finally, I believe that if you want to live the life you truly feel you deserve, you kinda have to believe in something, even if it's just yourself. I've always believed in myself, but we all have off days. I'd have days where I'd feel unstoppable, and other days where I'd feel like I just couldn't do it. Whenever I felt down, I would always talk to myself like I'm my own best friend or hype woman. If I didn't get the audition, I'd say, "It's okay babes, what's for you won't go by you!" If a TV producer didn't think I was right for his show, I'd say, "It's fine, just watch, one day they'll be begging to have you on it!" The hype woman in my head always worked eventually, but the closer I got to my dreams, the more I stopped needing her, because I started seeing signs. EVERYWHERE.

Now, look, I don't know if it was God or angels or divine intervention or manifestation, but things kept happening to me that let me know I was on the right path, and it was so bloody scary. In fact, these moments happened to me so much I had to start doing my research. It's called "synchronicity." You know when you're thinking of someone and then they randomly call you, or you haven't heard a song in ages, and then that's all that's playing everywhere you go? That was happening to me tenfold. One day, I was driving down the street randomly singing Corrine Bailey Rae's song "Put Your Records On," and just as I was wondering to myself what had happened to her, Corrine Bailey Rae herself literally crossed the street in front of my car. If I fixated on a word or phrase I hadn't heard before, it would then come up on every TV show I watched that week, or I'd think about a person I hadn't seen in ages, and then bump into them on the street. It was like my life was an iPhone that had been listening to all the conversations I had with my brain. It started to happen to me every week. But as much as it freaked me out, it also reassured me. When something is too much of a coincidence to be a coincidence, I believe that that's something to do with a force greater than what humans understand.

I was driving to an audition and running late. I was at a low point: frustrated and overthinking everything. Some people like to live in the past, some people live in the present, but I'm always daydreaming about the future. I'd spent so much time thinking about this amazing life I was going to have in America, but now that I had a US manager and things were actually in motion, I had a tiny freak-out. I was in my car, eyes on the road, mind completely elsewhere thinking, *What if my visa doesn't come through? What if it does come through, but then I don't get any work in the US? What if American audiences don't get me? Living in LA is expensive, plus they don't even have free health care! Did I really think I can do this, what if I can't do this, I'm not sure I can do this!* Total freak-out, still not paying attention to the road, when all of a sudden the car in front of me stops out of nowhere, and I quickly slam on my brakes. I lurch forward and my car comes to a stop. When I lift my head, there's a massive billboard staring back at me. In giant black letters, are the words:

DREAM BIG, LONDON.

That's all the billboard said, just that.

The traffic all around me had come to a complete standstill, and that giant billboard was staring me in my face for the next half an hour. Now, it was actually a sign advertising a car, but I took it as a personal sign for me to stop doubting the process. Everything in America was going to work out just fine, and pretty soon the universe was about to provide me with all the ammunition I needed to trust the process and leave the UK for good.

LOOKING FOR WHOOPI

Sister Act 2 is a genius classic film that literally transcends race. It's a film that's 85 percent Black talent—including a Black female lead and Black female co-star, but nobody would call it a Black film, or an "urban" film, or a BAME (that's what the television industry calls things that star Black, Asian, or Minority Ethnic people) film. It was just a film. That was the Whoopi Goldberg effect. Whoopi was so huge in her day, and so talented, that it didn't matter to anyone that she was a dark-skinned Black woman with no eyebrows. She was just funny. She was just Whoopi and the world loved her for it. I wanted to be Britain's answer to Whoopi Goldberg so badly that I even talked about it in my Edinburgh show.

I said:

In the history of the world there's only been one Black woman that's achieved the comedy success that I want and that's Whoopi Goldberg! She started doing comedy before I was even born and she's the only Black female in comedy to ever become a world-renowned household name!

So just a year later, when my TV producer cousin, Paul Hughes, said the following to me, I understandably lost my shit.

"We've spoken to Whoopi's manager, and she loves the idea of doing a travel show with you."

My cousin is a great bloke. When I was much younger, Paul had been a researcher on *The Jeremy Kyle Show*, Britain's guilty pleasure and answer to *The Jerry Springer Show*. I was so proud of him! Paul had worked his way up the TV ladder behind the scenes, and I had worked my way up in front of the scenes, and now we were finally teaming up to work together for the first time on a new project that we wanted to pitch to Sky. A travel show, starring yours truly.

In our first meeting, he had asked me, "Who would you love to do a travel show with, London? If you could choose anyone in the world?" I said the name Whoopi Goldberg out loud and laughed at how stupid I sounded. As if one of my Hollywood heroes, a living legend, an icon from across the pond, would agree to do a travel show with me . . . but reader she did, she bloody did!

The show was called *Looking for Whoopi*, a mockumentary-style travel show where I would go to Los Angeles with dreams of making it big as a comic and Whoopi Goldberg would be my coach, helping me reach my goals, showing me the comedy ropes, and traveling the country with me. We even filmed a little teaser film for it. Whoopi recorded all her parts from the US. I screamed when I saw her face on film, saying my name for the first time:

"London Hughes, it's Whoopi! Now, if you're gonna be Britain's answer to me, then I'm gonna need you to get in shape . . ."

I knew how important this show would be for the culture— for funny women and for Black women. At that time, travel shows were huge in Britain, and pretty much every male comic had one. It didn't matter if it was male comics traveling with their dads, or male comics traveling with their mums, or male comics traveling with their male comic mates, or male comics traveling by themselves, they all still got made. Funny men, will travel. Meanwhile no female comedians had travel shows.

Apparently, women weren't allowed to travel around the world on TV unless they were selling houses.

I knew this show would be groundbreaking. Two Black female comics, one at the top of her game and one just starting out, an American and a Brit, one fish out of water and one big fish, just sharing stories, learning life lessons, and being bloody funny. It had HIT written all over it! We took the show to Sky first, as that's who we were developing it for. They said no... and then so did every other TV channel in Britain. Some of the feedback suggested that the channels didn't believe Whoopi or I were "bankable enough stars." Okay, say what you want about me, I was a comedian turned kids presenter turned reality TV star... BUT WHOOPI "the EGOT winner" Goldberg wasn't a bankable enough star!? How fucking dare they!? I'd had my TV shows rejected enough times now that I'd grown a thick skin, but something about that rejection sucker punched me in the face. I finally threw in the towel. If I can't even get a TV show with Whoopi Goldberg off the ground, then I have no business believing that I will ever make it in this industry.

In that moment, every inch of my spirit was drained. I thought about the little Black girl who'd watched *Sister Act* back in 1993. How could I tell her that one day she'd have the chance to work with one of her heroes, but unfortunately she chose to be a Black female comedian in Britain in the year 2018, so it couldn't happen? I let all hopes of the show go and tried to forget about it. Whoopi and I never even got a chance to meet in person. I thought I'd handled the situation quite well. I didn't cry when I got the news even though I was devastated (#growth #maturity) and I tried to keep myself busy focusing on other projects. Sadly, that growth and maturity did not last, because on New Year's Day 2019 a very hungover London Hughes was in bed, and when *Sister Act* came on Channel 4, she got angry all over again and fired off one tweet that changed everything.

London Hughes ✓
@TheLondonHughes

Sister Act is on, and I'm still a tiny bit pissed off that in 2018 a whole Whoopi Goldberg agreed to do a travel show with me but no TV channels wanted it.

In 2019 let's have more female comedians travelling and making TV and not just male comedians and their mums please. Thnx

11:30 AM • Jan 1, 2019 • Twitter for iPhone

That tweet launched a few more tweets, and a few thousand more after that. It went viral as female comics all over Britain started coming forward with their stories about all the amazing travel shows they'd pitched to various TV producers over the years that had been turned down.

That then led to this interview in the *Guardian* with the headline:

WHO WOULDN'T WANT WHOOPI?

Which included the following paragraph:

The comedian-travel show format is now well trodden, commonly involving a comic taking a trip with either their family (Jack Whitehall's *Travels With My Father*, Romesh Ranganathan's *Asian Provocateur*, *Russell Howard & Mum*) or friends (*Joel & Nish vs the World*, *Dara Ó Briain's Three Men in a Boat*). Notice anything about these comics? All of them are men. In fact Sue Perkins seems to be the only woman in British comedy with a passport.

I couldn't have said it better myself, mate. It went on:

But Hughes believes that commissioners are too heavily influenced by the lack of diversity in the industry to understand why a female travel show might appeal. "The people making the comedy went to university with the people starring in the comedy," she says ... "I don't want to sound ungrateful," she adds. "I've had a great career and I'm actually making loads of other shows with the very channels that rejected the show with me and Whoopi. It's not an attack, but a comment on the state of comedy right now."

It was now clear in black and white that the UK comedy industry had a race issue and a gender issue. This was something that people working within the industry always knew, but now the public knew, and they were pissed! I read through all the angry tweets; the public just couldn't understand why a show like this wouldn't be made!

Not even a month later, Tiffany got an email from a production company claiming that they were now actively looking for females to front travel shows! (As if they'd just come up with that amazing idea all on their own.) They wanted to know if I was available, but I wasn't. It was too late, I was already in America. At that point I knew I was done with British television. Up until then, I'd still flirted with the idea of having my own show on British soil one day. While a part of me always knew that I'd have to leave Britain and go and make it in America, another part of me wished I didn't have to. We all want a chance to be celebrated in our hometown, and I wasn't any different. Whoopi was the last straw. That, plus ten years of continually being overlooked, undervalued, and unappreciated by the British television industry. London Hughes was finally done, America here I come.

I asked my extremely talented/genius friends Sir Lenny Henry, Daniel Kaluuya, and Phoebe Waller-Bridge to sign my O-1 Visa letters, and got Krish Majumdar (chair of BAFTA), Joe Mace (ITV entertainment commissioner), and Jon Mountague (head of Comedy at Sky) to sign them, too! With an all-star talent lineup like that Donald Trump just had to let me in to 'merica! My visa was finally approved. I could now legally live and work in the States, and I would soon be off to live the life of my American dreams.

TO CATCH A D*CK

But before I left, I had one more thing to do: I still hadn't achieved number 3 on my list: have a hit show at the Edinburgh Comedy Festival.

I was in Marbella on my cousin's hen do. There were about fifteen of us, and I was one of the bridesmaids in charge. I had all these drinking games and scavenger hunts planned to entertain the rowdy ladies. Unfortunately, it rained—all day, nonstop, honestly it was biblical; as we stayed inside to keep dry, I had to revert to old-fashioned forms of entertainment and decided to tell the girls some stories. Real stories all about my love life, past boyfriends, my thoughts on children, my dating disasters. I was an open vagina. The girls lapped them up. They were laughing, screaming, cringing, hanging on my every word. They wanted more sex stories, the more salacious the better, and I gave it to them, I gave it to them good! In the middle of telling a story about this guy with a foot fetish that I used to date solely because he gave me free shoes, a light bulb went off.

I had unfinished business with the Edinburgh Comedy Festival. There was still a part of me that couldn't leave the UK for good without first conquering that fucking festival. It was hanging over me, like a bad smell. The doors that had begun opening up for me in America meant that now I really had a point to prove to the UK comedy scene. I AM A SUPERSTAR, GUYS, AND YOU LOT DID NOT REALIZE IT.

I wanted to go back to the Edinburgh Comedy Festival one last time. Third time's a charm! The festival is in August and by September I planned to be in America anyway, so it felt like I had nothing to lose. I didn't NEED anything from the festival, I didn't want my own TV show in the UK anymore, I didn't care about getting on any comedy panel shows, I didn't want to be famous in Britain. This time around, all I wanted was some goddamn RESPECT. I stripped my whole show back, no props, no lighting guy, no director, no voice-over artist; just me, my mic, and some jokes. I wrote the show in my flat in London. It physically poured out of me. I sat on the floor, stuck on some Kevin Hart in the background for inspiration, took out the notebook that that loser Daniel gave me for Valentine's Day (thanks, babe), and I just wrote and wrote and wrote about my sex life. Pages and pages of dick jokes.

Phoebe Waller-Bridge's show *Fleabag* started out as a show at the Edinburgh Comedy Festival, and now the Amazon series was a huge success that had won like seventeen thousand Emmys the year before, so I had a feeling that some of the female shows at the festival would probably be *Fleabag* inspired—darkly funny, moving, and gritty emotional pieces. I didn't want to do any of that. I wrote the type of show that I would never see at a posh arts festival. A Black woman joyfully and happily talking about sex and dating. I didn't care if people wouldn't find the show clever or witty or emotional enough, I wanted to do some dick jokes, so the festival was getting dick jokes. I named the show *To Catch a D*Ck* and told Tiffany I was ready to go back to Edinburgh.

Now that I had a bigger social media following and a bigger name for myself, I was approached by a promoter who wanted to put on my show. This was new for me, I was so used to doing all the hard work myself—paying for everything out of my own pocket, finding a venue, marketing, flyers, the lot. It felt extremely surreal that this time I had a team of people whose job was to do all that for me. I just had to focus on creating the funnies. I ended up getting the exact venue I wanted, the Pleasance, the same venue I'd tried to get when I did *Superstar*. I had the choice of a 6:00 p.m. or an 8:00 p.m. prime-time slot. If I went on at 8:00 p.m., my show would be going up against all the Edinburgh festival favorites and comedy heavy hitters (basically white dudes with a much bigger following than me) and sure, it might be hard to compete with all that, but I didn't care. I had a point to prove. I told them to put me up against the best of the best.

The first time I previewed *To Catch a D*ck* in London, it was about two hours long, and I want to thank anyone who was in that audience that night. All I remember is it getting to 10:00 p.m. and realizing there was still an hour of the show left to go, but you lot stayed all the way to the end—God bless you, you bloody heroes. It's always a good sign when you have too much material, and I did, I had so much! My sex life was way too juicy. I recorded the first preview, listened back, reworked it, and then did another preview the very next day. I invited Tiffany and her assistant at the time, Camilla, to the second preview, and I could tell they were impressed. When I came offstage they gave me a huge hug and said, "That was fucking great, mate! Well done!" My friend and stylist Rebekah had seen it for the first time also, and she said she could see it as a Netflix special. Until then, I hadn't even considered that, but as soon as she said it, I knew she was right.

This whole time I was merely doing the show to prove a point, but when Rebekah mentioned it becoming a Netflix special, my whole energy shifted. No British female comics had ever had an original Netflix special, only Brit dudes, like Jimmy Carr, Ricky Gervais, Russell Howard, James Acaster, and Mo Gilligan. They say you should always trust your gut, and my gut never steers me wrong (except when I eat too much cheese). I can't explain how I knew it, but that night my gut told me that *To Catch a D*ck* was going to be a Netflix special.

In August, I took it up to the festival. The hour-long show

was all about my dating history. The premise stemmed around me turning thirty and still being single. "I can't believe I haven't even been proposed to; there's bitches in Croydon with no teeth that have been proposed to!" I then take the audience on a look back through my dick-catching history, to see where it all went wrong. There's tales about the foot fetish dude, jokes on how I feel about children ("My mum wants me to settle down and have kids. Chill out, Mum, I haven't even had an abortion yet!"), a story you might be familiar with about the time I got sacked from a major porn channel, the white dude I dated who wanted to reenact *12 Years a Slave*, and the investment banker who had a heroin come-down whilst on a picnic date with me in Hyde Park. The show was high-energy, in your face, and filthy, and the audience loved it. The entire month-long run sold out within the first two weeks.

The reviews came flying in and as I prepared myself for the first one, I kept telling myself it didn't matter what it was, getting three stars for *Superstar* in 2017 hadn't stopped my dreams then and a middling review wouldn't stop them now. I was just happy the show was sold out. It didn't matter if the critics didn't like it, I was a woman of the people, their opinion of me was the only one that mattered and OH MY GOD I GOT FIVE FUCK-ING STARS!!! Words like "dynamite," "iconic," "feminist," "powerful," "mesmerizing" were all being used to describe me and my little show about catching dick. I couldn't believe it. You all should know by now that I cried like a baby, but these were actually unhappy tears; I was crying for previous me. I felt sorry for her. In 2017 I knew things were going badly, but it didn't really sink in how bad they were then, until now, two years later as I sat there reading all this praise. I couldn't help but think about how much 2017 me needed to hear those words.

The reviews kept coming in, five stars, five stars, four stars, five stars, five stars (my only three stars was from the *Times* but we'll ignore that), five stars, five stars, sold out! Extra date added! Extra date sold out! I slowly started to become the talk of the festival. It was my turn to receive the rock-star treatment. The show was the hottest ticket of the festival, and because it was sold out and people couldn't get tickets, it made people want to see it even more! The whole comedy industry was buzzing over it! Tiffany was responsible for getting tickets for all the industry execs, from Sky to BBC, ABC to Amazon—everyone wanted to see the show, but there wasn't enough room for all of them! Tiffany would have to turn away HBO so she could seat NBC or turn down Sky to fit Netflix in. I was being wined and dined, having dinners with bigwigs. Halfway through the run my mate Daniel Kaluuya said his friend was in town and wanted to see the show. "Daniel, I love you, but I can't get anyone in, it's sooo tight, we're turning away people every night."

"Please, London man . . . is there anything you can do?"

"Daniel, I'm sorry, you know I would if I could! My hands are tied!"

"London, it's Lupita Nyong'o . . . she's the friend, she's in town and wants to see it."

". . . Tell her to be there at seven forty-five p.m."

Lupita Nyong'o came to watch my show!? Just casual super-star actors watching you sweat your tits off in a fifty-seat room at an arts festival in Scotland, no biggie. I want to stress to you that I did not expect all of this, I was just doing it to prove a point!

It was the most five-star-reviewed show of the festival that year.

Things heated up during the last week of the festival because the nominees for best show would be announced. I went through the names of every nominee in the history of the festival, a sea of white dudes here, a couple white women there. I'm sure it'd be no surprise to you to learn that if I got nominated for best show, I'd be the first-ever Black British woman to do so in the festival's entire seventy-five-year run. I sat on the floor of my Edinburgh flat, just waiting, and when I couldn't wait anymore I took myself out to lunch for a steak (medium rare) and some hot chocolate, and I kept telling myself to breathe. I took a long walk home, then sat back on the floor again, opened up the festival website and kept refreshing the nominees page over and over and over again, waiting for the results to go live. I thought of every scenario and my inner hype woman kicked in: "Hun, if you don't get nominated it is fine, *Fleabag* didn't get nominated and that didn't stop Phoebe Waller-Bridge from being an Emmy-winning queen!" I knew that I would be okay regardless, I didn't NEED this nomination, but oh God, I wanted it, I wanted it so badly. Click, refresh, click, refresh, click, refresh ... then my phone rang. It was Tiffany.

"YOU FUCKING DID IT, MATE! YOU GOT NOMI-NATED FOR BEST SHOW!!!!!!"

I screamed. And you know I cried.

I was the first-ever Black British woman to be nominated for the Edinburgh Comedy Award, but to be honest, I felt like a winner already. The congratulations poured in from all my peers. I really felt the love; it felt like people were rooting for me.

I was in all the papers the next day—interviews, double-page spreads, so much press that I actually started to feel sorry for the other nominees, because every newspaper broke the story of the awards with a picture of me. The Edinburgh Comedy Festival has a huge problem with diversity—it's seen as a very white and very middle-class festival (because it is) and let's just say the organizers were thrilled to now have a new Black face to show off. It made them look good. The festival organizers provided me with a separate photo shoot from all the other nominees, and the headline of a piece in the *Sunday Times* was "Young, Gifted and Black." The words "first British Black woman to be nominated for the comedy award" appeared after every mention of my name. They were laying it on thick, but I won't lie, I didn't mind. I celebrated my nomination the best way I knew how—by partying! The night before the winner was announced, I was out with some mates at a bar, and Ryan, the head organizer for the Pleasance, offered to buy me a drink.

"London fucking Hughes! All your shows sold out! You're the biggest hit of the Fringe! You've made this a great festival for me and the Pleasance! Let me buy you a drink!?" Ryan clearly didn't remember that in 2017, I had emailed him asking for a slot at this very venue, and in that email I stated how much of an asset I'd be to him, how I'd be a hit for him. I basically told him all this would happen if he took a chance on me, but he simply didn't reply.

Reader, I didn't want to be petty, but I had to do it.

"Don't you remember me, Ryan? Two years ago, I emailed you asking for a spot at the Pleasance and you didn't even bother replying to me. It's funny how life works out, innit, but sure, I'll have a tequila and apple juice, thanks." Ryan went bright red, and he apologized and brought over my drink. The next day, I got an email from him, a reply to the one I'd sent him back in 2017. He apologized again and said he should have had the common decency to reply to me, and this incident made him think twice about how he treated new talent in the future. Lesson to be learned here: the girl you ignore today could be the one you're buying drinks for two years later, but fair play to him for replying.

As I sipped my tequila and apple juice, a comedian I knew named Adam Rowe approached me and asked about the comedy awards.

"Do you think you're gonna win?"

To be honest, I did think I would win. I deserved to win. I had the highest reviewed show of the festival, why wouldn't I win? Adam continued, "I'm not saying you don't deserve to win, but don't forget that this is Edinburgh. They're probably going to give it to a white guy. I'm just saying, don't be surprised if Jordan Brookes wins."

Jordan Brookes was a comic I knew, we were mates. He'd been nominated for best show at the festival a few times, but had never won. He was an alternative comic, very talented, but apparently when the show he worked really hard on last year didn't win, he decided to come back to the festival and just give it his... nothing. His show this year was literally called *I Have Nothing*. It was a show about the fact that he didn't have a show. During some parts of it he just stood there. I didn't like what Adam said, but I knew deep down he had a point. Now, I'm not saying Jordan didn't deserve an Edinburgh win, he was a talented comic. I actually thought he deserved a win for his show the year before, but him winning this year would be, in my opinion, quite laughable! In 2019, the nominee selection was the most diverse it had ever been in the history of the awards! It would be seen as the epitome of white male privilege if, after all that progressiveness, the judges went ahead and gave the best show award to a white dude anyway, and for a show where he literally didn't do anything! What would it say? If you're Black and female you can have a five-star sold-out show and lose, but if you're a white man you can have a lower-rated show about nothing and win?

I didn't think the judges would do that . . .

But they did, and Jordan Brookes won best show! I wasn't surprised and I wasn't upset, I was frustrated for the culture. Winning wouldn't necessarily have changed my career trajectory, but it would have done something for the Black community. Funny little Black girls all over the UK would've considered the Edinburgh festival a viable option, instead of the white men's club it was and still is. In hindsight, I'm glad I didn't win. My nomination was deserved, but the pomp and circumstance around it all looked a bit performative, and I don't think the festival deserved the promo. If the Edinburgh Comedy Festival really wanted to become diverse, it should do the work, not just parade me around like, "See, we're not racist! Honest!" I was happy that my losing meant the festival couldn't use me as its diversity poster child.

I took my tiny nominee trophy and hopped on a train home, triumphant. I'd done it, I'd slayed the beast, I'd made my mark and did what I set out to do in 2017. The UK comedy world certainly know the name London Hughes now—I think at that point they were probably sick of it! I was so proud of myself, job done, chapter closed. I was a Superstar and they all finally realized it, plus in a few weeks I'd be back in Los Angeles, and I'd never have to concern myself with the Edinburgh Comedy Festival ever again.

CALIFORNIA DREAMING

Pilot season in LA is when the big TV networks cast actors to star in their new yearly TV pilots. Every new actor has dreams of landing a role in a big pilot, the show going to series and making them a TV star, and I was no different. I was in LA auditioning and having meetings with anyone who would see me. They call it "the water bottle tour." I'd hop in and out of Ubers all over LA, going from West Hollywood to Santa Monica, Santa Monica to Burbank, Burbank to Beverly Hills, up to my eyeballs in business cards and bottles of water.

Before leaving for LA I made sure I was fully prepared. I wrote ten movie ideas, ten TV show ideas (to be honest, most of them were just ones the UK had rejected), and ten unscripted TV show ideas, all focusing on me and my passions. Britain wouldn't allow me to be the funny girl I never saw on TV growing up, but part of me hoped that America would. In these meetings I told my story, pitching my ideas to any producer that would listen. America listened, and pretty soon I was getting somewhere.

Tiffany rang me: "Okay, you've got a meeting with UTA . . ."

UTA looks after some of the biggest writer-comedians and

performers in the world. They were the company Phoebe Waller-Bridge had just signed to when we filmed *Fleabag* together. They also represented Issa Rae, Tiffany continued. "Issa Rae's agent, Jay Gassner, wants to meet with you. Now look, he doesn't want to sign you... BUT hopefully you can convince him to get you and Issa on a project together."

Issa Rae is the creator and star of *Insecure*, a hit show on HBO that I was absolutely obsessed with. Tiffany had read somewhere that Issa was a bit of an anglophile and felt we needed an introduction, and Jay Gassner was just the man to do it. It was my job to charm him into making it happen. I walked into Jay's office in Beverly Hills, which was hands down the fanciest office I'd ever been in. I felt like I was in an episode of *Entourage*! We spoke for about twenty minutes and then he said, "London, I think you're going to be a massive superstar, and I'm never wrong... I want to be your agent." This man was responsible for the careers of stars like Kevin Hart, Kate McKinnon, Amy Schumer, Bill Hader, Kristen Wiig, and Aziz Ansari and now he wanted to add London Hughes to that list! The same London Hughes who hadn't been good enough to be a captain on *Don't Hate the Playaz*, the same London Hughes who couldn't get on *8 out of 10 Cats*, the same London Hughes who just had her ninth TV show rejected, even though it starred Whoopi Fucking Goldberg! Tiffany had sent Jay Gassner my *No Filter* sketches, and after watching the "One of the Lads London" sketch he had made the impulsive decision to sign me on the spot. I was in complete and utter shock. I cried like a baby (again, probably like the fiftieth time I've cried in this book alone).

I now had a Hollywood manager, a top Hollywood agent,

and I was spending all my time in Los Angeles. FYI, living in Los Angeles is EX-PEN-SIVE! This town is the only place where you can have a friend who just bought a house for four million and another friend who's living in her car. I was staying in hotels and it was costing me thousands a week. I was slowly running out of money so my manager, Chanell, suggested I live with her mother-in-law, Gwen.

Gwen was a seventy-three-year-old tap-dancing, cocktail-drinking actress who did background work on *General Hospital* and stand-in work on *Dancing with the Stars*. I lived with Gwen (or Gwenny as I like to call her) rent-free in her two-bedroom bungalow in Burbank. I'd come home from auditions, and she'd make me a mint julep and we'd sit and watch *Jeopardy!* together. Gwen was so much fun. She was an older white lady from New Jersey and I was a young Black girl from Croydon, but we had so much in common! You hear these stories of what actors had to do before getting their big break. Idris Elba lived in his car, Tiffany Haddish was physically homeless, and I was living in Burbank drinking cocktails with a retired tap dancer. Gwen and Chanell soon became my LA family, and California was starting to feel more and more like home every single day.

THE TALK OF TINSELTOWN

The one thing I love about the TV and film industry in the US is that all the people involved in it are a bunch of go-getters. There's money to be made, awards to be won, projects to be green-lit—stop dicking around and let's go! Working in the US made me feel like anything's possible, that people were hungry for my ideas. By the time my narrow size seven feet landed in Los Angeles, I was already the talk of Tinseltown. Word of me smashing it in Edinburgh had reached stateside, and now all the US TV execs wanted to see the show, too. I performed *To Catch a D*ck* in LA for two nights, which was the springboard to my US success. Those shows led to a movie deal with Will Packer and Universal Studios, they led to my first sitcom pilot with Universal Television and NBC, and they caught the attention of a certain world-famous comedian by the name of Mr. Kevin Darnell Hart.

The TV Show

Let's talk numbers. I'd had nine TV show ideas rejected, all concepts I came up with, developed with a production company, and then failed to sell to a TV channel. Out of those nine failed projects, I'd only been paid for one of them, one thousand pounds to develop *28 Dates Later* for Comedy Central. I was pleased about that money; I felt like a proper writer. That script ultimately got rejected by Comedy Central, causing me to get frustrated and then write *No Filter*. *No Filter* was the reason Jay Gassner signed me to UTA. UTA then set up a meeting with Larry Wilmore. Larry Wilmore co-created *Insecure* with Issa Rae. Larry wanted to team up and create a show starring me, and we pitched that show to a room full of executive producers and commissioners at NBC Universal. It was called *London Calling*, about a young Black British girl heading to LA with dreams of being a star.

I walked out of the meeting room in a trance. I couldn't believe what had just happened. Larry and I were in the room for about twenty minutes. Our pitch was half a page long. Larry read the outline for the show and I gave a little speech about what the show meant to me, tried to make them laugh a bit, and that was it, done! They bought it. We'd just sold a show to NBC. I skipped all the way home to Gwenny's place. I hadn't even been in Los Angeles a month and I'd already sold my first show. Larry and I would now have to write the show, but no worries, they were paying me SIX FIGURES—yes, one, two, three, four, five, SIX FIGURES for my troubles! I'd really leveled up from a thousand pounds! Ah, God bless America.

I didn't even recognize my life anymore. I was going to work at the NBC Universal lot every day, having writing sessions with the man who created *Insecure* and *The Bernie Mac Show*, learning so much about the ins and outs of show business. I'd drive the golf buggies around the lots, drive past Steven Spielberg's offices, have lunch in the staff cafeteria, then go home to my bungalow in Burbank and stay up late watching *Succession* with Gwenny, my Caucasian cocktail-making mother figure.

Only a year before all this, I was on set dressed as an inflatable duck!

The Netflix Special

I had Kevin Hart playing in the background whilst I was writing *To Catch a D*ck*, for good vibes and inspiration. It was his *Let Me Explain* Netflix special. I watched as he worked the crowd up into a frenzy, studying his facial expressions, the cadence in which he delivered his jokes. The man was at the top of his game, the biggest comedian on the planet. What were the chances that that same comedian would want to work with me? After *To Catch a D*ck*'s success, Netflix offered me a comedy special. My gut already knew that this would happen so I wasn't too shocked. I was ecstatic, but not shocked. What shocked me was that Kevin Hart wanted to meet with me to talk about executive producing that special. Kevin saw a clip of me performing *To Catch a D*ck* at the festival, and members of his production company Hartbeat productions watched me perform the show live in LA . . . Kevin and his execs saw something in me that a lot of UK execs didn't: they saw a future star.

"What the fuck, London, Kevin Hart?! That's insane!" is what my LA bestie Yazmin said when I told her the news. It felt weird even saying it out loud. It's like even I didn't believe the words that were coming out of my mouth. A part of it felt like karma: Maybe I had to go through the hard times in the UK so I could come out on the other side. Those rejections made me work harder and forced me to be a better writer, a better comic, and a better performer. I was grateful for where the journey had led me, and looking back on it, I'm glad it happened this way. It was tough, definitely soul breaking at times, but I would have happily done it all again.

The first time Kevin called me, I was in my mate's car driving through LA. We put Kevin on speaker, and his voice boomed out of her car stereo.

"Heyy! London, it's Kevin! How are you!?"

My friend looked like she was going to faint. I tried to play it so cool, but I wasn't cool, I was the opposite of cool, I was very, very hot and sweaty! So hot that moisture had started building up under my armpits and my hands felt like lead. Kevin told me he had no doubt in his mind that I was going to be a massive star, and he wanted to help make it happen. Kevin was so warm and kind and inviting, he made me feel like he really believed in me. I knew that with Kevin Hart on my side, I could take over the bloody world. I couldn't truly take stock of what was happening to me; before leaving the UK I'd prepared myself to try to break down doors in the US, but maybe I didn't need an ax after all. The door was swinging open for me, and I just couldn't wait to walk inside.

I WANT MY OWN SITCOM. IF YOU CAN'T GIVE ME THAT THEN DON'T RING MY PHONE.

Okay, chicken merry, hawk di near. Things were going ridiculously well for me in the US, so of course here comes the drama from the UK. I was the most famous I'd ever been in the UK, but it didn't matter to me; Tiffany was turning down jobs for me left, right, and center. Everyone wanted to give me a TV show! But oh no no no, it was too late to come running to London Hughes now, huns, you had your chance babe, she's gone stateside now! I did a lot of press, making sure to let all the UK journalists know that I was the talent the UK missed out on. I didn't even need to spell it out for them, they knew it, too. I saw what people were saying about me on social media: "The industry is so racist, London Hughes had to move to the US just to get noticed!" "Our loss is America's gain!" "I still can't believe she didn't get a show with Whoopi Goldberg!"

Now, I'm not sure if I believe in star sign traits, but what I do know is that I'm a Gemini and I like to speak my mind. No matter how uncomfortable it is, I will always speak my truth. Other "truth"-speaking Geminis include Kanye West and Donald Trump; make of that what you will. I have no problem with putting my neck on the line and taking a stand for something that I think is right. I've often used Twitter to voice my opinions of the unjust way British television treats Black talent, I've used my Twitter fingers to speak out against injustices women in comedy face, I've spoken up for Black women in the music industry, and of course for Black women in comedy. I have attacked racial stereotypes on British shows, I've called out tokenism, I've taken aim at the BBC for their portrayal of Black people in their TV dramas. I have no problem ranting and raving about what's wrong with British television in 140 characters. I spoke out ALL THE TIME. Only back then, people weren't listening to me. Now they were, and everything I said was being put under a microscope.

In 2011, there was a show on Channel 4 called *Top Boy*. It was a gritty and violent drama about Black boys, gangs, guns, and council estates. I watched it as a few of my friends at the time were in it. I instantly hated it. I've never been into Black trauma porn. I personally don't enjoy shows that glorify the Black struggle for predominantly white audiences. Sure, this is the reality for some Black people, but it's damaging to depict a huge diaspora of people *only* this way. At the time, we'd been oversaturated in the UK with stories about Black pain, Black death, Black crime, and I was tired of it. On the BBC alone, the only dramas involving people of color all had "murder" in the title. There was *Murdered by My Boyfriend*, about a Black girl murdered by her Black boyfriend; *My Murder*, about a Black girl who set up her boyfriend to be murdered by her ex and his friends; and *Murdered by My Father*, a story about a Pakistani girl living in London who was, you guessed it, murdered by her father in an honor killing for having a boyfriend. Anything to do with Black people and drugs or guns, I'm out mate, not interested. I personally found *Top Boy* to be extremely unnecessary, whereas some of my Black friends were just happy to have Black people on the screens at all. Why was this type of show the only Black show being made? Why did we need it? When the original series of *Top Boy* got canceled after two seasons, I was relieved . . . but then years later rapper Drake (yes, Drake the rapper) rediscovered it and decided to help revive the show for Netflix. Welp, you know this Gemini had to speak their truth.

I fired off one tweet about my distaste for *Top Boy*. I even made a joke, saying of all the Black British shows they could revive, why did it have to be that one? Why couldn't they have brought back *Desmond's*! For the uninitiated, *Desmond's* was a happy comedy about a barbershop in South London owned by a happy Black man. Same vibe as *Good Times*. That tweet got the attention of the press, and I was asked to write a piece for the *Independent*. I wrote a fun and lighthearted piece about my issues with the show, highlighted all the great shows that Black creatives were making, and spoke about the fact that *Top Boy* was written by a now-rich white man, and that maybe we should commission new Black stories from Black writers instead of reviving old Black stories by white writers. The article was extremely divisive—some people understood my point entirely, while others didn't want to hear it. *Top Boy* was a beloved show for some members of the Black community and speaking out against it was a big no-no.

A week after the *Top Boy* article came out, I was on the cover of the *Guardian*'s weekend guide, dressed in a pink ballgown, looking fiercely at the camera with a sparkly phone in my hand. The headline read, "The Rise and Rise of London Hughes," which was placed underneath a quote from me in big black letters which read: "I want my own sitcom. If you can't give me that then don't call my phone." That statement was exactly how I felt at the time, and it was aimed specifically at all the UK execs now clamoring to get me on their TV shows. Inside the magazine was an in-depth interview. By now, I'd done many interviews for the press, and I'm always completely honest. I never hold my tongue; I speak my truth no matter who wants to hear it and this interview was no different. The online version dropped the night before the Emmys. I immediately posted it on my Twitter and then went to bed. I woke up the next morning thinking that my friends and fans would be happy for me. It was my first-ever cover, and I'd revealed the exciting new projects I was involved in stateside. It was a real local hero story. I wanted to make Black Brits proud—the girl from Croydon that done good! Instead, I woke up to floods and floods of abuse.

THE BLACKLASH

Ever wondered what it feels like to have hundreds of Black people calling you anti-Black on Twitter? Not fun. I guess timing is everything. My *Top Boy* piece had angered many Black fans of the show, and in my *Guardian* interview, I said, "There are no Black female household names, bar Naomi Campbell." It was a completely true statement. At the time of the interview, there weren't any. I'd said it plenty of times, I've even said it in this book! To me, that statement wasn't offensive. It was aimed at all the gatekeepers, the people in charge who make the decisions yet fail to recognize and celebrate Black British talent. It was very clear to me that I was trying to fight the problem, but some Black people believed I WAS the problem. The tweets about me were truly horrible; I was being completely misunderstood. They thought I was saying there weren't any Black female household names in Britain because no Black women were talented enough! Angered, some blue-tick Twitter users even decided to list talented Black women in the industry who they'd believed I'd left out and insisted that I was "trying to silence the achievements of the Black women that came before me." I thought it was pretty obvious that I was highlighting the fact that there should be more Black female household names in Britain but because of systemic racism, there were not. That misconstrued quote, along with my public disliking of *Top Boy*, meant that I was now seen as anti-Black to a lot of Black people.

I had never received this much hate in my life for openly disliking a TV show. For the record, I also dislike a lot of white TV shows and loathe Caucasian limited series! I refuse to watch *The Office* UK because it's way too white for me. I've grown up for most of my life mainly consuming white content, so now I have to be picky. In my opinion, if a show's not giving me any diversity, then the writing has to be beyond top tier, and that's why the only all-white show that I'm okay with watching is *Succession*. I didn't deserve the hate I got on Twitter that day. I got called words like "coon" and the Black British female online magazine *gal-dem* wrote an extremely slighting think piece on why I was "so problematic." I saw former friends, and Black women I'd worked with in the past, all take to the internet to jump on the "I hate London Hughes" bandwagon. I laughed at first. Thought to myself, you really can't be serious. After all that I've been through in my career, I finally got to a place where I hoped my sheer existence in this space would be seen as an inspiration to all Black British women, and now Black British women were the ones using their platforms to tear me down!

Things got so bad for me that activist and actress Jameela Jamil was in my DMs offering advice. I bloody love Jameela Jamil. She's so used to being attacked online that she held my hand through my first-ever Twitter cancellation. I called her gasping through tears. I couldn't even breathe properly. She calmed me down and made me feel like I wasn't alone. There's something so upsetting about people from your own race turning on you. I could withstand abuse from white people all day long, but Black British women—the women I've always used my platform to speak out for, to fight for, the very women I want to inspire—were attacking my character and I was completely heartbroken.

The night of the Emmys had arrived, and Chanell took me to the NBC party. It was the fanciest soiree I'd ever attended in my life: ice sculptures, canapés, live band, rooftop panoramic view of Hollywood, it was insane. Pearlina Igbokwe, a gorgeous Black woman and the president of Universal Television, took me by the hand and paraded me around, introducing me to Adam Sandler, Lorne Michaels, and Dave Chappelle as "the future of comedy." I was supposed to be having the night of my life, but my phone would not stop pinging with more Twitter abuse from the UK. I went to the beautiful toilets and cried.

For a moment, I was taken back to my school days, getting bullied by the girls I lived with, my character under attack, being called something I wasn't. I gasped for air again. "Get it together London, get it together!!" My inner hype woman was letting me know it would all be okay. I looked in the mirror and stared long and hard at my face. I stared so hard I saw deep into my soul. Even though I was upset, I knew that this was a pivotal moment in my life. I wasn't the same girl that boarded the plane from Heathrow. I told myself that this was all a part of the journey. You wanted to be famous, babe, well this is the type of stuff that comes with it. I dried my eyes, sucked it up, and enjoyed the party. I refused to let those bastards get me down. That night I remembered the famous Brené Brown quote, the one she uses about haters on the internet:

IF YOU'RE NOT IN THE ARENA GETTING YOUR ASS KICKED, I'M NOT INTERESTED IN YOUR FEEDBACK.

Yeah, babes, I'll listen to your opinions once you've walked a mile in my inflatable duck costume.

Take a Bow, Babes

Despite all the Twitter abuse, I flew back to London with my head held high and I landed in Heathrow a legend. I had ten sold-out dates of *To Catch a D*ck* at the Soho Theatre, and two sold-out nights at the Bloomsbury Theatre in London's West End. It felt amazing performing the show for a London audience—the energy was unlike anything I'd ever experienced. I finished my last joke and got a standing ovation. I looked out at the roaring crowd and saw my family, friends, fans, and I was overwhelmed, completely overcome with emotion. This would be my last time performing that show for a UK audience, because things were going so well in LA that in two weeks' time, I'd be moving to America for good. I took a deep breath, exhaled, and just soaked it all in. I thought about how far I'd come. That little girl performing in her living room pretending it was a stage had been preparing me for this moment. The little girl who wrote herself into episodes of *The Fresh Prince of Bel Air* had been preparing me for my life as a writer in the US. I called it popstar training, but it was just training for the life I had now. Everything made sense, it had all been leading up to this very moment. I'd finally become everything I said I would be all along. I looked out into the audience at the Blooms-bury Theatre and when I told them that *To Catch a D*ck* was being recorded as a Netflix special, they all roared with applause. I mentioned the special was being executive produced by Kevin Hart and they roared even louder. You already know I cried my eyes out. I was a wonderful and emotional mess.

The next month, Kevin flew me to Las Vegas to meet him. We spent the whole day together, and I was so nervously excited I didn't go for a pee once! Kevin asked me what I wanted to be, and I told him it was my plan to be Comedy Beyoncé. He laughed and said, "I love it. Okay, well, I'm gonna drive this train; call me the captain! Get on this train and I promise you, I'll drive you to stardom!" And he was definitely a man of his word. In December 2020, my very first Netflix special *To Catch a D*ck* dropped on Netflix in 194 countries, executively produced by the one and only Kevin Hart. I was lucky enough to film my first special in Los Angeles at Universal Studios the day before Halloween, and that will be etched into my memory banks for the rest of my life. There are no suitable words to describe that feeling; none of them will do it justice, but shout-out to my manager Chanell and my executive producer Tiffany Brown at Hartbeat productions for holding my hand throughout the whole thing and making sure I didn't pass out from excitement and exhaustion! When the special dropped on Netflix, my social media went crazy! Honestly, my DMs looked like the United Nations of Dick! People from all over the world were complimenting me and my comedy, and I was completely taken aback by the response. The night the special came out I decided to book myself into the presidential suite at the Beverly Wilshire hotel in Beverly Hills. It's the hotel where *Pretty Woman* was filmed, and my suite was the same one where Beyoncé filmed her famous "7/11" music video. Hey, if it's good enough for actual Beyoncé, then it's good enough for Comedy Beyoncé! My suite was huge, the height of luxury with an enormous wraparound balcony that showed off a 180-degree view of Beverly Hills. The morning after the special came out, I stood on my balcony alone and looked down at the whole of Los Angeles. I poured myself a glass of Dom Pérignon champagne, took a sip, and then yelled out with all the breath in my lungs: "I DID IT! I DID IT, LOS ANGELES!! SO MANY PEO-PLE SAID I COULDN'T DO IT, BUT I DID IT! LOOK AT ME NOW!!!!" I took a moment and remembered all the times I almost gave up, all the times I'd been rejected, all the times I'd been defeated. I remembered driving to all my auditions, stuck in London traffic and daydreaming about future me sipping champagne on a beautiful balcony in LA. I had now become that girl. I was no longer daydreaming about my life in the future; I was literally living my dreams right now.

That comedy special completely changed my life, Hollywood was starting to take notice, job opportunities opened for me, movie and TV deals came rolling in. Top movie producer James Lopez, the then-president of Will Packer Productions, had seen me perform live and was so impressed he literally GAVE ME A MOVIE!…"It's called *Hot Mess* and I want you to star in it," he said to me over lunch at a swanky Beverly Hills hotspot; I nearly choked on my spicy mango margarita! We sold *Hot Mess* to Universal Studios a few months later—a Hollywood movie for little old me?! Not too shabby for the girl who was cut from *Bridget Jones's Baby!* I'd also landed several Netflix jobs including *The Netflix Afterparty*, which I got to host alongside comedians Fortune Feimster and David Spade! I'd been living in America for ten months, during the height of a global pandemic, and yet in that short and crazy time I'd had more career success than my whole eleven-year career in the UK. I was so happy I moved! My life was completely unrecognizable, and my heroes were now starting to become my friends. Just six months after that special aired, I was celebrating my thirty-second birthday at Dave Chappelle's house in Ohio eating weed-infused macaroni cheese goodness and dancing the night away. His chef made me a beautiful cake in the shape of the British flag, which had my name on it in gold with stars. My new LA bestie, R & B queen Estelle, held my hand as she and all my friends and the partygoers sang "Happy Birthday" to me. It was the best birthday I've ever had. Every part of my life was completely unrecognizable from that of the girl with mild eczema and tiny wrists waiting at Pizza Hut for her birthday guests, who never arrived; and even though I had all the belief in the world, I still couldn't imagine that things would turn out this way. I was truly LIVING MY BEST LIFE, HUN.

I'm so grateful that I never gave up on my dreams, and hey, if you're reading this, please take this as a sign that you shouldn't give up on yours, either.

So whenever life gets you down, just yell out, "Plot twist!" And think to yourself: *What would London Hughes do?*

Acknowledgments

I would like to thank every single British comedy exec who rejected me—if wasn't for your lack of taste in comedy, I wouldn't be living it up in America right now and this book would not be possible, so truly, thank you. My wonderful family, for consistently keeping me grounded. When I told my mum I was writing this book, she said, "Are you sure you know how to write a book? You sure you don't want me to help you with it?" Appreciate you, Mum! I want to thank my life partners, aka my support system, aka Team London for life, aka my managers Tiffany Agbeko and Camilla Cole at Curtis Brown and Chanell Hardy, Amy Slomovitz, and Jesse Hara at Haven Entertainment. Shout-outs to Jay Gassner and my team of special agents at UTA, and to Gordon Wise, my literary agent, for making this book possible. Also Quercus and Grand Central Publishing, you are legends, thank you! To all the men I've dated: Thank you for all the content over the years; I couldn't have done it without you! I want to thank all the bullies for giving me the best revenge story ever, to quote my queen Beyoncé, "Always stay gracious, best revenge is your paper."

I want to thank all the heroes in this book: James Lopez, Tiffany Brown, Dave Chappelle, Jameela Jamil, Whoopi Goldberg, Larry Wilmore, Kevin Hart, Alan Carr, Sir Lenny Henry,

Stephen K. Amos, Phoebe Waller-Bridge, Daniel Kaluuya, you're all a permanent part of my success story, and I'll be forever grateful.

I wrote this book in two months, without drinking any alcohol, going on social media, or leaving the house, so I want to thank my willpower and Chips Ahoy! cookies for getting me through those really dark days... And finally, thank you to all my fans and supporters for sticking with me on this fourteen-year-long journey! Wow, this is only the beginning, huns; I really hope to continue to make you proud.

And to twelve-year-old me... you told me so.

About the Author

LONDON HUGHES is a stand-up comedian, writer, actor, and host who was the first British Black woman to be nominated for the Dave's Edinburgh Comedy "Best Show" Award for *To Catch a D*ck*, which was recorded as her debut comedy special for Netflix. London was awarded a Royal Television Society Award for "Best Entertainment Performance" for her work on ITV 2's hip-hop comedy quiz show *Don't Hate the Playaz*, and at the beginning of her career received the prestigious Funny Women Award at the London Comedy Store. London has been interviewed by Jimmy Fallon for *The Tonight Show* on NBC and has appeared in the BBC/Amazon award-winning and critically acclaimed series *Fleabag*. Further credits include performances on *The Russell Howard Hour* on Sky Max, *The Stand-Up Sketch Show* on ITV 2, and *Mock the Week* for BBC Two. London also created, wrote, and starred in her own YouTube comedy series, *No Filter*, which featured some of the UK's brightest new talent. She has also co-hosted Netflix's first ever chat show, *The Afterparty*, alongside David Spade and Fortune Feimster, and hosted Channel 5's *Extreme Hair Wars*.